# TYRANNY OF THE BOTTOM LINE

# TYRANNY OF THE BOTTOM LINE

Why Corporations Make Good People Do Bad Things

## Ralph Estes

Berrett-Koehler Publishers
San Francisco

Berrett-Koehler Publishers, Inc.
155 Montgomery Street
San Francisco, CA 94104-4109
Tel: (415) 288-0260   Fax: (415) 362-2512

ORDERING INFORMATION

Individual sales. Berrett-Koehler publications are available through most bookstores. They can also be ordered direct from Berrett-Koehler at the address above.

Quantity sales. Special discounts are available on quantity purchases by corporations, associations, and others. For details, contact the "Special Sales Department" at the Berrett-Koehler address above.

Orders for college textbook/course adoption use. Please contact Berrett-Koehler Publishers at the address above.

Orders by U.S. trade bookstores and wholesalers. Please contact Publishers Group West, 4065 Hollis Street, Box 8843, Emeryville, CA 94662. Tel: (510) 658-3453; 1-800-788-3123. Fax: (510) 658-1834

Printed in the United States of America

 Printed on acid-free and recycled paper that is composed of 50% recovered fiber, including 10% post consumer waste.

Library of Congress Cataloging-in-Publication Data

Estes, Ralph W.
    Tyranny of the bottom line : why corporations make good people do
bad things / Ralph Estes. — 1st ed.
        p.    cm.
    ISBN 1-881052-75-3 (alk. paper)
    1. Social responsibility of business.    2. Corporations—Moral and
ethical aspects.    3. Business ethics.    I. Title
HD60.E784   1995
658.4'08—dc20                                                                95-25473
                                                                                 CIP

First Edition

99  98  97  96  95                          10  9  8  7  6  5  4  3  2  1

*Tyranny of the Bottom Line* is dedicated to those who have been sacrificed on the altar of the bottom line, in the hope that these sacrifices will not have been in vain.

# Contents

# Preface

I began to research this book because I saw too many people needlessly hurt by corporations, and I wondered if business had to be that way.

Once I was testifying (as an expert witness on economic loss) in a case involving a young woman who had died from toxic shock syndrome. Her husband's description of the unspeakable pain she suffered in her last days and hours was almost unbearable, for me and the jury. But what bothered me the most was the discovery that this woman suffered such agony because of an impersonal corporate decision, a decision that favored its bottom line over her life.

I saw honest, productive people turned out of their jobs in a spasm of corporate "downsizing," many at an age when they would never again have a decent job, never earn a livable wage. And I asked again: are higher corporate profits reason enough to produce human misery, broken families, even suicide? Is this the only way to run our businesses?

Doing business ought to make us feel good. We ought to have a feeling of accomplishment—providing goods and services that people like and that help them and seeing employees become friends and sharing in their success as they advance in the organization. There ought to be opportunities for everyone in a company, from the top to the bottom, to experience self-satisfaction. Business ought to be fun. Today it is usually just the opposite.

Like you, I have known of many employees who were injured at work or contracted a serious illness because their company decided to run the machines without adequate safeguards or to skimp on product testing and quality.

I've had friends die from cancer that I believe was caused by emissions from local corporations, corporations that were held up by the chamber of commerce as great assets to the community. And as I hurt for my friends and others like them, as I talked with them about what had happened to them, what the corporations had done, I began the research for this book. Through that research I slowly came to the conclusion: most of this harm was needless.

All of us—from top business executives to politicians to reporters to average citizens—have been conditioned to think that business must do these things to make a profit, and it must make a profit to stay alive.

That sounds good, but it turns out to be specious. Yes, business needs to make a profit. But we no longer examine this idea. How much profit? For whom? At what cost to others? Just what counts as profit and what doesn't?

My research began with trying to understand why corporations were first created. Was it to "make a profit," as we understand that today? Is that why Queen Elizabeth and her successors, sovereigns and states granted precious charters of incorporation to a select few companies?

What I found, what historical records show clearly, is that corporations were first chartered in the public interest, to meet a public need, to provide a public service. They were seen as extensions of the government, doing government—that is, state or public—business. Investors were allowed a return for the use of their capital, just as workers were allowed compensation for their labor. But the reason for granting the charter was the public purpose. Then corporations turned from serving the public purpose to serving private interests.

How did this happen? What was the instrument that led to this perversion of corporate purpose? What harm has it produced? What does "maximizing profits" cost corporate stakeholders—employees, customers, suppliers, communities, and our nation—in externalized social costs?

All these questions are answered in *Tyranny of the Bottom Line*. But the real question is what can we do about it. Are we damned from now on with a corporate system that puts "profits" first and people last, that devastates communities by moving operations to Mexico and Malaysia in pursuit of a few dollars more on the bottom line? A system that presents a respectable corporate face but that answers to no authority, in any nation of the world?

No, we are not. It does not have to be this way. Business can be run successfully, with a fair return not only to stockholders but to all stakeholders, and still be humane. It can be competitive, it can be financially strong. And it can be fun.

To make it that way, we will first have to understand what really drives the corporation—what it is about business that makes good people do bad things. We will see that it is an archaic scorekeeping system that does not do what it is supposed to do: it doesn't measure and report the real performance of the firm.

Once a problem is accurately diagnosed, the prescription often becomes obvious. We need a new, fair scorekeeping system, one that will send different messages to corporate managers. A scorekeeping system that simply shows the effects of a corporation's actions on all its stakeholders, not merely its stockholders, and then tells managers that they will be responsible for these effects.

*Tyranny of the Bottom Line* lays out this prescription in an effective and workable program that can make corporations safer and more rewarding for all of us, and more enjoyable, more honorable, for the people who run them.

This prescription is a product not only of my research and reflection but also derives substantially from a lifetime spent working in and with business, as well as studying and teaching about business. My work as a CPA, auditor, and systems consultant with a "Big 6" accounting firm gave me an opportunity to get deep inside of client firms, large and small. There I met many hard-working, honest, wonderful people— people who were being tyrannized by the bottom line and whose lives were dominated and made miserable by the strange morality demanded by the corporate system.

And I have to admit that I've designed and helped put into place bottom-line-oriented business systems that undoubtedly led other good people to make corporate decisions that caused harm, not only to the victims of corporate actions but to the souls of the decision makers themselves. That's not surprising since I was a product of the education, training, and cultural system that has taught so many the perfidious corporate theology: anything and anyone are expendable for the bottom line.

More recently, I've been the chief financial officer of a software development and publishing company. This responsibility doesn't allow for a lot of naivete or innocence about the corporate system; we do have to meet a payroll. But it has reinforced the view presented in this book that you can "do well while doing good," that humane and socially responsible management is not only consistent with financial success but may very well, in the long run, be necessary for financial success.

*Tyranny of the Bottom Line* is structured to be read straight through. But that may be an author's conceit. If you're in a hurry, or want to cut right to the chase and return to the whole story later, here's how you might read this book:

- You know the problem and want to get on with the solution: Read Chapter 9, skim Chapter 10, and read Chapter 11.

- You're skeptical about this idea that corporations were first created to serve the public purpose and not to make a profit for stockholders: Read Chapter 2.

- As a corporate executive, you're most interested in moving ahead promptly with a stakeholder report; or you're a stakeholder and want to see what information you ought to be receiving from corporations: Read Chapter 10 and Appendices 2–5.

- You pretty well understand the problem and the solution, and you want to move on to implementing that solution: Read Chapter 11.

Some may misread this book as an attack on corporations. It is not meant to be an attack on the corporate form of business, but it *is* an attack on the abusive behavior that is driven by the tyranny of the bottom line. Corporations can make a positive contribution to our society, but the corporate *system* needs to be restored to its original, its founding, purpose.

Neither is this book an attack on corporate managers, although it is concerned with those managers' decisions that, driven by the bottom line, cause harm to stakeholders. Except for what is undoubtedly a small minority, corporate managers were not born bad people. They are, by and large, ordinary persons who have become hostages to the "bottom line" culture.

*Tyranny of the Bottom Line* is for these good people in business who feel, deep down inside, that there should be a better way, who want to go home at night feeling good, not bad. It's for the executives, the middle managers, the clerks, and the wage earners who have been victims of downsizing, or who find it impossible to give the loyalty to their employer they would like to give, or who have been asked—explicitly or implicitly—to do something they haven't felt quite right about. It's for all the other people, all the other corporate stakeholders, who have suffered from actions that were driven by the tyranny of a perverted corporate scorekeeping system.

*Tyranny of the Bottom Line* is a book for everyone who wants a better, fairer, more humane business system in America.

RALPH ESTES
Washington, D.C.
July 1995

# Acknowledgments

*Tyranny of the Bottom Line* was a joint effort at every stage with Martha Burk. Those who know her will not be surprised; they will simply say, "of course."

This project has been informed by the concerns, experiences, and generous contributions of many other people, especially over the past ten years during which it was researched and written. Each deserves the fullest acknowledgment, but unfortunately that would fill another book. You were unstinting with your help, kind in your praise, and constructive with your criticism. Your enthusiasm kept me on track when other concerns interfered. As sincerely as I can, I say thank you. And I'll do better than that when we are together.

The ideas which are here expressed so laboriously are extremely simple and should be obvious. The difficulty lies, not in the new ideas, but in escaping from the old ones, which ramify, for those brought up as most of us have been, into every corner of our minds.

John Maynard Keynes
*General Theory of Employment, Interest and Money*

# 1

## *The Manager Held Hostage*

### WHY CORPORATIONS MAKE GOOD PEOPLE DO BAD THINGS

"UNDER YOUR DIRECTION, your company has continued to allow women, tens of thousands of them, to wear this device—a deadly depth charge in their wombs, ready to explode at any time."[1] Judge Miles Lord had the top executives of A. H. Robins, producers of the Dalkon Shield intrauterine device, in front of him, and he was incensed. Women had suffered sterility, spontaneous abortions, and pelvic infections from the Dalkon Shield.[2] Some had died.[3]

"The only conceivable reasons that you have not recalled this product are that it would hurt your balance sheet and alert women who have already been harmed that you may be liable for their injuries," Judge Miles scolded. "You have taken the bottom line as your guiding beacon and the low road as your route."

The bottom line as their guiding beacon! Isn't that what business is all about?

Well, yes it is—today. And that's why corporations, like A. H. Robins and so many others, often cause serious harm.

Isn't there a better way to do business?

This is the question now being asked by thousands of corporate managers and employees—decent people who find that their jobs

1

seem to require them to do indecent things. Of course they usually do not ask these questions aloud since such doubts are not well received in the corporate culture.

But corporations have always worked this way, haven't they?

Actually, they haven't. Corporations were not originally created to "maximize profits to stockholders." From their creation until well into the 1800s, that notion would have seemed bizarre; a person proposing it would have risked being seen as a bit "off."

Corporations were first chartered by governments to serve the public purpose. The story of the first corporations is told in the next chapter. There we will see that sovereigns issued corporate charters to achieve a public purpose without permanently expanding the government bureaucracy—a genesis not well known today. Later democracies and states adopted this tradition to obtain needed public services—water systems, turnpikes, stage lines, colleges.

For over two centuries, corporations were viewed as fairly benign servants of the public good. But they are no longer our servants, and they are often not benign.

Though many of their products are good, even excellent, many also cause harm. Workers may be injured, poisoned, or brutalized on the job, and then "downsized." Neighbors and taxpayers in surrounding communities pay to undo the damage corporations do to the air, water, and neighborhoods. Corporations lobby and buy their way into the halls of Congress, the offices of the administration, and the national budget.

Instead of striving for better products and better service, corporations often focus on mergers and takeovers. Obsession with bottom-line profit drives a short-run outlook that leads corporations to skimp on training, service, maintenance, and research and development—even though there is growing evidence that such a short-run approach hurts long-term financial performance.

Employees are worried, and rightly so. Jobs earned with sweat and loyalty are eliminated with the stroke of a pen. A lifetime of work, once thought to earn job security and a comfortable retirement, is abruptly arrested with a layoff or a plant shutdown. The worker, who may now be past middle age, can be on the street with no job, no career, no resources, and no hope.

Workers lucky enough to have jobs often fear for their health and safety. "What are these chemicals and what effect will they have on my body in twenty years?" "This machine will take off an arm if I'm not careful, but the pace is fatiguing, and it's easy to slip up." "I breathe these fumes every day—will my baby be born deformed?"

As consumers, we may shop carefully and then learn we've spent our money on defective or dangerous products that can turn against us, such as death by fire in an exploding car, toxic shock syndrome from superabsorbent tampons, or "hot" batches of DPT vaccine that destroy a child's brain. Other examples could include tires that explode at sixty miles an hour, food with carcinogenic additives or coated with toxic pesticides, or cancer and nerve damage from products rushed to market with inadequate testing or with incriminating test data suppressed.

The problem isn't our people. We are as good—and as bad—as we've ever been. We are still inventors, builders, pioneers, thinkers, workers, fighters, and dreamers.

And the problem isn't government. Some politicians and bureaucrats are good, some crooked, some mean, some courageous, and some wise. But in the main they come and go, while the problem has been with us and building for more than a century.

The problem is that our large corporations have lost their bearings. (Although small corporations are driven by the bottom line and may also do harm, our concern here is primarily with the larger enterprises, and especially with corporate "giants." Most are multinational, with facilities, sources of materials, and markets all over the world.) They no longer admit to a public purpose and to public accountability. Nor, as we shall see in Chapter 3, are stockholders, government, or the marketplace able to effectively hold them accountable.

Unfortunately, unaccountable power will always, sooner or later, be abused.

Is there a better way to do business?

We all know, in our hearts, that there has to be. Business doesn't have to be exploitive or destructive. It should be, and can be, good for all stakeholders, not just for stockholders. At the end of the day, business people should feel that they have done something good, and not have to go home guilt laden.

## Stakeholders: Investors All

Some will say that only stockholders are investors in the corporation and that it is proper for management to act in the stockholders' exclusive interest, that the stockholders' bottom line is the appropriate measure of corporate performance. They will argue that stockholders make the investment, they take the risks, they deserve the profit. But the corporation has other constituents as well: the workers, customers, suppliers, the community, and the greater society. These other stakeholders are investors too, and they often risk far more than financial investors.[4]

Employees invest in the corporation. They bring their education, skills, and experience—often gained at substantial personal expense—to the job. They invest time, energy, and too often their health. They invest their careers, careers that can be effectively wiped out in a casual layoff or relocation decision. And sometimes, like the workers at Manville (described in Chapter 6), they invest their lives.

Customers invest in the corporation. Their monetary investments are often greater than those of stockholders; the buyer of an automobile, for example, invests more in that car than the average stockholder invests in the corporation that makes it.

And the customer may invest much, much more. If an automobile is defective in design or manufacture, canned goods are adulterated, or a child's clothing is highly flammable, the customer's loss can become enormous.

Like workers, suppliers are investors too. They may commit production facilities, install special equipment, redesign products, and provide financing to their corporate customers. They have a right to expect fair treatment and a fair return on their investment.

## Who's the "Investor"?

Investments can take different forms: money, equipment, experience, intellectual capital, labor. All may benefit the corporation.
Jack and Jill form an oil exploration and development partnership. Jill just completed a special course of study in geology that cost her $25,000, and she brings these valuable skills to the partnership. Jack has no such training or experience, but he has $25,000 to invest. How should these investments be counted? Should both receive a fair return on investment, or is only Jack so entitled?

In other words, should workers be viewed as investors the way stockholders are? Or should workers' investments not count?

Communities—neighbors, towns, cities, counties, and states—invest in corporations. They provide much of the infrastructure, such as streets and bridges, water and sewer systems, and police and fire protection, without which the corporation could hardly function. Communities, along with the workers themselves, pay for the educated labor force on which the corporation relies. Citizens pay taxes for the benefits of living in a community; but large corporations, with their great power, often get tax exemptions and rebates to the point where they pay only a small fraction of the cost of the facilities and services they use. Citizens and smaller businesses have to make up this tax deficit. Communities are investors and deserve a fair return on investment as much as stockholders.

The nation—society—invests in the corporation. It provides the social capital and structure, without which we would face the brutal anarchy of the cave dweller. Our society supports the democratic system that allows the corporation, and the rest of us, freedom of movement and action. It provides protection for the free enterprise system. Nations also grant specific benefits to corporations, such as

> The responsibility of management is "to maintain an equitable and working balance among the claims of the various directly interested groups—stockholders, employees, customers, and the public at large."
>
> **Frank Abrams, speaking in 1951 as chair of Standard Oil Company[5]**

investment incentives, tariff protection, research subsidies, defense contracts, and tax benefits including investment tax credits, accelerated depreciation, and foreign tax credits.

Employees, customers, suppliers, communities, and society are all investors, but the corporation is not accountable to them. It reports regularly and comprehensively to stockholders, almost never to other stakeholders.

## Questioning Conventional Wisdom

Plato said, "the life which is unexamined is not worth living."[6] Yet much of what we do—and believe—in the practice of business is unexamined, accepted, and repeated as a sort of gospel without critical analysis. Let's inspect some of these notions that guide our decisions every day in business.

### Maximizing Profits

Take the top banana of these, perhaps articulated most famously by Milton Friedman: "the business of business is to maximize profits."[7] Is this correct? And what exactly are "profits"?

The Bible asks, "For what is a man profited, if he shall gain the whole world, and lose his own soul?" Here, and frequently in other contexts, profit is used in a general sense to mean betterment, gain, or benefit. Economists speak more narrowly of increase in resources or capital over a period of time. Accountants are more specific still, and usually mean the excess of revenues over expenses.

Not very interesting so far, but what happens when we ask, "profit for whom?" The prior section discussed how workers, customers, communities, and the nation all invest in businesses; they risk these investments (and incur other risks with the corporation as well); and their contributions and investments are essential for the survival, much less the "success," of the business enterprise.

So does maximizing profits mean maximizing gains only to stockholders? Or does (should) it mean maximizing gains to all those who make the enterprise go? Most of us are prone to respond to such questions reflexively, without careful examination, and in this case may never have even considered the second formulation.

In recent years Corporate America has gone through a spasm of "downsizing"—cutting jobs, "laying off" workers (but permanently, not temporarily), demanding wage/salary givebacks and other concessions, and identifying previously "permanent" jobs as temporary or "contingent." While some firms unquestionably had too many employees, many had been profitable in recent years and were profitable at the time of downsizing.

At the beginning of 1995, for example, American Home Products reported annual sales up 8 percent and quarterly sales up 22 percent, net income up 4 percent, earnings per share up 5 percent—and elimination of thousands of additional jobs, bringing the total for the year to over 10 percent of the company workforce.[8] And toy manufacturer Mattel made the following announcements just before Christmas 1994: The company would have record-high sales and earnings for the sixth year in a row, the balance sheet was strong and getting even better, dividends would be raised, stockholders would get a five for four stock split—and oh yes, the company was going to eliminate 4 percent of the employees' jobs.[9] Were these companies truly benefitting anyone with their downsizing, or were they following a fashionable business dictum without examination?

The evidence, in fact, suggests that the spate of downsizing may have hurt companies on all levels. MIT's Lester Thurow notes that workers in such an environment will see no point in working hard, undergoing training that benefits only the firm, and accepting transfers when they know they will be downsized no matter what their contribution.[10] Many companies have thrown away employee loyalty, experience, morale, productivity, and commitment in the name of cost-cutting; in return they have reaped, in Thurow's words, "an inferior work force." Eric Greenberg, research director of the American Management Association, states flatly that, "the facts show that the mid- to long-range effects of downsizing are not good." The AMA's survey supports this observation; it found that fewer than half of the companies that downsized reported an increase in profits afterward.[11]

The responses of workers are informative. S. P. Joyce of Northborough, Massachusetts, wrote to *Business Week*:

> Wait. Let me get this straight. While Digital Equipment Corp. employees cannot expect salary increases for the foreseeable future and while thousands of them have lost, or will lose, their jobs as a result of mismanagement, two members of senior management have received 18 percent and 35 percent increases? Do these guys know how to lead, or what?[12]

Another writer tells *Time:* "The operative word in the American workplace these days is fear."[13]

## Competitiveness

Another part of the business dogma goes something like this: "We've got to [shave quality] [close the Peoria plant] [cut back on testing and inspection] [fudge the accounting numbers] in order to be competitive." Just what does it mean to be competitive?

If a company cuts corners in manufacturing and produces a shoddy product that it sells at a lower price than other companies, is

> Just talk about restructuring as positive and investors will buy it. It's really an admission of failure: We're closing this operation and firing these people so that we can stay in business. But we ain't paying the price. The employees, the community, they pay the price. Meanwhile, the executives' salaries go up and their benefits increase because they are making the "hard decisions."
>
> **Jerry Sterner, businessman turned playwright**[14]

it competitive? If a company sells more than anybody else in the industry and makes less "profit," is it competitive? If a company survives through government subsidies, tax breaks, and wage reductions, is it competitive? If a company is able to report high profits by underfunding its pension liabilities, but in the process risks its employees' retirement security, is it competitive? If American industry is earning unprecedented profits while American workers' earnings are declining, is our economy competitive?

Corporate actions are often defended in the name of global competitiveness, sometimes with patriotic references to the national interest. Getting business by bribing foreign government officials? Got to do it to compete globally! If the competition is relying on slave labor in a Third World country, should we follow suit to "compete"? Where do we draw the line—or do we? Will we stoop to any level in the name of global competition?

Different people might give different answers to all these questions, but most would agree that they deserve thoughtful examination, not knee-jerk reactions.


## Productivity

Productivity is another word that is bandied about without much thought: "We've got to be more productive!" We might think a person is productive who produces a lot, who gets a lot done. But if we think

> What do we mean by "competitiveness" anyway? Rarely has a term of public discourse gone so directly from obscurity to meaninglessness without any intervening period of coherence. Surely the ultimate test of competitiveness should be the standard of living of Americans.
>
> Labor Secretary Robert Reich[15]

just a little bit deeper, we might ask whether that person's production was of high quality, or was it of such low quality that the output was unusable. And if we take a further step, we might ask whether it was the right kind of output. If we hire a crew to repair our roof, it doesn't help us if they do a nice job of repairing the roof next door.

How should we measure the productivity of a company—or is this even a relevant concept? The Department of Labor assesses national productivity by calculating the average output per hour of all persons. This calculation has some obvious utility in assessing aggregate economic performance, but is it the only logical way to calculate productivity, and is it relevant for business?

What about calculating a company's output per dollar of investment? A company that achieves a high level of output from a relatively low investment base would seem to be a productive company, wouldn't it? Note that such a company would, relative to other companies, tend to spend more on labor, training, and research and less on plant and equipment.

Or we could calculate taxes paid by a company per dollar of sales. This could be a relevant measure of productivity from the perspective of the community in which the company is located.

How many jobs are generated per tax dollar invested? Many tax dollars go to corporations through investment tax credits, government contracts, and subsidy programs such as enterprise and empowerment zones. Similarly, "tax expenditures" in the form of corporate tax credits and deductions benefit business as fully as direct payments and cost taxpayers accordingly. Most of these benefits are provided by the government and taxpayers in hopes of stimulating job creation and economic growth, so a measure of productivity related to job creation would appear to make sense.

We could consider several other notions of productivity, but what is more important is that we stop and think about these and other such abstract concepts, which are often used to justify corporate actions that end up hurting someone. Thoughtful examination will lead most people to question several practices of modern corporations. A growing number of business leaders, in fact, are challenging the notion that harmful actions can be justified by the bottom line. They are raising the possibility that business can be a win-win proposition, one in which all stakeholders get a fair return. They are asking: Isn't it possible in business to do well while doing good?

Based on a substantial body of research I have reviewed, I am convinced that business can do well while doing good. In fact, businesses that follow this path will probably do better in the long run on *all* dimensions, including their financial performance.

## Business Can Do Well While Doing Good

So how do we get there?

We begin by changing the way we keep score.

The only score that counts today is the bottom line—the gains and losses to stockholders. Effects on everybody else, all the others who make the enterprise run smoothly, are counted only in terms of how they affect that bottom line. A job eliminated, a worker terminated, may bother management, but the scorecard says "this is good." No matter how great the pain to employees and their families, it is not acknowledged in the corporate scorecard, the profit and loss statement.

Compare a corporation to a basketball team. Its five players would be the employees, customers, suppliers, communities, and stockholders. In the scoring system used in basketball, every player's goals count; the *team* benefits when anyone scores. But if coaches used the kind of system that corporations use, they would insist on the other four players always passing off to the stockholders; only stockholder goals would count. Here's how the scorecard affects action:

- New safety equipment will protect workers from injury, but the cost means a minus on the bottom line. So safety will suffer.

- If selling adulterated baby formula means a plus to stockholders, after allowing for probable lawsuit losses, the formula will probably be sold.

- If "laying off" senior workers several weeks before they become vested in their retirement benefits would produce more pluses than minuses on the scorecard, then out they will go.

If an action increases the stockholders' bottom line, this arcane corporate calculus calls it good. If it decreases that bottom line, it's bad. Period.

Coaches of athletic teams know they will rarely win if a single player is supported while the rest of the team is sacrificed. They can see this clearly, because they have a rational scoring system. But business managers are now stuck with an irrational scorecard, the profit and loss statement. It shows only the return for stockholders and makes it very difficult to see the effects of putting stockholder interests above those of all other players on the team.

Since a business exists through the investments and efforts of several constituents, it needs a better scorecard, one that will report the performance of the enterprise and its managers in providing a fair return, a profit, to all stakeholders. And with such a scorecard, workers, customers, and communities could more wisely "vote with their feet" in channeling their contributions and resources into the companies that represent good investments and away from those that exploit these constituencies in favor of financial investors only.

When top executives find that the more capable workers are going with competitors, customers are drifting away, and communities are unwilling to tolerate toxic emissions without offsetting gains, they will hold managers at all levels responsible for balancing the returns to these several constituencies. As managers are held personally accountable, they will change their decisions. Not all harm will be eliminated, but business will move toward a balance among the several groups that make it work, instead of concentrating all benefits in the basket of the stockholders.

Many believe additional regulation is necessary to control business. Some would go so far as to explicitly regulate decisions made at all levels—decisions such as product content and performance specifications, packaging, production layout, office and shop lighting, individual job descriptions, waste recycling procedures, personnel placement and promotion procedures, plant location, even the number of operating days per year.

Such an approach would require costly, cumbersome, and intrusive monitoring, policing, and enforcement efforts, yet would almost certainly not prevent new and unanticipated problems. In contrast full and fair disclosure to stakeholders will give them the information they need so the marketplace can effectively provide much of the necessary regulation of business; we'll outline such a system of disclosure later in this book.

## Imagining a Society With Accountable Corporations

We have not seen accountable corporations, not in our or our parents' lifetimes. Yes, we may sometimes observe that a particular corporation seems to be a responsible citizen or a good place to work. We may come to like, and develop a loyalty to, particular products. The better corporations will look good on one or another dimension, but it would surely be difficult to identify a corporation that is accountable on all fronts, to all stakeholders—one that provides meaningful, secure, and fair employment; products we trust and want to keep buying; fair returns to suppliers, lenders, and stockholders; a good citizen to the community and the nation.

But even if we found such a corporation, we know it could change virtually overnight. Regardless of how good it looks today, or how committed the CEO is to social responsibility, sooner or later the inexorable tyranny of the bottom line will work its power.

Later in this book we will see how to achieve corporate account-ability. But it might be helpful to first imagine how an accountable corporation would look. Call it Quality Corporation. The stated purpose of Quality Corporation is to serve all its stakeholders: its customers, workers, stockholders, community, suppliers, and society.

Quality Corporation manufactures and sells automobiles. That is the present product line, but its research and development department is constantly seeking ways to better serve society's transportation needs. In the meantime the automobiles it produces have safety designed in. They are fuel efficient and are priced and sold to represent fair values. Different models appeal to different needs and wants, but Quality Corporation does not engage in the kind of advertising that creates the perception of need where none exists. It does not, for example, promote speed and excessive horsepower as symbols of virility.

For long-term growth that will enable it to continue to provide a fair return to all stakeholders, Quality Corporation is operated to generate more resources (cash, materials, labor, equipment) than it uses. It uses resources to design better products, ones that customers want. It uses resources to pay fair wages and benefits to its employees. It uses resources to pay fair prices to suppliers, with fair terms. It uses resources to pay the community and society for the roads, police and fire protection, education system, and other public services they provide. It uses resources to pay lenders and stockholders for the use of their capital.

In other words, Quality Corporation pays a fair return on the investments of all its stakeholders. When the surplus of resources generated over resources used builds to a level that is beyond the needs of prudent growth and expansion, "dividends" are distributed equitably to all stakeholders through price discounts, worker bonuses, payments to stockholders, contributions to charities, even rebates to especially reliable suppliers (a number of court cases have sanctioned such distributions to stakeholders).

It is often said that business must make a profit to survive. This is an oversimplification, but it's true enough that, over time, a business must obtain as many resources as it uses. Quality Corporation readily meets this standard. It operates at a profit—but a profit to *all* its stake-holders. This is different from saying that Quality Corporation operates at a profit in the traditional sense—the traditional accounting profit that ignores effects on stakeholders other than stockholders.

What makes Quality Corporation behave responsibly toward its stakeholders? The key is its scorekeeping system, a new system that is more rational and more useful than the traditional "bottom line."

Quality Corporation is accountable through standard, periodic reports to stakeholders. Executives, managers, and other decision makers at Quality Corporation know that the effects of their decisions will be reviewed by stakeholders. A decision to charge customers more in order to raise wages will be carefully audited by the regular customers and by consumer groups when they receive their stakeholder report; it will also be audited by workers and their unions. A decision to avoid spending money on air pollution control in order to raise stockholder dividends is certain to be audited by public interest groups and community leaders—and of course by stockholders too.

Quality Corporation's managers do not operate behind closed doors, accountable to no one. They have freedom to run the company, but their actions become known to stakeholders, and the stakeholders communicate their views to management and to the media.

Quality Corporation's managers are sort of like your city council members. They have substantial power as well as freedom to exercise their judgment on issues that come before them, but they can also count on hearing from their constituents when they do wrong.

A few of Quality Corporation's managers are so thick-skinned and insular in their thinking that they disregard this feedback, but most are well attuned to it. They have learned that their performance is rewarded when they successfully balance stakeholder interests, and they are liable to be called to account if they favor one group while disregarding the others. The obtuse managers generally receive poor performance ratings, and don't stay around long.

That is why Quality Corporation behaves responsibly to its customers, employees, suppliers, stockholders, community, and society—it *accounts* to them, and they in turn hold the corporation *accountable* for its actions. Laws don't tell Quality Corporation's managers how to act; the managers make their own choices, but they make them in an environment of accountability. In this environment customers have the information they need to fairly evaluate products, workers can see which companies have the best employment records, and communities can assess the costs of corporate pollution and the returns from giving business tax breaks. And managers have full freedom to make ethical decisions that don't sacrifice jobs, quality, safety, or public resources on the altar of the bottom line.

This is the way all corporations could behave. But we must first have accountability.

For accountability we need a new scorecard, one that will measure corporate success in terms of the corporation's public purpose. It must show the effects on, the returns to, all stakeholders and not just the returns to stockholders. Management—and corporate—performance will be tallied up in terms of the effects on all stakeholders; with adequate information, stakeholders, acting in their own best interests, will reward responsible corporations and penalize irresponsible ones.

Does this sound utopian?

Was it utopian when Congress required manufacturers to make public the quantities of toxic chemicals released into the atmosphere (the Toxic Release Inventory, or TRI)? This disclosure led to a 35-percent reduction in toxic emissions in just four years.[16] Was it utopian when we required airlines to report their on-time performance? Once that information started getting out, their performance certainly improved. Was it utopian when community right-to-know laws were passed that require reports on toxic and dangerous substances? Ask the firefighters who are still alive because they were able to know before going into a burning warehouse whether those barrels were filled with explosive toxics. Was it utopian when we required corporations to provide audited financial reports, or would we rather go back to the financial shenanigans of the 1920s and suffer another 1929?

Now imagine this scenario: You turn on the evening news and hear, "Ajax Corporation released its stakeholder report today. It shows that 25,000 workers were exposed to asbestos poisoning during the past year!" Or "Despite claims to the contrary, Behemoth Corporation continues to lag far behind industry standards in affording equal opportunity for women and minorities. This station's analysis, compiled from Behemoth's stakeholder report and those of other companies in the industry, shows Behemoth is dead last in promoting women and minorities to the ranks of management." And "We have the CEOs of these companies with us in the studio. Gentlemen, how do you explain these deplorable results?"

Information is a powerful tool. Full and fair disclosure will not solve all of the problems with our business system, but it *can* empower the marketplace to discipline corporations and bring about more responsible behavior.

And it can be a giant step toward restoring corporations to their original and rightful purpose—serving the interests of the public that grants their charters and life, instead of serving the narrow special interests of financial investors. Business can be fun, and it can be "profitable" to us all. But first we have to overcome the tyranny of the bottom line.

## Notes

1. Courtroom statement of Judge Miles W. Lord, Chief U. S. District Judge for Minnesota, on February 29, 1984, cited in Morton Mintz, *At Any Cost: Corporate Greed, Women, and the Dalkon Shield* (New York: Pantheon Books, 1985), 267.

2. Catherine Breslin, "Day of Reckoning," *Ms. Magazine*, June 1989, 46–52.

3. For details on the Dalkon Shield issue, see Morton Mintz, "A Crime Against Women: A. H. Robins and the Dalkon Shield," *Multinational Monitor* (15 January 1986): 1–7; "For Many Dalkon Shield Claimants Settlement Won't End the Trauma," *The Wall Street Journal*, 9 March 1988; "Judge Ready to Approve Robins Plan," *The New York Times*, 19 July 1988; Russell Mokhiber, *Corporate Crime and Violence* (San Francisco: Sierra Club Books, 1988), 149–62.

4. W. E. Halal, "A Return-on-Resources Model of Corporate Performance," *California Management Review* (summer 1977): 23–33, has

proposed calculating a return-on-resources (ROR) for investors, employees, customers, the public, and associated companies. Resources invested by employees, for example, would include upbringing, education, training, and health. He suggests that, in at least one hypothetical case, the ROR would have been around 4.5 percent for employees, 17.3 percent for customers, and a negative 1.4 percent for the public.

5. Robert L. Heilbroner et al., *In the Name of Profit* (Garden City, N.Y.: Doubleday, 1972), 241.

6. Plato, *Dialogues, Apology,* Cited in *Bartlett's Familiar Quotations,* 15th ed. (Boston: Little Brown, 1980), 83.

7. Milton Friedman, "The Social Responsibility of Business Is to Increase Its Profits," *The New York Times Sunday Magazine,* 13 September 1970, 146.

8. "American Home Plans to Cut 4,000 More Jobs," *The New York Times,* 25 January 1995.

9. A. M. Rosenthal, "The Real Revolution," *The New York Times,* 6 January 1995.

10. Lester Thurow, "The New World of Work," *The Boston Globe,* 16 August 1994.

11. Lisa Baggerman, "The Futility of Downsizing," *Industry Week,* 18 January 1993, 27, 29.

12. Readers Report, *Business Week,* 24 October 1994, 14.

13. Letters, *Time,* 13 December 1993, 11.

14. "We Forgot to Write a Headline, But It's Not Our Fault," *The New York Times,* 19 February 1995.

15. "Reich, Redefining 'Competitiveness,'" *The Washington Post,* 24 September 1994.

16. "An Embarrassment of Clean Air," *Business Week,* 31 May 1993, 34.

# Part One
# The Root of the Problem

# 2

# *The Perversion of Corporate Purpose*

THE STORY OF a benign creation that turns on its maker has been told many times, in many ways.

It is the story of Pandora's box from Greek mythology, which released all the mortal evils and was so difficult to close. It is the story of the jinns, or geniis, of Arabic tales who could not be put back into the bottle; of Rabbi Löw's *Der Golem*; Goethe's "*The Sorcerer's Apprentice*"; Frankenstein's monster; Capek's *R.U.R.*; the 1993 movie *Jurassic Park*. It is even the story of the sheriff in our Old West history, especially as portrayed in the movies: the frontier town in desperation hires a gunslinger to rid it of the outlaws, but when that job is finished, the new sheriff stays to tyrannize the townfolks.

And it is the story of this book: how we created the corporation for the public good and how that creation on occasion has turned and abused us. Most importantly, it is the story of a perverse scorekeeping system that is the engine that drives corporate misbehavior.

◆ ◆ ◆ ◆ ◆

There were no giant corporations 150 years ago; now they dominate our nation. Just five generations past, this arrangement would have been incomprehensible. Our forebears would be astounded to learn that the simple corporate system they created had swollen until it was out of control of the society that created them.

For more than two hundred years after Plymouth Rock, corporations were chartered to serve society.[1] They were created for a specific public purpose, to perform a task that individual citizens or the established but limited governments could not do better. Even then they were usually limited to twenty or fewer years of life.

Corporations still do good and necessary things. However, when they do good now, they do so not as an end, not as their reason for being, but as a way of increasing the bottom line. When we benefit, we know this is merely a fortunate by-product. But too often we do not benefit; we do not get fair value for our purchase price or our work; or we are even directly harmed.

There have been backlashes against the abuses produced by the concentration of corporate power, including Teddy Roosevelt's trust-busting; the organization of labor unions; standards for financial reporting; and regulations on pollution, discrimination, workplace dangers, and adulterated and dangerous products. But in spite of these, the corporation has greater power today than ever and is little constrained by legal or social controls.

We charter our corporations through state action, and state action can only be justified in the public interest. But corporations no longer claim to serve the public interest. Their purpose has been perverted to where they now seek only profit. When the public loses, the explanation is a glib "that's the way the economic system works." This chapter tells the important story of how this occurred.

## In the Beginning

In the beginning corporations were chartered by monarchs to serve the interests of the state. These sovereigns may have harbored less-than-noble objectives, and they may have abused their powers, but in their time (and still today in monarchies) they embodied the political power and the interests of the society. Democracies later adopted this tradition

> Early in the century it was not considered justifiable to create
> corporations for any purpose not clearly public in nature.
>
> John P. Davis, *Corporations*,[2] writing in the 1800s

of chartering corporations to serve a public interest. "The development
of the corporation," according to business historian Ross Robertson,
"was in reality the transformation of an instrument of communal service to accommodate the demands of a new industrial age."[3]

Investors were allowed a return as an inducement to fund the corporation, but providing a return to financial investors was secondary to
the corporation's real purpose, which was to provide a *public* return, a
public benefit. (When the early commonwealth of Massachusetts chartered a turnpike company, for example, this was not done to benefit the
corporation's investors; it was done to benefit the citizens of Massachusetts.) The elevation of stockholder interests above those of the
state, of the public, came later. According to David Finn in *The Corporate Oligarch*, "It was not until the middle of the nineteenth century that
a profit-making commitment to stockholders was formulated as the
major corporate goal. In the process, what was once management's
obligation to contribute to the public good became a matter of [the
manager's] personal taste."[4]

The early corporations were created essentially as extensions of the
government, to carry on public functions that the state did not have the
organization or resources to perform. As Mark Green and Joel Seligman testified before Congress, "They were created for the purpose of
enabling the public to realize a social good without direct government
participation."[5] This objective was to be accomplished without a permanent growth in the state bureaucracy. (Today governments still "del-
egate" certain public functions to private corporations in areas such
as waste disposal, transportation systems, experiments with privately
operated prisons, production of military weapons, and development of
nuclear power.)

The earliest corporations to deserve the name were ecclesiastical organizations, in a time when religion was very much a concern of the state. Next came municipalities, universities, guilds, and livery companies. These were followed by corporations chartered to exploit foreign lands—the Russia or Muscovy Company, the Levant (Turkey) Company, the Jamestown Company, the East India Trading Company (whose purpose was "to supplement the spice trade of the Levant Company by opening a direct trade route to the Indies by way of the Cape of Good Hope"[6]).

A corporation's charter was subject to revocation when the state became able to assume the function or when the corporation overstepped its franchise. Hence the Turkey Company's charter was revoked in 1825, and the East India Trading Company's in 1874.

America's colonization was accomplished largely through corporations: the Jamestown Company, the Massachusetts Bay Company, the Plymouth Company, the London Company. "The government of England . . . aimed to secure the development of colonies, a public purpose, through the stimulation of private interest by grants of political and commercial privileges."[7] The governmental function of these colonizing corporations is seen clearly in the subsequent adoption of their charters as state constitutions.[8]

As the colonizing corporations metamorphosed into colonies, the weak colonial governments in turn looked to chartered private corporations to meet public needs. These early American corporations mainly provided transport, water, insurance, library, and banking services.[9] "At its origin in Massachusetts the corporation was conceived as

The Virginia Company was considered a patriotic enterprise whose mission was to extend the bounds of English civilization by finding wealth, providing jobs for England's unemployed, civilizing and Christianizing the Indians, and developing new products for sale at home.

Jamestown (Virginia) Museum display[10]

an agency of government, endowed with public attributes, exclusive privileges, and political power, and *designed to serve a social function for the state*"[11] [emphasis added].

Inevitably corporate charters were extended, especially as the nineteenth century progressed, to other types of enterprise less concerned with the public interest, such as manufacturing. Many, including legislators, saw such corporations as dangerous.[12] Fearing this "nonhuman person, without conscience or soul, who could roam the world at will,"[13] they demanded that corporations be restricted. Limitations imposed on corporate charters by state legislatures included a time duration, usually twenty years or less, full liability of stockholders for corporate debts, a narrow interpretation of charters, and a reserve clause that allowed the legislature to amend any charter at any time for any reason.[14]

The people feared big corporations, but they were sought by developing states to stimulate settlement and growth. Interstate competition quickly altered the climate, and soon states were prostrating themselves before corporations with inducements, benefits, and a general relaxation of restrictions. Populist concerns were swept aside; the corporation was king. States would seemingly stop at nothing to woo them, until Delaware finally outran the rest in the race to the bottom. By becoming the easiest and most hospitable state for incorporation, Delaware established the lowest common denominator of restrictions.

What states were doing in the 1800s, cities and communities continue today. Dowries are offered to corporations far out of proportion to possible community benefits. Citizens and other, usually smaller, businesses pick up the tab. Corporations are bribed, pampered, wooed, and worshipped. They are protected by the law, granted benefits through their charters, and courted by communities. No longer are they held to a standard of public service.

How did we go from the useful instrument of public will to the twentieth century corporation that seeks only to maximize its bottom line? How was the corporation's purpose perverted from serving the public interest to exploiting that public interest for private ends? This is an important story that has gone largely unrecognized and untold by historians, economists, and politicians.

The prevalence of the corporation in America has led men of this generation to act, at times, as if the privilege of doing business in corporate form were inherent in the citizen; and has led them to accept the evils attendant upon the free and unrestricted use of the corporate mechanism as if these evils were the inescapable price of civilized life and, hence, to be borne with resignation. Throughout the greater part of our history a different view prevailed. Although the value of this instrumentality in commerce and industry was fully recognized, incorporation for business was commonly denied long after it had been freely granted for religious, educational and charitable purposes. It was denied because of fear. Fear of encroachment upon the liberties and opportunities of the individual. Fear of the subjection of labor to capital. Fear of monopoly. Fear that the absorption of capital by corporations, and their perpetual life, might bring evils similar to those which attended mortmain. There was a sense of some insidious menace inherent in large aggregations of capital, particularly when held by corporations.

Justice Brandeis, in *Ligget vs. Lee*[15]

## The Loss of Accountability

In the beginning sovereigns, or their personal agents, monitored corporations and decided whether they were adequately serving their public purpose and whether their charter should continue. Were trade routes being opened successfully? Was the intended ferry or water or postal service being provided? "The accomplishment of the corporate purposes was ensured by the visitation of civil corporations by the king through the court of king's bench. . . ."[16] If further performance information was desired from the corporation, its production could be ordered at will.

Sovereigns could demand accountability; they held the power of life and death. Early financial investors had no such power. To protect their investments early stockholders—capitalists with money at risk in the corporation—hired accountants to monitor and report on their investments. This was especially important with trading companies and other corporations operating in foreign lands, far removed from the investor's home.

The investors' agents did little more than count what came in, what went out, and how much was on hand.[17] Even as enterprises grew in size, this did not change substantially. It was easy enough to count (or weigh, or measure) gold coins, sheep, horses, bolts of cloth, or bushels of grain. One could not so readily "count" the success of an enterprise, the quality of goods, or something like job safety, especially in a time when placing a value on a worker's injury would have presented even greater moral and religious questions than it might today.

In the first part of the nineteenth century, corporations increased in number but not so much in size. The new states, competing with each other for growth, passed more and more liberal incorporation laws. Meanwhile Americans were becoming egalitarian in their attitude toward corporations. Followers of Andrew Jackson and other small-*d* democrats were saying, "If this is such a good way to do business then we ought to let everybody in on it. It should not be just for the rich."

The years following the Civil War saw almost explosive growth in the size of some businesses. Rapacious, predatory tycoons, men like Cornelius Vanderbilt, Jay Gould, John D. Rockefeller, Daniel Drew, Andrew Carnegie, and J. Pierpont Morgan—all celebrated in Matthew Josephson's *The Robber Barons*[18]—were building giant corporate empires as often as not through unscrupulous, violent, and criminal means.

These robber barons were secretive and distrustful. They wanted to be accountable to no one. Vanderbilt, for example, "carried all his book-keeping accounts in his own head and trusted no one with them." Drew did likewise.[19] Much like earlier sovereigns, they assessed the performance of their enterprises by personal observations and by calling subordinates to account. Formal procedures and formal structures were disdained.

But corporations grew ever larger, too large for one person to oversee and comprehend. As the corporations spread westward with the nation, decentralization became necessary and inevitable. The tycoons' wealth and greed and appetite for power produced an acquisition spree that later came to be known as the merger movement, not greatly unlike the takeover frenzy of the 1980s.

The simple structure of the early corporations had now evolved into a complex entity organized into many divisions and branches, territories, and subsidiaries. These had to be monitored, evaluated, and scored. The tycoons, the owner-managers, may have disdained a formal scorekeeping system; the professional managers whom they hired to run their far-flung empires were more bureaucratic. They didn't manage by "gut" feel or the seat of their pants. They believed in numbers. They wanted performance reports. But there was no mechanism in place for scoring the corporation, for assessing and reporting its performance in fulfilling its chartered purpose.

There was, however, another mechanism already in place. This was the simple system that stockholders' agents had first set up to report to their principals on how well their investments were doing. It was never intended to show the performance of the corporation as a whole, in terms of its chartered purpose. But it *existed*. It was on hand. And it looked reasonable. So the professional managers of these expanding corporations turned to this simplistic and inapplicable system as a measure of corporate performance.

It was as if a teacher, lacking a grading system for a class, turned to the record of attendance. Then in short order, attendance alone became the criterion of performance.

The system to which they turned did not count accidents on the job, or reports from customers of defective or dangerous products, or the amount of coal soot and smoke emitted over a city. It counted benefits and costs to only one of the groups affected by the corporation's activities, the stockholders, and not the effects on the corporation's other constituencies.

Its scorecard looked like this:

| | |
|---|---|
| Benefits to stockholders | $xxx |
| Costs to stockholders | xxx |
| Net profit/loss to *stock*holders | $xxx |

It did not look like this:

| | |
|---|---|
| Benefits to employees | $xxx |
| Benefits to customers | xxx |
| Benefits to stockholders | xxx |
| Benefits to suppliers | xxx |
| Benefits to lenders | xxx |
| Benefits to neighboring communities | xxx |
| Benefits to society | xxx |
| Total benefits generated | $xxx |
| | |
| Costs to employees | $xxx |
| Costs to customers | xxx |
| Costs to stockholders | xxx |
| Costs to suppliers | xxx |
| Costs to lenders | xxx |
| Costs to neighboring communities | xxx |
| Costs to society | xxx |
| Total costs created | $xxx |
| | |
| Net profit/loss to *stake*holders | $xxx |

Some of these benefits and costs may appear to be included in the traditional profit and loss statement, but they are always counted in terms of their benefits and costs to stockholders, not to the other stakeholders. Interest paid, for example, is a benefit to lenders, but it is not counted; it is listed only as a *cost* to stockholders.

This superficial, incomplete scorecard produced a bottom line that came to be accepted as the measure of the corporation's performance, although it reflected only the performance for stockholders and not performance in terms of the corporation's public purpose—or for the other investors or stakeholders.

Thus a crude arithmetic calculation developed by early accountants to serve the outside capitalists who employed them came to be accepted, not only by stockholders but by everyone, including corporate managers, workers, and the rest of society, as the *standard measure of corporate performance*. The rough measure of results arbitrarily called profit is now everywhere taken as the corporation's *score*. And all the effects on other stakeholders that were left out of these early, special-purpose calculations are left out of this corporate scorecard today as well.

(The deficiencies of this scorecard, this corporate profit and loss statement, may be better understood by going through the "quiz" in Exhibit I toward the end of this chapter. You may want to take a short break now and see how you do on it.)

*The bottom line is not now and was never a rational measure of the corporation's performance.* We need to do now what should have been done at the outset: develop a new and valid scorecard that measures corporate performance against the purpose for which the corporation exists.

## The Purpose of the Corporation

But what is that purpose?

Since corporations were at first chartered by the sovereign, and this role was then assumed by the newly democratic states, we must look to the sovereign state for its purpose in chartering corporations. States and state governments, like national governments, are formed to "promote the general welfare." Their actions, including the chartering of corporations, are taken (or are supposed to be taken) in pursuit of that broad objective. We saw at the beginning of this chapter that, historically, charters were granted to corporations explicitly for a public purpose, and not to serve the narrow interests of the few at the expense of the many. Clearly, then, corporations were chartered and their charters are allowed to continue to promote the general welfare, to serve the broad public interests of the state and its people.

The public interest may be served in several ways: providing needed products and services at fair prices, creating jobs, and paying taxes. The public interest can also be harmed in a variety of ways, such as through discrimination, adulterated products, pollution, congestion, bribery, and other illegal activities.

This, then, is how corporations should be evaluated, how their performance should be measured and reported: *We should ask how well and in what ways the corporation has served, and how it has harmed, the public interest—because there is no other reason for us to charter corporations and to grant them special business privileges.* To begin to restore corporations to their public purpose, we need a new corporate scorecard that will measure the corporation's performance against this standard. As long as the scorecard is incomplete and counts the wrong things, corporate managers will direct their behavior and decisions so they look well on that irrelevant scorecard.

This may be easier to see with a professional sports team, such as the basketball team that was introduced in Chapter 1. The team is the entity in which we are interested; neither the owner nor the individual players constitute the entity, the team. From the owner's perspective, it is of course interesting to know how much profit or loss was earned by the team (although this may not be the only or even the most exciting result). Players might want to know how much each earned and how each player's reputation and future prospects were affected by a season's play. But neither the owner's nor the players' perspectives adequately reflect the purpose of the team. The team exists in the first place to win games, perhaps the playoffs and the league championship. This is its primary objective.

To measure and report on an organization's performance, we must know its objectives. For the basketball team, we report the win-loss record and relative standing in the league. We also occasionally hear that a team is or is not profitable, or that a player was signed for a record sum, but these do not represent the primary measures of the team's performance as an entity.

So it must be for a corporation as well. Its objectives, as an entity, cannot be found by looking to the stockholders; that will reveal the *stockholders'* objectives, not those of the entity.

It may be tempting to say that we must look to or inside the corporate entity for its objectives, but that is also a fruitless line of reasoning. The corporate entity, beyond its physical components, its employees, its contracts, exists only as a social construct, an abstraction, an artificial being—albeit one now granted specific rights and privileges.

The objectives of corporations must be sought in the reasons we, as citizens acting through our governments, grant them charters and special privileges. By examining these reasons, we may determine that a corporation's primary objective is to provide safe and useful goods or services at a fair price. Another objective, sometimes secondary but not always, may be to provide jobs. This may become evident as we listen to city commissioners and civic leaders speak of attracting industry. A third objective, related to the second, may be to contribute to the overall economic well-being of a city or region—profit to all, but not solely to the corporation's stockholders.

With an appropriate scorecard, we could evaluate corporations the way we do basketball teams—in terms of the *purpose* of the organization. A relevant scorecard would tell us how well corporations serve their public purpose, and not simply the return paid to one group.

We created corporations to serve the public interest; return to investors was only a means to that end. Now we accept profit to stockholders—the "bottom line"—as the end objective, and any good that may come to the rest of us, as customers, workers, and neighbors of the corporation, is only a by-product at best and too often accompanied by costs we would rather avoid.

## The Manager Held Hostage

When the public learns of corporate abuse, some think of scheming, greedy corporate managers. Terms like "fat cats" and "robber barons" may be used. There are undoubtedly corporate managers who are mean, selfish, and narrow-minded; some may be cruel, even capable of great evil. But corporate managers, for the most part, are like you and me, except that they've spent a good part of their lives in the corporate system. That system, and the peculiar way it keeps score, holds them hostage.

Let's go back to our basketball team. The coach is giving a pep talk before a game.

> All right, if we win today we've got a shot at the playoffs. Let's go out there and play the way we know how . . . mentally alert . . . no letdowns on defense. Concentrate on your assignments. I don't want to see any solo hot-dogging—this is a *team*. We're gonna win this thing and go all the way, but everybody has to pull together. And we're going to win it clean. I see anybody starting a fight, you've got a $1,000 fine. Now let's go!

Well, maybe I'll never make it as a basketball coach, but you get the idea. If you're a player you know what's expected of you. You know what you're supposed to do, how you're supposed to play. Now let's listen to a different pep talk.

> This franchise is not making enough money. We need to draw more fans, and to do that we've got to put on a show. Winning's fine, but excitement is what brings the fans out. I want some really high-flyin' jammin' tonight. Every slam dunk's worth a $500 bonus. It you can break a backboard, that's just fine with me—fans love it. We may be a stronger team when we slow it down, but the fans really don't like that. So we're gonna run, run, run. And we're gonna be aggressive. I want to see you get tough out there. Show some spirit, maybe get mad a little. You get into a fight, I'll back you up. There's nothing like a good free-for-all to get the crowd's adrenalin flowing. Our attendance jumps whenever we have a brawl. So get out there and *kill!*

It's clear what this coach is looking for, what he's going to count. If you're a player you'll know what you're supposed to do when you get out on the floor.

What we count when we keep score tells the players how to act. This is as true for corporate managers as it is for basketball players. And in corporations, the scorekeeping system now in use establishes one clear goal: "maximize the bottom line." This is translated into subgoals for every division and unit in the corporation, all of which say, in essence, "always take that action that will be best for the bottom line; nothing else counts." If people lose their jobs or communities get poisoned, but earnings per share go up, by the present corporate scorecard the manager has done well.

◆ ◆ ◆ ◆ ◆

Let's see just how the scorecard defines the corporate ethic as it works its way on some pretty decent people. Say your next door neighbor, Ed Casey, is the personnel manager of a national manufacturing company; he's been with his company twenty years now. Ed has always seemed to be a nice guy with an upstanding family, one kid in college and one a year away.

Ed has been called to a meeting with "Hank" Dale, the company president; Gertrude Burk, marketing vice president; and Mark Clayton, the controller. Dale opens the meeting.

HANK:  I called this meeting to make a decision about our plant in Dodge City, Kansas. Let's go over the numbers I asked you to put together, Mark.

MARK:  Okay. Dodge City's revenue has trended upward steadily over the past ten years. In that same time it's managed to reduce variable costs about 10 percent. Fixed costs have stayed pretty constant. So the profit has been growing and is not bad in absolute terms. I guess a lot of businesses would like to have its profit.

The problem is with how that profit relates to the investment in assets, the return on investment. The plant is producing about 18.5 percent, while our corporate average not counting Dodge City is 20 percent. Dodge City has been improving, but with its labor and shipping costs, I don't see how it's going to be able to get over about 19 percent in the foreseeable future.

HANK:  So if we stay in Dodge City, we get an 18.5-percent ROI, and that drags us down overall. Now what did you get when you ran the Dodge City operation in with our plant in Mexico?

MARK:  Our Tijuana plant has been running pretty close to the figures
we projected when we opened it five years ago. Mainly because
we don't have to have the same degree of pollution control
and the labor costs are much lower, its ROI is just under 21 percent, the highest of any of our five plants. With the present setup
I don't see any reason for that rate to go down in the near
future.

You asked me to also project what Tijuana would look like
if we moved the Dodge City operation down there. Tijuana
would have to increase its labor force by about a third, and
that would push its labor costs up some—not too much,
though, because Tijuana is a pretty big labor market and any
new growth there brings in new entry-level workers from the
boonies. And we get a good tax deal from Mexico. So our best
estimate is that moving the Dodge City operation down there
would bring the Tijuana return on investment down just a little, probably to around 20.5 percent.

GERTRUDE:  So the present Tijuana ROI is 21 percent, and it would go
down to 20.5 percent if we move Dodge City's business down
there. Since the Dodge City work would bring the Tijuana average down, that means Dodge City's share would be producing
even less than 20.5 percent. How much would you expect the new
business in Tijuana, the Dodge City business, to earn.

MARK:  We ran the numbers on that. We estimate it at approximately
19.4 percent.

HANK:  From the numbers it looks clear to me: we need to close Dodge
City and move its work to Tijuana. But first we need to be sure
there would be no unexpected marketing problems, Gertrude.

GERTRUDE:  Just from the marketing standpoint, I wouldn't see any
problems. We've digested the operation in Tijuana pretty well,
and now with NAFTA the Tijuana and San Diego transportation
arrangements can easily handle the increase in volume.

HANK:  And Ed, would you see any problem in getting the labor we
would need in Tijuana?

ED: Well, no, I don't think there'd be any problem there. We've got our own management team well installed in Tijuana. The line workers are basically unskilled, and like Mark said, Tijuana seems to attract as much labor as it needs.

But we haven't talked about another problem. What about the workers in Dodge City?

HANK: Yeah, what do we have there, about 2,000? Well, we can give those that want to an opportunity to transfer, can't we?

ED: Transfer? Pack up their home and family and move to Tijuana to earn less than our minimum wage?

HANK: Well what the hell, nobody's gonna *make* them. That's their choice. But if they don't want to transfer, then they can't complain about losing their job. Besides, they'll have sixty days notice. The government makes us give them that.

ED: Wait a minute, Hank. Be reasonable. Nobody's gonna transfer. There will just be 2,000 human beings out of work in Dodge City. They'll get sixty days notice, but no severance pay. Some will find other jobs there, but look, it's not that big a town, only about 18,000 altogether, I think, and the labor force is just some fraction of that. Besides, the Dodge City economy is already depressed. The oil business is in the dumps and the big meat packing plant is laying off a new bunch every month. Sixty days notice or a one-day notice, our people—or at least we used to call them our people—are still just gonna be 2,000 new names on the unemployment roles. The young ones will have to hit the road and a lot of the older ones are going to be out of work from now on.

MARK: Ed, all that may be true, but look at the numbers. Our responsibility as executives is to run this company *to maximize profit*. If we can get a higher return in Tijuana than in Dodge City, then, by George, I think we have to take it.

ED: Mark, you know we've got plenty of discretion in decisions like this. We can take into account the effects on our workers and their communities, even if the profit is reduced. The courts have said so. And in this case we're only talking about the difference between, what was it, 18.5 percent or 19 percent in Dodge versus 19.4 percent in Tijuana. If anybody complained, and I doubt if they would, the courts would certainly uphold a decision to sacrifice a mere 1 percent or less in return on investment if it meant preserving 2,000 jobs in this country and not wrecking a community.

HANK:  Yeah, that may be what the courts say, but the courts don't write our balance sheet. And if we can make that sucker look better, that's what we're hired to do. I'm not going to preside over a company that didn't earn every damned dime it could!

ED:  Even if we earn it over the wrecked lives of our own employees? Even if we devastate a town like Dodge City in the process?

HANK:  Hey, Ed, you work for the same company I do. You've got a pretty fine job here. It's that old balance sheet that pays your salary and is gonna put your kids through college. I'm sorry as hell for those Dodge City employees, and I'm sorry for Dodge City. It's gonna be rough out there. But that's the way the cookie crumbles. They all know that. We're not an employment agency, and we're not social workers. Our job is to pay attention to the bottom line. If we can get it up, we'd better damned well do it.

ED:  Maybe so, Hank. I guess we don't have any choice, if Mark's figures are right. But, gee, I'm sure not gonna sleep well over this.

HANK:  Wait till we get the profit and loss statements after the move, Ed. They'll help you sleep. Now, all in favor of closing Dodge City in, say, ninety days and moving the operation lock, stock, and barrel to Tijuana?

MARK:  Aye.

GERTRUDE:  Aye.

ED:  Aye, I guess.

HANK:  Good. It's unanimous. Ed, better get the notices out right away.

◆ ◆ ◆ ◆ ◆

This scenario could be repeated and expanded a thousandfold, always with the same conclusion. When the scorekeeper counts points scored, the team tries to score points. When the scorekeeper counts slam dunks and fights, the team plays by a different standard. So too in the corporation. If the scorekeeper counted benefits to workers, to customers, and to communities, then managers would behave one way. But if the scorekeeper counts only profit to stockholders, then managers—at all levels in the company—will play by that standard.

The manager is held hostage by the scorekeeping system. And the manager's decisions determine the corporation's behavior and its effects on us. The corporation now is too often an amoral agent of iniquity, doing harm in the name of profit. Any good that might be done for society is a coincidental means to higher profits and not an end in itself. With a scorekeeping system that counted effects on all stakeholders, the corporation could be a powerful force for social progress, for a better life for everyone. *The corporation could regain its original purpose, its public purpose.*

The challenge we face is to restore our corporations to their public purpose, to redefine our measures of corporate performance so the bottom line is only one component of success and not the whole. This will require corporate accountability. At the end of this book, we'll lay out a plan for achieving *corporate accountability.*

At this point some will be troubled. Isn't the corporation controlled by its stockholders? Doesn't it derive its power from them? How can we talk about corporate accountability to anybody else? If the stockholders hold the power, why would they give any up in favor of other stakeholders?

We'll consider these questions in the next chapter. What we'll see is well known to serious students of the corporate form of business organization: large corporations are generally not controlled, except in rare circumstances, by their stockholders or by any other external entity. Powerful corporate enterprises are, in the main, unconstrained by any social, legal, or financial institution. They are accountable to no one for their substantial power.

## Exhibit I .  A Little Quiz

How well can you "read" corporations? Here's a little quiz. Based on the following data from the traditional scorecards used by Wall Street for a recent year, which is the best company?

|  | Company A | Company B | Company C | Company D |
|---|---|---|---|---|
| Net income ($ millions) | 232 | 152 | 1,842 | 116 |
| Earnings per share | $1.76 | $1.91 | $7.75 | $1.88 |
| Return on investment in assets | 3% | 18% | 10% | 7% |
| Return on stockholders' investment | 21% | 32% | 30% | 11% |

Ranking these companies, with 1 the highest, gives:

|  | Company A | Company B | Company C | Company D |
|---|---|---|---|---|
| Net income | 2 | 3 | 1 | 4 |
| Earnings per share | 4 | 2 | 1 | 3 |
| Return on investment in assets | 4 | 1 | 2 | 3 |
| Return on stockholders' investment | 3 | 1 | 2 | 4 |
| Composite ranking | 3.3 | 1.75 | 1.5 | 3.5 |

How would an accountant or a Wall Street analyst respond to our quiz? They would undoubtedly give higher ratings to Companies C and B and lower ones to A and D.

Now what are the companies? In alphabetical order, but not necessarily in the order shown above, the four companies are Maytag, Philip Morris, Polaroid, and Union Carbide. Before we see which is which, let's consider some information that the present scorecard does not provide.

**The Maytag Company** is lauded in *The 100 Best Companies to Work for in America* for its wages ("higher than the competition"), employee benefits ("one of the most generous in the industry"), incentive payments, and product quality control.[20] In *Rating America's Corporate Conscience*, the Council on Economic Priorities commends Maytag's community relationships ("like a mutual admiration society"), product quality, premium wages, benefit packages, union harmony, and employee participation and communication.[21] Maytag appears as a company managed for the benefit of all of its stakeholders.

**Polaroid Corporation** is another firm that appears to rank high on stakeholder management. According to the Council on Economic Priorities, "whether it concerns involvement in South Africa, employee relations, charitable giving, or job training for youth, Polaroid's initiatives have been imaginative, innovative, and forceful."[22] This company directly subsidizes employee child-care expenses and reimburses 100 percent of worker tuition costs. It was an early supporter of "right-to-know" laws requiring companies to inform employees of the presence and potential dangers of toxic chemicals used in the workplace. These programs, coupled with a strong record on equal employment opportunity, also earned Polaroid a ranking as one of the 100 best companies to work for in America.[23]

The investigative magazine *Multinational Monitor* charged that **Philip Morris**'s products killed 75,000 people in 1987, justifying this company's ranking among their "10 Worst Corporations of 1988";[24] it was still on the magazine's "10 Worst" list in 1994.[25] Philip Morris makes cigarettes. It vigorously opposes legislation regulating smoking in offices and public places, legislation that, according to its supporters, seeks only a fair balance between smokers' and nonsmokers' rights.

Critics blame Philip Morris for seducing youth into smoking by glamorizing cigarettes through sponsorship of youth-oriented music and sporting events. With lung cancer now the leading cause of cancer deaths among women, the company has been especially faulted for its sponsorship of the Virginia Slims women's pro-tennis tour. Additionally, through its Miller and Seven-Up subsidiaries Philip Morris has fought legislation to promote recycling of beer and soft drink bottles.[26] But Philip Morris was also ranked among the 100 best companies to work for, primarily on the basis of its employee benefits—benefits that include the dubious perquisite of a free carton of cigarettes every week.[27]

**Union Carbide** is of course the company charged with leaking toxic gases that caused thousands of deaths and hundreds of thousands of injuries in Bhopal, India, the company that then rushed to sell off many of its assets, distribute the proceeds to stockholders, and thus deprive the victims of fair compensation.[28] And in a similar incident on a lesser scale in Institute, West Virginia, Union Carbide became the company charged with OSHA's largest fine up to that date.[29]

Like Philip Morris, Union Carbide earned the questionable distinction of being named to *Multinational Monitor*'s list of "10 worst corporations."[30] The magazine cited Union Carbide for running a plant in Bhopal that was inadequately designed and incapable of containing or neutralizing a methyl isocyanate reaction; for inadequately training its workforce to cope with emergencies and leaving it understaffed; and for using methyl isocyanate as an intermediate in the production of carbamate pesticides when a less hazardous method was available.[31] Union Carbide also made the Council on Economic Priorities' rogues gallery of U.S. corporations for its role in South Africa.[32] Not surprisingly, Union Carbide did not make the list of the 100 best companies to work for in America.[33]

Now which is which? Recall that the composite rankings from the Wall Street scorecards, with 1 the highest, were:

| Company A | Company B | Company C | Company D |
|-----------|-----------|-----------|-----------|
| 3.3 | 1.75 | 1.5 | 3.5 |

Company C, with the highest ranking based on these data, is Philip Morris. U.S. Surgeon General C. Everett Koop called its tobacco products a twentieth-century plague. This company's effects on its customers have led it to be labeled a "merchant of death,"[34] but its workers and stockholders like it.

Company B is Maytag. It gets a high rating from just about every-one—customers, workers, neighbors, and stockholders.

Company A is Union Carbide. Wall Street would call it a so-so company. Its neighbors in India and West Virginia would use harsher terms.

Company D is Polaroid. It gets a good rating from workers, but not so good from financial investors.

What do these rankings reveal? They show that the scorecard now being used does not tell customers, workers, or neighboring commu-nities anything useful about how good a corporation is. The so-called profit and return on investment numbers might be of interest to the corporation's stockholders, but they offer no significant information to other stakeholders.

This scorecard is biased. It might say a company is doing great even though it is killing its workers, and it could give a truly good employer a poor rating. It shows only a fraction of a corporation's full performance.

# Notes

1. See John P. Davis, *Corporations: A Study of the Origin and Development of Great Business Combinations and of Their Relation to the Authority of the State* (New York: Capricorn Books, 1961), I: v, 29, 34, 159, 241–42; II: 72–73, 158, 200, 211, 248–49, 269; James Willard Hurst, *The Legitimacy of the Business Corporation in the Law of the United States: 1780–1970* (Charlottesville: The University Press of Virginia, 1970), 15; Ronald E. Seavoy, *The Origins of the American Business Corpora-tion: 1784–1855* (Westport, Conn.: Greenwood Press, 1982), 47–48, 73–74, 254, 257–58.

2. Davis, *Corporations*, II: 269.

3. Ross M. Robertson, *History of the American Economy*, 2nd ed. (New York: Harcourt, Brace & World, 1964), 243.

4. David Finn, *The Corporate Oligarch* (New York: Simon & Schuster, 1969), 53.

5. Senate Committe on Commerce, *Corporate Rights and Responsibilities: Hearing before the Committee on Commerce,* 94th Cong., 2nd sess., June 1976, 216.

6. James Ole Winjum, *The Role of Accounting in the Economic Development of England: 1500–1750* (Urbana, Ill.: Center for International Education and Research in Accounting, 1972), 214.

7. Davis, *Corporations,* II: 158.

8. Ibid.

9. Hurst, *The Legitimacy of the Business Corporation,* 15.

10. Visited by Ralph Estes and noted, March 1992.

11. Oscar Handlin and Mary F. Handlin, "Origins of the American Business Corporation," in Donald Grunewald and Henry L. Bass, *Public Policy and the Modern Corporation* (New York: Appleton-Century-Crofts, 1966), 3-24.

12. Dow Votaw, *Modern Corporations* (Englewood Cliffs, N.J.: Prentice-Hall, 1965), 21.

13. Ibid., 24.

14. Seavoy, *The Origins of the American Business Corporation,* 237.

15. Henry A. Wallace, *Whose Constitution—An Inquiry into the General Welfare* (New York: Reynal & Hitchcock, 1936), 165–66.

16. Davis, *Corporations,* II: 212.

17. Peter Ramsey, "Some Tudor Merchants' Accounts," *Studies in the History of Accounting,* ed. A. C. Littleton and B. S. Yamey (Homewood, Ill.: Richard D. Irwin, 1956), 185–201.

18. Matthew Josephson, *The Robber Barons* (New York: Harcourt, Brace & World, 1962).

19. Josephson, *The Robber Barons,* 14–15, 18.

20. Robert Levering, Milton Moskowitz, and Michael Katz, *The 100 Best Companies to Work for in America* (Reading, Mass.: Addison-Wesley, 1984), 203–05.

21. Steven D. Lydenbert, Alice Tepper Marlin, Sean O'Brien Strub, and the Council on Economic Priorities, *Rating America's Corporate Conscience* (Reading, Mass.: Addison-Wesley, 1986), 156.

22. Lydenbert, Tepper Marlin, and Strub, *Rating America's Corporate Conscience,* 156.

23. Levering, Moskowitz, and Katz, *The 100 Best Companies,* 272–74.
24. Russell Mokhiber and E. Virgil Falloon, "The 10 Worst Corporations of 1988," *Multinational Monitor* (December 1988): 12–20.
25. Russell Mokhiber, "The Ten Worst Corporations of 1994," *Multinational Monitor* (December 1994): 7–16.
26. Lydenbert, Tepper Marlin, and Strub, *Rating America's Corporate Conscience,* 156.
27. Levering, Moskowitz, and Katz, *The 100 Best Companies,* 262–65.
28. David Dembo, Ward Morehouse, and Lucinda Wykle, *Abuse of Power: Social Performance of Multinational Corporations, the Case of Union Carbide* (New York: New Horizons Press, 1990).
29. "Carbide Violations Draw Fine," *The Wichita Eagle-Beacon,* 2 April 1986; "Criticism of Leak Increases," *The Wichita Eagle-Beacon,* 13 August 1985; and "Carbide Chief Says Company Took Too Long to Tell of Leak," *Reno Gazette-Journal,* 17 August 1985.
30. Mokhiber and Falloon, "The 10 Worst Corporations of 1988," 12–20.
31. Ibid.
32. Lydenbert, Tepper Marlin, and Strub, *Rating America's Corporate Conscience,* 156.
33. Levering, Moskowitz, and Katz, *The 100 Best Companies,* 1984.
34. Larry C. White, *Merchants of Death: The American Tobacco Industry* (New York: Beech Tree Books, 1988), 11.

# 3

# Power Without Accountability

## WHO CONTROLS THE CORPORATION?

When Mary Wollstonecraft Shelley's hero, Frankenstein, endowed his synthetic robot with a human heart, the monster which before had been a useful mechanical servant suddenly became an uncontrollable force. Our ancestors feared that corporations had no conscience. We are treated to the colder, more modern fear that, perhaps, they do.

A. A. Berle, Jr., *The 20th Century Capitalist Revolution*[1]

THE POWER EXERCISED by the larger corporations can be substantial—even greater, sometimes, than government (as we'll see in Chapter 4). If corporate power is controlled by one or another institution in our society, then we should look to that institution to ensure that this power is not misused. Or if this power is always exercised benignly, with only beneficial effect, it might not be an issue.

But the tyranny of the bottom line too frequently causes corporate power to be exercised in ways that harm stakeholders. So we need to examine the source of corporate power. Where does it come from? And who—if anyone—controls it?

The corporation, perhaps more than most institutions, is based on a series of myths. Managers serve owners. . . . Shareholders elect representatives to the board of directors. The free market disciplines winners and losers. All the myths have a purpose: to make us believe the corporation is accountable and efficient.

The truth of the matter is that the public corporation has generally been a benevolent autocracy for decades. Managers have run the show. Shareholder meetings have been elaborate ceremonies. Proxy votes have been foreordained rituals. People who have served as directors on boards have usually been friends of the boss.

*Business Week*[2]

In olden times we spoke of the divine right of kings. We laid that notion to rest in the United States with our Revolution. We proclaimed that all power proceeds from the people, that government (but no king, thank you) receives its power from the consent of the governed.

The power that corporations exercise is derived from their charters, granted by the state—that is, by citizens, acting through their state governments. *Thus, the fundamental privilege of existing, and all other privileges of corporations, are bestowed by the people.*

The corporate charter bestows not only power but also great privilege and benefits not available to other business forms such as partnerships and proprietorships. For example:

- A corporation can make contracts in its own name; in partnerships and proprietorships these must be made in the name of a real person.

- A corporation can sue in court to enforce its contracts, just like a human being.

- Corporations have been given many of the rights of citizens, such as freedom of speech. Although corporations aren't mentioned in our Constitution, these rights have been extended through congressional action and court interpretations.

◆ A corporation has unlimited life. A partnership or proprietorship ends when any principal dies or withdraws.

◆ Owners of businesses organized as partnerships and proprietorships face unlimited liability for their companies' actions; creditors can go after the owners' personal assets if the business doesn't pay. But state statutes have provided corporate stockholders with the special privilege of "limited liability." This means that stockholders can only lose the money they put into the corporation; creditors can't look to stockholders' personal assets.

◆ Corporations can issue ownership shares (stock) that may be freely exchanged. In a partnership one partner's interest can't be sold without every other partner agreeing.

Perhaps most importantly, a corporation has the ability to disguise itself, to run and to hide, or to reorganize into a whole new entity. It can sell off divisions and subsidiaries, be taken over and absorbed into a different company, or reorganize and rename itself and emerge as, seemingly, a completely different company. Today's corporation often wasn't yesterday's and can't be counted on to be tomorrow's. It may be better or it may be worse, but it is sure to be different.

Drexel Burnham Lambert, Inc. is a good example. Its image befouled with six felonies plus the legacy of junk bond king Michael Milkin, Drexel used a tax loophole to give itself a whole new identity as the spanking clean New Street Capital Corporation. Drexel, with its felonies, couldn't get a license to run a gambling casino in Puerto Rico it wanted to take over. New Street could—even though it emerged out of Drexel's hide. This special corporate benefit is of course not available to ordinary humans.[3]

Although stockholders, like employees, customers, and communities, provide resources the corporation requires, corporate power and privilege come from the charter granted by the state, not merely from the investments of stockholders. Stockholders don't give the corporation its power, and neither do they control that power.

## Do Stockholders Control the Corporation?

The general view is that corporate power comes from the stockholders because this is what we have been taught.

Corporate management tells us repeatedly that the stockholders control the corporation and have full power over it and them. Some executives may believe this, but for many it is little more than a smoke screen to obscure the fact that *no one* has direct, significant control over top management. There are, to be sure, occasional examples of stockholders turning management out, contesting for control, even rejecting a management recommendation at a stockholders' meeting. For example, the stockholders of Kmart Corporation were able to prevent the sale of interests in its specialty outlets.[4] But we read of such occurrences because they are exceptions and thus newsworthy. Stockholder uprisings that realize any degree of success are exceedingly rare in large corporations. The CEO or a few top executives exercise autocratic control in the great majority of these colossal enterprises.

Accountants have for hundreds of years produced reports for stockholders (although many critics, from both the investment and the accounting communities, find these reports to be sorely lacking). From the very beginning, these accounting statements have measured the corporation's performance in terms of its effects only on stockholders, while ignoring effects on other stakeholders. Through these many years, this practice gradually has elevated the stockholder to a position of absolute primacy.

> Essentially the stockholders, though politely called "owners," are passive. They have the right to receive only. The condition of their being is that they do not interfere in management.
>
> A. A. Berle Jr. *Power Without Property*[5]

We have been taught that stockholders provide the funds that fuel the corporation, and from the funds comes the power. But this is incorrect. Only a small portion of the funds used by the corporation comes directly from stockholder investments. Most funds—most corporate capital—come from the retention and reinvestment of profits from operations, which are realized through purchases of goods and services by the corporation's customers; when additional funds are needed, the corporation usually borrows instead of selling stock. As John Kenneth Galbraith has put it:

> In the large corporation ... capital is all but exclusively provided out of earnings or by borrowing. The stockholder ... has no power and hence no role in the running of the firm.[6]

While accounting teaches us that these reinvested profits, or "retained earnings," belong to the stockholders, they are more precisely the fruit of the corporation's own efforts. Stockholders do not produce the goods or make the sales, and stockholders have little say, except in extraordinary situations, over what happens to the profits.

If stockholders are so unimportant, what is all that activity on Wall Street about? The daily paper and the evening news give a lot of attention to individual stock prices, price movements, and averages. This seems to tell us that stocks are important.

So they may be, but mainly to the individuals who trade them and the Wall Street industry that makes money on the trades. The corporations themselves generally are not involved or even affected. For

> More and more people are coming to the realisation that the shareholders are really a bunch of 26-year-olds sitting behind their trading desks, and that the people who have the best interest of the company and its employees at heart are really those in management.
>
> A corporate director[7]

example, millions of shares of Ford Motor Corporation stock can be bought and sold on the stock exchanges every day, without Ford getting or paying a dime. The president of Ford and some other executives may follow these transactions with great interest,[8] but the trades still do not directly affect the *corporation* itself. The corporation is rarely involved in any of those millions of daily stock trades.

Corporate stock transactions are sort of like used car sales. Ford is affected when it sells new cars. Later, when these cars are traded, maybe a number of times, in the used car market, Ford is not involved. The company does not receive a dime, and it is hardly affected by the prices its cars bring in the used car market. So too with Ford stock: after a stock issue is first sold (and for most outstanding stock that would have been years ago), all the stock market transactions we hear about have no direct effect on Ford. And if Ford never issues new stock again—which is more than a possibility—then the market price of its stock can go sky high or sink to the cellar without changing a dollar on Ford's balance sheet.

New stock issues are rarely made by large corporations and are, in the aggregate, an insignificant source of corporate funds. This is shown clearly in the Federal Reserve Board's report on sources of corporate funds, which reveals that in 1993, the latest year reported, corporate funds came from the following sources:[9]

| | | |
|---|---|---|
| Funds from operations (profits retained in the business, plus depreciation, etc.) | $476.1 billion | 82% |
| Borrowing (bonds, notes, trade credit) | 81.5 | 14% |
| Equity issues (sale of stock) | 23.0 | 4% |
| Total | $580.6 | 100% |

Funds from the sale of stock were only 4 percent of total corporate funds. In fact, in seven out of the last ten years reported *corporations bought back more of their own stock than they issued!* This phenomenon can be better understood when we think of the takeovers, lever-

> Companies rarely, if ever, raise capital through the stock market. Since 1983, in fact, companies have been buying back their shares, at the rate of about 5 percent of the total value of listed stocks each year.
>
> Charles R. Morris, Wall Street consultant[10]

aged buyouts, and cases of companies "going private" that have occurred in recent years.

In a nutshell, stockholders provide funds for startup companies and other, generally small, corporations. Big corporations get their funds from sales and from borrowing. Their power today comes from sources other than stockholders. As Robert Heilbroner says:

> ... No longer even a significant source of venture capital, the stockholder is now merely a passive holder of certificates of varying degrees of risk and potential return. As to the actual operation, the available choices, even the real performance of "his" corporation, he knows little, being guided in his estimate of the corporation's activities by the collective judgment of the stock market, largely comprised of other holders as blind as himself.[11]

There are of course likely to be exceptions to any such observation about an issue as complex as control of corporations. In smaller, nonpublic corporations stockholders and management may be identical. And even in some larger corporations stockholders may, because of tradition or the personal disposition of management, have substantial influence, but the overwhelming predominance of corporate actions are not seriously constrained by stockholders or stockholder desires.

Managers in large corporations know that the popular view of stockholder sovereignty is a myth. They manage stockholders as readily as they manage cash, inventory, and employees.

> ...some oil industry executives are into what I call an empire syndrome. Anything that threatens them and helps the shareholders is a threat to their empire. A lot of them think shareholders are nothing but a nuisance....
>
> T. Boone Pickens[12]

## Managing Stockholders

Of course stockholders would like to have power. Many try, every year, to influence the behavior of "their" corporation. Some write to management, some introduce resolutions at stockholder meetings, some undertake proxy battles to replace management. But most, sooner or later, accept reality and settle into a passive role, resigned to selling their stock if the corporation's behavior or management is unsatisfactory. John Kenneth Galbraith, in *The New Industrial State*, describes the stockholder's condition as follows:

> ...to change control more stockholders must be persuaded, against the advice of management, to vote their stock for someone whom, in the nature of the case, they do not know and will not be disposed to trust. The effort must also contend with the tendency of the indifferent to give proxies to management. It is also in face of the requirement that the loser of a proxy battle, if he is an outsider, must pay the cost. And it must contend finally with the alternative, always available to the dissatisfied stockholder, of simply selling his stock. Corporate size, the passage of time and the dispersion of stock ownership do not disenfranchise the stockholder. Rather, he can vote but his vote, if for management, is unnecessary and if against, futile. In other words, it is valueless.[13]

Even institutional investors, whom we might expect, because of their large stock holdings, to have much greater leverage than the individual stockholder, are often frustrated. Two of the largest, most powerful institutional investors, the California Public Employees' Retirement System (Calpers) and the College Retirement Equities Fund (the equities part of TIAA-CREF), opposed the reelection of the board of directors of Borland International. They charged that the board and the company's CEO, Philippe Kahn, had failed to protect shareholder value. But that didn't matter. The board was reelected with 94 percent of the vote. Why? Because, as in virtually all such contests, the bulk of the votes were actually controlled by management through proxies returned by stockholders.[14]

The corporation's top management and its stockholders do come face to face once a year in an anachronistic ritual—the shareholders' meeting—whose primary function might appear, at least to a cynic, to be abuse of the stockholders. What stockholders view as input or a democratic voice, management sees as disruption and protest. A big business group, The Conference Board, has even provided a textbook, *Handling Protest at Annual Meetings,*[15] for keeping stockholders under control. It suggests:

- Physical arrangements that might facilitate management control such as the design, operation, and protection of the public address system.

- Advance preparation of careful responses to the issues management thought the protesters might raise.

It approvingly cites tactics that have proved effective in dealing with "protesters":

- Prompt and firm action in removing unruly persons.

- Firmness in sticking to the agenda and channeling the protest into the general discussion at the end of the meeting [to dilute the effect of stockholder presentations].

- Advance presentation of the company's record of accomplishments in the areas of expected protest.

- Restricting discussion of political matters and government policy.

The stockholder who expects to be treated with appropriate respect at the annual stockholders' meeting may be in for a rude surprise, encountering tactics such as being ruled out of order, facing a suddenly dead microphone, or belittlement of questions by the chair. According to The Conference Board:

> Participating companies gave special attention to microphone placement, control, and protection. Microphones were used not only as amplifiers but also to help in keeping control of the meeting. Placed strategically throughout the auditoriums, they could be switched on or off by the chairman, either by controls at the podium or by signals to a control operator. On occasion chairmen found it convenient to be able to overpower shouting demonstrators by increasing the amplification on their own "mikes."[16]

The Conference Board also gives a clear picture of the way some corporate managements view their stockholders:

> Another company's management had misgivings about the annual meeting as a forum on other grounds. It considered the average stockholder, as well as the general public, poorly informed about the capitalistic system and the function of corporate enterprise in American society. Consequently, it believed that a public forum, such as an annual meeting, was not likely to provide an audience sufficiently informed on economic matters as to be capable of appraising management's policies and decisions fairly.[17]

But it could be worse. According to *Newsweek*, Japanese corporations have hired yakuza, or mobsters, "to suppress questions at shareholders' meetings."[18] There is much admiration in the United States for Japanese management; we can hope this is one technique that will not be imported.

[Stockholder] Evelyn Y. Davis said Roche, GM chairperson, was responsible for the bear market, and went on to describe him as "stupid." He then cut off her microphone. Then when Harvard professor and Nobel laureate in biology George Wald was seconding the nomination as director of Stewart Mott, Roche first tried to "rein him in" and then cut off his microphone.[19]

Why do corporate executives claim stockholders control them if it is not so? Why do they appear to give so much attention to such statistics as stockholder profit, return on investment, earnings per share, and price-earnings ratios?

Although some managers accord stockholders appropriate respect, many bow to stockholders publicly to create the impression that the stockholders, not management, are in control and are responsible for the company's actions. If people understood that corporate executives wield the power with no real external check, the public might demand changes, possibly new laws or regulations, that would impose restraints. Understandably, management prefers to be free to do what it wants.

If stockholders don't control the corporation, then does anyone else? What about the marketplace, the customers? Does government effectively regulate? Do the workers and labor unions keep the corporation in line? Or do the corporation's neighbors—the city and county commissions and the state legislatures? Let's take these one by one.

## Does the Marketplace Rule?

Economists like to say that the corporation is controlled by the marketplace. This is partly but not generally true. The marketplace—you and I, as consumers—can impose outside limits on what the corporation can do. But within these somewhat loose margins, the corporation exercises the power and the control.

This is especially so for the giant corporations that we are concerned with here; less so for the smaller ones; and generally not the case for the little companies, the "mom and pop" stores. Even the giant corporation may not be able to control the market when the "market" consists of other large corporations. Large corporate *buyers* have or can afford the expertise to fully evaluate and test major purchases, and they often have leverage with the seller to obtain desired product modifications.

But when a large corporation sells to individual consumers, it has great power—through its advertising and marketing budget—to induce us, in the aggregate, to respond to its bidding, to buy its product.

As individuals we consumers are independent and often stubborn. We will resist persuasion. We will reject one vendor's wares and buy another's, or buy none at all. But only as individuals. Collectively, when we represent the "marketplace," we are malleable in known ways. Our behavior as individuals is often inexplicable, but as a market we are persuadable and predictable.

Consider this. In the mid-1950s automobile manufacturers presented cars with rear fender fins, some truly outlandish. There is no record of consumers having petitioned for fins. No march on Detroit demanded them. Fins were merely a marketing ploy, to distinguish new and unimproved models from old. Consumers were accustomed to cars without fins; fins had no identifiable practicable value, and they did not suit our established tastes. And so we had to be "sold" on them.

If the marketplace ruled, this aberration in our cultural history could not have occurred. Archaeologists in the twenty-fifth century would be spared the bewildering discovery of these questionable appendages in automobile graveyards. The sequence would have been:

1. Cars with fins were introduced.
2. Finny cars were not accepted by the market and failed to sell.
3. Finny cars were withdrawn, at great loss to their manufacturers, and finless cars were offered. Market sovereignty ruled supreme.

But giant corporations are often able to control the consumer more than the consumer controls the corporations, so the actual sequence was:

1. Cars with fins were introduced.
2. Consumers were bombarded with advertising that promoted finny cars.
3. Some easily persuadable consumers bought finny cars; others held back.
4. Finless cars became scarce; even stubborn consumers had little choice but to give in to the combination of advertising, growing cultural acceptance, and unavailability of alternatives.
5. Finny cars became a success in the marketplace!

We can all recall other examples, from furniture to detergents to politicians, from toys to the latest style in jeans.

There are exceptions—as was said, the marketplace does impose limits. The Edsel, though now forty years past, is always mentioned. Others would cite several of IBM's personal computer models. Unquestionably, even great power can be neutralized by exceptionally injudicious decisions. But the conclusion is indisputable: in the aggregate, the larger corporations control the market far more than the market controls the corporations. Privately, their managers would be embarrassed were it otherwise. That is, after all, what they are trained, and paid, to accomplish.

Traditional economists often do not see things this way because they assume a world that does not exist. They define an *Alice in Wonderland* world and say, "This is how it works *given our assumptions*." One of their assumptions is that the consumer has "perfect information." We are supposed to know and understand everything—every ingredient, every chemical, every preservative—that goes into, for example, a frozen dinner. To make informed decisions, we are supposed to know what the test results have been, which products we are individually sensitive to, which will aggravate an allergy or swell a sinus or produce a rash, which causes cancer in lab animals, which ones a pregnant woman should avoid—and how each ingredient interacts with others that we have ingested.

The traditional economist further assumes that, with this perfect information, we will regulate the marketplace with our pocketbooks and chastise the mighty corporation when the contents or the construction are not what we would prefer.

This is a world that does not exist and probably never has, certainly not since the Industrial Revolution and certainly not in our lifetimes. Even so, customers can discipline the corporation by refusing to buy when three conditions exist:

1. The product is relatively simple;

2. Buyers have complete information, or can get it at a reasonable cost; and

3. There are many sellers (the market is not controlled by only a few corporations).

We can do okay with, say, clothes, insofar as quality of construction goes. But even with clothes, we cannot readily know or determine, without an expert's help, whether they are highly flammable and whether their chemical coatings and treatments are toxic or will aggravate allergies. You cannot look at a shirt and know what the dye might do to your skin.

Food is even tougher. The risk is greater and there are more additives. Even the seemingly simplest foods, such as fresh apples— uncanned, uncooked, unprocessed—can be treated with harmful insecticides. For processed and packaged foods, consumers must place their health in the hands of the corporation and the FDA (which admits it can test only a fraction of the products under its jurisdiction).

To a substantial degree, we must even buy our homes on faith. Few among us have the knowledge to judge whether a house is adequately fireproof; how safe and functional its roofing, wiring, plumbing, and foundation are; whether the subsurface is unstable or dosed with toxic waste; whether fireplaces and chimneys are usable; whether insulation is adequate; or whether plans for future neighborhood development will affect the property's value. We require considerable *expert* assistance at added cost.

A home is a good metaphor for much of our purchasing. We are vulnerable and at risk unless we personally obtain substantial expertise and information or unless we engage expert assistance, both at potentially significant cost that can be charged off against only the one purchase (or at best a few). Most of us do not have the technical expertise, or indeed the interest, to do a full evaluation on such products as automobiles, appliances, power tools, restaurant food, airline flights, medicines, or electricity.

For many goods and services, we face a single or a few providers. You cannot "vote with your feet" when there is no place else to go. Even when other sellers exist, corporate oligopolies so diligently standardize their products that our apparent choice turns out to be little choice at all. Ever wonder why automobiles, whether from Japan, Germany, or the U.S., now look so much like each other? Why you cannot buy summer clothes in the summer or winter clothes in the winter, but must conform instead to the sellers' schedules and buy your winter clothes in the heat of August? Why most cities have about two "brands" of supermarkets instead of a dozen or a hundred? This is not consumer sovereignty; it is corporate sovereignty. Taken collectively consumers are a reasonably predictable and reasonably manipulable mass, not a serious power over giant corporations.

So the large corporation rarely faces the three conditions required for consumer sovereignty—a simple product, complete information, and many sellers—although these may exist often enough for products sold by smaller companies. As Professor Galbraith showed in *The New Industrial State*,[20] great corporations *manage* demand; they *manage* the marketplace through planning, advertising, and marketing.

Consider a day in the life of an average person, maybe a secretary in an office. She wakes to the clock radio, and the first thing she hears is an advertisement. The radio commercials continue as she bathes and dresses. At breakfast her morning paper is chock full of display ads—not totally unwelcome, as she seeks ways of fulfilling wants previously induced by corporate advertising. As she drives to work billboard advertising competes with the commercials on her car radio. Mail deliveries at the office dump pounds of junk mail on her desk, while the occasional real document coming in on the office FAX is bracketed by a stream of promotional material.

The onslaught hardly diminishes when she returns home, where the "real" mail in her mailbox is outnumbered five to one by advertising pieces. Sample products and promotional flyers adorn her doorknob. Her telephone rings through dinner and beyond with telemarketing calls. The television assails her with its high-decibel and high-tech commercials scientifically designed and pretested to reach into her psyche— thank heavens, at least, for the "mute" button. Not until she settles into bed with a good book is she finally free of the corporation's efforts to influence and manipulate her—that is, unless it is one of those new books with advertising, and unless all the commercials and ads have not so subliminally intruded themselves that they now dominate her dreams.

The customer, as the marketplace, is hardly a match for the directed resources of larger corporations. Corporations do face another factor in their environment that can impose some discipline, and that is competition. Economists, in their theoretical models, usually assume a world of perfect competition. That means many firms are competing with each other for the consumer's dollar. Like their assumption of perfect information, this is a fantasy.

In the world of the giant corporations, there are rarely many firms competing directly. Business executives would prefer to have a complete monopoly; this would permit complete exploitation of the market. Since this extreme is usually thwarted, large enterprises usually have to settle for the next best thing: an oligopoly—few, rather than many, firms in an industry.

Oligopolies may occur when the larger firms in an industry gobble up the smaller ones until only a few, all large, are left. These few can then move to standardize products and styles, fix prices, and divide up the market. Think of interest rates. One megabank raises the prime rate a half point and before the sun sets every big bank in the country has done likewise. Or one steel company raises the price and all follow. It happens even among smaller businesses. How did every gas station in town know to raise its price ten cents a gallon when it opened this morning?

But in a world of global competition even an oligopoly may not provide as much insulation as management would like. An oligopoly in another country still might come in and knock your socks off. Even a large corporation, then, can face limitations from competition. The marketplace is not irrelevant and cannot be ignored by management, but it does not effectively *control* the large corporation.

## Are the Feds in Control?

Corporate executives often complain about government regulation, although Washington policymakers are quick to point out that much regulation is first demanded by business. (Back when banks were limited in the amount of interest they could pay on savings accounts to 5 percent or so, the public was generally not aware that these limits were imposed at the behest of *banks*, to prevent hungry competitors from pushing up rates to get new business.) Regulations set standards, bring order to markets and industries, restrict predatory trade practices, and protect American markets from foreign competition. Regulation also shelters the companies that dominate an industry by making it difficult, even next to impossible, for other companies to come into the industry. (This device has been used to particular advantage by CPAs and other professional groups.) Regulation is important and valuable to Corporate America, despite self-serving protests by some to the contrary.

Even when regulations benefit business, they do amount to government control over business, don't they?

Not according to the eminent scholar Robert Heilbroner. He writes of what might be called the "fox in the henhouse syndrome," the inexorable takeover of the regulatory agency by those it is charged with regulating.

> . . . if nearly a century of regulatory history tells us anything,
> it is that the rules-making agencies of government are
> almost invariably captured by the industries which they are
> established to control. Thus the ICC becomes the protector
> and promoter of the railways; the FPC, the ally of private
> rather than public power; the FCC, unable to define any

standard of "public interest" that might cut seriously into the profits of the broadcasting industry; the CAB, an agency whose primary aim is to limit competition among the airlines; the Pentagon, a guardian of the health of its client corporations; even the SEC . . . an agency characterized by a philosophy of benign neglect.[21]

If corporations are too powerful to be controlled by the federal government, then of course they are not likely to be called effectively to account by local or state government. Since states charter corporations, state governments have theoretical authority over them. But the history of state chartering has been a race to see which could charter the largest number of corporations by providing the greatest freedom, the least control and regulation. State law has now "been reduced to reflecting the preferences of the managers of the largest corporations."[22] As Professor Ernest Folk has observed:

> Corporation statutes and most judicial decisions largely tend to reflect the interests and orientation of management. . . . In short, state law has abdicated its responsibility.[23]

## What About Labor?

Individual workers in small organizations may be able to negotiate with individual managers. Fair working conditions and compensation may be thus arranged. There is no question in either party's mind, however, as to who is in charge in these negotiations. The decision authority, the power, and the position of strength are with management.

Even though exceptions and aberrations may exist, this is even more so for large corporations and their employees. The corporation—more precisely, its managers—is in charge. The managers, not the workers, have the power.

But what happens when workers organize into labor unions? Does labor then control the corporation?

Certainly labor that is organized has more leverage with management and more ability to protect itself. Worker benefits, safety, and security have advanced substantially during this century, a period concomitant with growth in the labor movement. But organized labor is not growing now. Union membership has declined significantly in recent years and dropped by a fifth in just the last decade.[24] The record of that decade has been one of labor concessions to management, not labor gains.

Clearly labor does not control the corporation and does not control management. It is, however, a constraining factor on particular issues. Management has the power, but this power is not without boundaries.

## Do the Directors Direct?

The popular view of corporate control is that the stockholders elect a board of directors that in turn appoints the corporate managers, sets their compensation, oversees their actions, and when necessary takes them to the woodshed.

This is the way it works with some, mainly smaller, corporations, but for the great majority and especially for the corporate giants, reality is quite different—in fact, almost the opposite. Comprehensive studies of corporations show that management—and often this means the chief executive officer acting alone—slates the directors. These are routinely affirmed by the stockholders; occasional opposition is easily overcome with proxies executed in management's behalf. Chief executive officers often set their own level of compensation, as well as that of the other executives. They even select their own replacements as CEOs. Directors do not make policy, and those who ask too many questions or otherwise annoy are replaced.

> Yielding to the wishes of Lee A. Iacocca, the directors of the Chrysler Corporation have agreed to name a General Motors executive to succeed Mr. Iacocca as chief executive. . . .
>
> *The New York Times*, 16 March 1992[25]

Harvard Business School professor Myles L. Mace spent thousands of hours in corporate board meetings and consulting with company top managements on board problems. His definitive findings were published in *Directors: Myth and Reality*.[26] Here's what he discovered.

Who picks the directors?

> Directors are generally selected and invited to serve on the board by the president of the company. . . . The stockholders, of course, unless their holdings are substantial enough to assure representation on the board . . . play no part in the selection of directors . . .[27]
>
> [Recent news stories reported that two veteran directors of IBM resigned so the new chairperson, Louis Gerstner, could "have the right to choose some people he knows, respects, and who are much more attuned to the industry."[28]]
>
> Directors as described in the literature represent the stockholders. Yet typically they are actually selected by the president and not by the stockholders. Accordingly the directors are on the board because the president wants them there. Implicitly, and frequently explicitly, the directors in point of fact represent the president.[29]
>
> [Or as Professor Galbraith acerbically put it, the stockholder "is represented nominally by a board of directors which is selected by the management and which, in one of the most predictable of political rites, then appoints the managers that appointed it."[30]]

Do directors establish objectives, strategies, and policies?

> I found that boards of directors of most large and medium-sized companies *do not* establish objectives, strategies, and policies, however defined. These roles are performed by company management. Presidents and outside directors generally agreed that only management should have these responsibilities.[31]

In most companies the allocation of capital resources, including the acquisition of other enterprises, is accomplished through a management process of analysis resulting in recommendations to the board and in requests for approval by the board.... Approval by boards in most companies is perfunctory, automatic, and routine. Presidents and their subordinates, deeply involved in analysis and decision making prior to presentation to the board, believe in the correctness of their recommendations and almost without exception they are unchallenged by the members of the board. Rarely do boards go contrary to the wishes of the president.[32]

Do directors ask significant, probing questions?

[Another] classical role ascribed to boards of directors is that of asking discerning questions—inside and outside the board meetings. Again it was found that directors *do not*, in fact, do this. *Board meetings are not regarded as proper forums for discussions arising out of questions asked by board members* [emphasis added].[33]

Many presidents stated that board members should manifest by their queries, if any, that they approve of the management. *If a director feels that he has any basis for doubts and disapproval, most of the presidents interviewed believe that he should resign* [emphasis added].[34]

Who sets the president's and officers' compensation?

The [board] compensation committee, and the board which approves the recommendations of the compensation committee, are not in most cases decision-making bodies. These decisions are made by the president, and in most situations the committee and board approval is perfunctory. The president has de facto powers of control, and in most cases he is the decision maker.[35]

Who picks the president?

> ... it was found that in most companies directors do not in
> fact select the president except under [two specific crisis
> situations]. ... The administrative use by the president of
> board committees to evaluate candidates for his successor in
> the presidency gives the selection process an appearance of
> careful evaluation and objectivity. But *in most cases the deci-*
> *sion as to who should succeed the president is made by the pres-*
> *ident himself* [emphasis added].[36]
>
> [The two crisis situations to which Mace refers are when
> the president suddenly dies or becomes incapacitated, or his
> performance becomes so unsatisfactory that a change must
> be made. In such situations the directors take one of three
> actions: hire a management consultant to evaluate the pres-
> ident, ask the president to resign, or resign themselves from
> the board. Mace found *that most directors, to avoid facing the*
> *unpleasant task of acting to replace a president, choose to resign*
> *themselves!*][37]

There are corporations in which the board of directors functions
in a manner closer to the classical concept wherein control of the corporation lies in its hands, but this is not the norm:

> Some presidents, but not many, are completely aware that
> they have de facto powers of control and that they can
> behave in their relationships with their board in any manner
> that they elect, but they choose to include the board as a
> major and important element in the management structure.
> ... Of all the companies studied over the years, including the
> last two of full-time intensive field research, only a relatively
> small minority of instances were encountered where the
> president felt this way.[38]

Other distinguished observers of corporate boards confirm Professor Mace's findings. In his comprehensive study of corporate control,

Wharton professor Edward S. Herman concludes that directors "are usually passive and do what management wants them to do."[39] William O. Douglas, later justice of the U.S. Supreme Court, grumbled back in 1934, "Directors do not direct."[40] Peter Drucker, in his classic *Management*, states coldly of boards of directors: "They do not function."[41]

As Professor Mace has so clearly shown, the board of directors is a formality, an atrophied appendage to the corporate body that has lost, except in rare instances, whatever function it may once have had. It may provide advice and counsel, but it does not *direct* and it obviously does not control.

## Corporate Managers: The Real Controllers of Corporate Power

Who controls corporate power? We have seen that it is not the stockholders. Not the market. Not labor. Not the federal government. Not the states. And not the board of directors. Does this mean that the corporation controls itself?

Subject to some constraints already mentioned, that is essentially the case. The corporation, or more precisely (since the corporation is not, as yet, human) its management, controls itself.

As we might expect, corporate executives say they see things differently. "By and large, American business leaders do not see themselves nearly as powerful as their critics do. On the contrary, they commonly contend that they are dominated by other forces, including public interest groups, labor unions, consumers, the news media, even the academics, and most of all by government."[42]

The extent of management control has been carefully researched by Professor Herman.[43] He determined that, as of December 31, 1974, 183 of the 200 largest, publicly owned, nonfinancial corporations were controlled by management.

Management control of large corporations has been growing throughout this century, from some 24 percent of large companies in 1901 to 41 percent in 1929 to 92 percent in 1974.[44] With the torrent of leveraged buyouts in the 1980s and the recent record of corporate

> The management, though its ownership is normally negligible, is solidly in control of the enterprise. By all visible evidence it possesses the power. Yet there has been great reluctance to admit of a significant and enduring shift of power from the owners of capital. Some observers have sought to maintain the myth of stockholder power. As in foreign policy and bad marriages it is hoped that incantation may save what the reality denies.
>
> John Kenneth Galbraith, *The New Industrial State*[45]

stock redemptions, management dominance has certainly grown further. The trend is clear: management control of larger corporations is virtually complete.

It may be appropriate to emphasize again at this point that we are not concerned here with the small corporations—the job shops, the mom-and-pop convenience stores and other small retailers, the quick print shops, the neighborhood dry cleaners—but with the corporate giants, the "Generals" (General Dynamics, General Electric, General Foods, General Mills, General Motors) and similar huge enterprises.

How did hired managers gain control of great corporations and their assets from the corporations' owners and the directors elected by the owners? The answer can be found in four factors: growth, aging, proxies, and power. As a corporation grows to a size that makes it no longer manageable by its founders, "professional" managers are hired. Pressure to bring in professional managers also comes from capital sources, banks and investors, when capital is sought for growth.

As the founders of businesses age, they eventually find it necessary to pass the reins of control. As one's children, with all their known foibles and weaknesses, are compared to idealized professional managers with imagined qualities, the outsiders often win out. And so begins the passing of power from the founder's family to the professional manager.

Proxies are stockholder votes signed over to another. This "another" is usually management, but sometimes a group of stockholders undertakes a proxy contest. They almost always lose. Why? First, challengers bear the cost of their proxy challenge, but the costs of management's proxy campaigns are paid by the corporation—i.e., from stockholders' funds. So the challengers have to pay twice, or more; management can wait until challengers have solicited proxies and follow with one, two, three, or even more solicitations—and the *last-dated* proxy is the only one that counts. Management can also hire professional proxy solicitors with corporate funds. Finally, management has access to corporate personnel including accountants, attorneys, economists, statisticians, public relations specialists, and other experts both to perform research and analysis for use in the contest as well as to campaign in management's behalf. The result: "During the eighteen years for which data are available, 1956–73, management has won 99.9 percent of all proxy solicitations in ten out of eighteen years."[46]

The final, and perhaps the most important, reason management retains and increases its power is *power* itself. From a near impregnable base of resources, management can beat down virtually any challenge. We do hear of managements being ousted, but this appears to require derelictions that go far beyond mere incompetence or moral turpitude, such as insider trading or other such heinous crimes. Power begets power. "Them that has, gets."

What do corporate managers do with their power? Do they exercise it in behalf of the stockholders, customers, employees, and the public interest? Or do they mainly take care of themselves?

Studies of corporate management invariably conclude that managers are driven toward growth—a larger market share, more assets, bigger corporation. Growth means even more power for the executive,

> It's not ownership that counts—it's control. And as Chief Executive that's what I've got!
>
> W. Michael Blumenthal, as head of Bendix Corporation[47]

more prestige—at least within the limited world of large corporations and country clubs—and more personal gratification. Growth also leads reliably to higher and higher levels of compensation for executives— and it does not much matter whether the growth is accompanied by higher earnings. Even poor performance is often not a threat to their jobs or their pay. A few examples of the many that could be cited:

♦ Northrop Corporation raised its chief executive officer's compensation from $681,250 to $795,721 in apparent reward for an $81 million loss, a $500 million drop in sales, and a 44 percent slide in the stock's price.[48]

♦ Washington's *City Paper* reports that Craig McCaw, chairperson of McCaw Cellular Communications, was awarded a bonus of $53.6 million in a year when his firm lost $289 million; in fact the firm had never shown a profit, with some years' losses exceeding $1 billion.[49]

♦ Notorious corporate raider and union buster Frank Lorenzo paid himself, as chairman of Texas Air Corporation, $1.25 million in cash compensation in 1989 when Texas Air was losing $719 million.

♦ How did Chrysler punish its chairperson, Lee Iacocca, when its profits plunged 66 percent? With a nice compensation increase of nearly $388,000, making his total $3,976,359.[50]

♦ Peter Cohen managed to do very well even when getting fired from Shearson Lehman Hutton. He walked away with a $10 million package just before the firm reported one of the biggest losses in Wall Street history. A stock trader on the floor of the New York Stock Exchange had a caustic reaction: "Ten million bucks for wrecking the company? Nice work if you can get it."[51]

Apparently no amount is too much for executive compensation. In 1992 the CEO of HCA-Hospital Corporation of America, Thomas F. Frist, Jr., topped the executive pay sweepstakes with a whopping $127 million. That one person's pay would cover the cost of employing over 4,000 workers at $30,000 a year. Imagine standing before 4,000 people and telling them, "My work is worth as much as that of all of you put together."

> "Point of order," yelled one shareholder as the [DWG Corp.] board considered a new bonus plan for [Chairman Victor] Posner and other managers. "This sucks."[52]

In 1980 the average compensation of corporate CEOs in the United States was 42 times that of the average worker, 39 times the average pay of teachers. Twelve years later, a period that culminated with massive firings throughout Corporate America while ordinary workers struggled to hold on in the face of a dangerous rise in the unemployment rate, CEOs averaged *157 times* as much compensation as the average worker and 113 times as much as teachers. Meanwhile, Japanese CEOs were receiving less than 32 times the average pay of rank-and-file employees.[53] Is it any wonder that American business is often seen in world markets as bloated and greedy?

Another way that corporate managers take care of themselves instead of the corporation: when their personal positions are threatened, they see to themselves before attending to the corporation.

Consider what happens when an unfriendly takeover looms. Takeovers, it is argued, are good for stockholders. They are often directed toward corporations that are not measuring up to their potential or that are run by inadequate or incompetent managers. The first effect is a significant increase in the market price of the target company's shares. What could be better for stockholders than an aggressive change?

Then takeovers, in most cases, should be welcomed. But unsolicited takeovers are invariably opposed by management. Management fights tooth and nail to prevent them, with an orchestra of devices: "golden parachutes," "poison pills," "greenmail," "white knights," (even "hushmail," a term used by some to describe the $700 million GM paid H. Ross Perot to get him off its board and out of its hair[54]).

**Some Terms Favored by Top Executives**

*Golden parachute:* A set of special benefits, often extremely generous settlement payments or retirement arrangements, established for present executives to ensure a soft landing in the event they are forced out following a takeover; some have called them "rewards for failure."

*Poison pill:* A "doomsday device" that may be adopted by management without stockholder approval and provides (theoretically) for stockholders to sell their shares back to the company at a price so exorbitant that the value of a raider's investment would be diluted to an unacceptable level. Since no raider has ever been willing to proceed in the face of the poison pill device, stockholders have never gotten the benefit of the exorbitant stock price—but management has been completely protected from hostile takeovers.

*Greenmail:* Payment to a hostile bidder to stop an attempted takeover. It protects management, but works against the interests of stockholders.

*White knight:* A friendlier acquirer, invited in by management to stymie a hostile raider.

Unfortunately, as *Business Week* has noted, there are no golden parachutes when the twenty-year lower-level employee is forced to bail out.[55]

When faced with a possible takeover, management often shows little concern for stockholders.[56] They may show concern for earnings per share and share prices, but this appears to be done as much to increase the value of management's stock options and to protect their jobs as to benefit stockholders.

Management has the power to provide itself with golden parachutes, with no real accountability. But when challenged to invest in safer products, provide workers with healthier and safer workplaces,

> [Threatened by takeovers] corporate managers . . . are beseeching
> Congress to help them keep control. They are proposing many
> silly, self-serving remedies. One oil company executive has sug-
> gested that raiders be required to write impact statements before
> being allowed to complete a deal. Management, meanwhile,
> would still be free to close plants, sell assets, or do whatever it
> wants without such constraints. Other managers want to make
> shareholders hold stock for six months before they're allowed to
> vote on proxy resolutions or bids, yet still feel free to lay off 20-
> year employees.
>
> *Business Week*[57]

reduce pollution, or protect a community by keeping a plant running,
corporate executives often respond: "Our responsibility is to stockholders; this would reduce stockholder profit and would be a violation of our fiduciary responsibility." Thus they create the appearance of
responsibility and accountability that does not correspond to reality.

## Summing Up: Power Without Accountability

As we have seen, the corporation was initially responsible to the sovereign and was chartered, at least ostensibly, for public or state benefit. Stock companies then evolved; these were still responsible to the
sovereign, but also had stockholders.

We retained government chartering in the United States, but allowed
it to lose its meaning—the chartering function atrophied.

Like the state chartering function, the stockholder's role as owner
also atrophied, leaving the stockholder with only an invest/disinvest
choice but exercising none of the powers and prerogatives of an owner.
Stockholder initiatives and resolutions are not evidence to the contrary;
they almost never obtain even a 5 percent vote. Stockholders rarely can
muster the power to force management to do anything (although the

> The salary of the chief executive of the large corporation is not a market reward for achievement. It is frequently in the nature of a warm personal gesture by the individual to himself.
>
> John Kenneth Galbraith[58]

publicity surrounding stockholder resolutions will sometimes embarrass management into taking the desired action).

The board of directors, workers and their unions, the government, and the marketplace do not effectively control large corporations either. In virtually every large corporation, actual control is exercised by a small, self-perpetuating coterie of top executives, often dominated by a single individual.

Who are these people? What moves them?

They start out, by and large, like you and me. Some come from Brahmin families; many do not. Typically in college they major in business or later get an MBA; here their indoctrination into the bottom line mentality begins. Once they enter the corporate world, they are exposed to role models who further bequeath the corporate morality. Before they know it, they have become full-fledged members of the corporate culture, following the dictates of the bottom line even when it doesn't quite feel right. While they are operating in the corporate world, they suppress their personal morality. (How frequently and how painfully this must tear at a manager's insides!)

Business people, when functioning outside the corporate world as individuals, are responsible to themselves and to their conscience, their sense of morality, their families, and their religion; all of these act as a check on personal behavior. They are also, as individuals, responsible under the law and subject to personal sacrifice for violating the law.

But when acting in their corporate capacity, managers are, practically speaking, not subject to sacrifice or to any significant personal costs under the law. Recklessly unsafe products traceable to the individual, working as an individual and not in a corporation, might result in severe personal penalty. When a corporation does the same thing it is, at the worst, fined, typically in an amount that is hardly noticeable, and managers, at least at the top, are left untouched. (Managers down the line might suffer some internal consequences, perhaps as scapegoats, but they likewise are not likely to pay any external price, such as jail or a personal fine.)

Even when there are no external penalties, why aren't corporate managers responsible to their personal sense of morality—to their conscience? Because, when they accept and adapt to the corporate culture, they adopt its mores and morality. The corporation, without a religion, a guiding parent, a personal philosophy, a soul, or a conscience, receives its moral standards from the balance sheet. This becomes the soul of the corporation. In accepting their position in the corporation, and their rewards from it, managers often feel bound to put their personal morality aside and to act on the corporation's moral standards—at least while they are acting in their capacity as managers of the corporation and not separately as individuals.

This contradiction between personal and on-the-job morality was remarkably confirmed in an experiment by J. Scott Armstrong. He asked almost two thousand management students from ten countries to play the roles of board members of a transnational pharmaceutical company. The decision facing the board was a real-life situation that had confronted the Upjohn company: should it remove from the market a drug that had been found to endanger human life? In acting as board members, 79 percent of the students not only refused to withdraw the dangerous drug but also undertook legal or political maneuvers to forestall efforts of the government to ban it—the same action

> Rather than think of corporate actors as individual personalities, they should be viewed as actors who assume certain roles. The requirements of these roles are defined by the organisation, not by the actor's personality.
>
> John Braithwaite [59]

the Upjohn board itself had taken. Yet when Armstrong asked a sample of his students about the actual Upjohn action 97 percent classified it as "socially irresponsible."[60]

In smaller corporations, there may be less of an established corporate culture, and the tyranny of the bottom line may have less force than in a large bureaucracy. The owner-manager may be in personal contact with employees and customers, and may therefore be more likely to follow the golden rule. But in the large organization customers and employees are often only means to an end—the maximization of the bottom line.

John Z. De Lorean, formerly a General Motors executive (and intermittently of other fame), recognized this.

> The system has a different morality as a group than the people do as individuals, which permits it to willfully produce ineffective or dangerous products, deal dictatorially and often unfairly with suppliers, pay bribes for business, abrogate the rights of employees by demanding blind loyalty to management or tamper with the democratic process of government through illegal political contributions.[61]

Thus we have a small group, not elected by the populace but chosen *by* themselves, from *among* themselves, a managerial elite whose members hold great power, and whose personal morality is kept on hold while acting in their corporate roles (which for some is practically twenty-four hours a day). To a substantial extent they collectively decide where and how we will work, how safe our job will be, when we will lose our jobs (possibly for the rest of our lives), what we will eat, what we will wear, how we will clean it, how we will get around, how we will communicate, how much we will make in wages and as a return on our investments, what we will do for entertainment, and yes, through control of the media with its influence over our culture, even what we will think.

This sounds rather like pre-perestroika Russia. There the government controlled the quality, price, purity, safety, and choice of food, and

Power corrupts; unaccountable power corrupts absolutely.

of all other consumer products. It ordained the quality, safety, and wage rate of the job. The government was not one of checks and balances, not seriously constrained by a constitution, and not elected by or accountable to the mass of citizens. It was chosen and perpetuated largely by itself.

Strangely, in a society that opposed the Russian communist system throughout its existence, we appear to have come to accept a very similar arrangement in the United States (as have other capitalistic countries). Our system is marked by a relatively small number of individuals, with no accountability, controlling great power for the benefit of narrow interests, while the broad public interest is carried along as a captive passenger, a hostage.

We would not long tolerate a government without accountability, a dictatorship answerable to no one. But we allow unaccountable corporations to control more of our lives than government has ever attempted.

Corporations—or more precisely, their managers—have great power. Because there is no system of accountability for that power, public harm often results. In the following chapters, we will examine the extent of that unaccountable power and consider the nature and cost of the harm that results.

# Notes

1. Adolf A. Berle, Jr., *The 20th Century Capitalist Revolution* (New York: Harcourt, Brace & World, 1954), 183–84.
2. Bruce Nussbaum and Judith H. Dobrzynski, "The Battle for Corporate Control," *Business Week,* 18 May 1987, 76.

3. Allan Sloan (column), "Drexel Wiggles Through a Tax Code Loophole to Shed Its Felonious Past," *The Washington Post*, 30 March 1993.

4. "Shareholders Block Kmart Stock Issue," *The Washington Post*, 4 June 1994.

5. Adolf A. Berle Jr., *Power Without Property* (New York: Harcourt, Brace & World, 1959), 74.

6. John Kenneth Galbraith, *Annals of an Abiding Liberal* (Boston: Houghton Mifflin, 1979), 79.

7. Corporate director quoted in "Bored Directors," *The Economist*, 27 January 1990, 74, 76.

8. Bonuses and stock options for senior corporate executives may be tied to the stock price, so these individual executives may have a strong interest in what happens to the stock price. But this has no direct bearing on the fortunes of the company. Similarly, the stock price may be used as a measure of performance for lower-level managers; in such usage the stock price is a surrogate measure that, again, does not reflect anything about the actual performance of the company.

9. Bureau of the Census, *Statistical Abstract of the United States 1994*, Table 838, "Corporate Funds—Sources and Uses: 1980 to 1993" (Washington, D.C.: U.S. Bureau of the Census, 1994).

10. Charles R. Morris, "The Stock Market Is Far Removed from Reality," *The Wichita Eagle*, 6 November 1989.

11. Robert L. Heilbroner et al., *In the Name of Profit* (Garden City, N.Y.: Doubleday, 1972), 240.

12. "T. Boone Pickens: 'Clearly a Phenomenon,'" *The Wichita Eagle-Beacon*, 24 February 1985.

13. John Kenneth Galbraith, *The New Industrial State*, 4th ed. (Boston: Houghton Mifflin, 1985), 84.

14. "Borland's Board Re-elected Despite 2 Funds' Opposition," *The New York Times*, 31 August 1994.

15. The Conference Board, *Handling Protest at Annual Meetings* (New York: The Conference Board, 1971).

16. The Conference Board, *Handling Protest at Annual Meetings*, 17–18.

17. Ibid., 41.

18. "The Yamaguchi-gumi Goes to the Mattress," *Newsweek,* 11 February 1985, 49.

19. E. J. Kahn, Jr., "We Look Forward to Seeing You Next Year," *The New Yorker,* 20 June 1970, 40–2+.

20. Galbraith, *The New Industrial State.*

21. Heilbroner et al., *In the Name of Profit,* 239.

22. Ralph Nader, Mark Green, and Joel Seligman, *Taming the Giant Corporation* (New York: W. W. Norton, 1976), 60.

23. Ernest Folk, "Does State Corporation Law Have a Future?" *Georgia State Bar Journal* (February 1972): 311–12.

24. Bureau of Census, *Statistical Abstract of the United States 1994,* Table 683.

25. "A Top G.M. Official Is Reported Chosen to Succeed Iacocca," *The New York Times,* 16 March 1992.

26. Myles L. Mace, *Directors: Myth and Reality,* rev. ed. (Boston: Harvard Business School Press, 1986).

27. Ibid., 195.

28. "These Board Members Aren't IBM-Compatible," *Business Week,* 2 August 1993, 23; "2 Expected to Leave I.B.M. Board," *The New York Times,* 22 July 1993.

29. Mace, *Directors: Myth and Reality,* 188.

30. Galbraith, *Annals of an Abiding Liberal,* 76.

31. Ibid., 185.

32. Ibid., 186.

33. Ibid.

34. Ibid., 187.

35. Ibid., 181.

36. Ibid., 188-89.

37. Ibid., 183

38. Ibid., 194.

39. Edward S. Herman, *Corporate Control, Corporate Power* (Cambridge, Mass.: Cambridge University Press, 1981), 31.

40. Nader, Green, and Seligman, *Taming the Giant Corporation,* 95.

41. Ibid., citing Peter Drucker, *Management: Tasks, Responsibilities, Practices* (New York: Harper & Row, 1973), 628.

42. Leonard Silk and Mark Silk, *The American Establishment* (New York: Avon Books, 1980), 264.

43. Herman, *Corporate Control, Corporate Power,* 58–59.

44. Ibid., 62, 64.

45. Galbraith, *The New Industrial State,* 52.

46. Nader, Green, and Seligman, *Taming the Giant Corporation,* 81.

47. Alvin Toffler, *The Third Wave* (New York: William Morrow, 1980), 79.

48. "The Pay-for-Performance Myth," *The Washington Post,* 22 July 1990, H3.

49. "News of the Weird," *City Paper,* 22 June 1990, 11.

50. "Iacocca Pay Climbs to $4 Million," *The Washington Post,* 14 April 1990, C10.

51. "$10 Million Severance Package," *The Washington Post,* 28 June 1990, C1, C6.

52. "The Posner Principle: When Goliath Controls the Company, Look Out," *Business Week,* 29 October 1990, 34.

53. "Executive Pay: The Party Ain't Over Yet," *Business Week,* 26 April 1993, 56–79.

54. Nussbaum and Dobrzynski, "The Battle," 70–77.

55. Nussbaum and Dobrzynski, "The Battle," 77.

56. When corporate management puts its own self-interest above that of stockholders, management scholars call this an *agency problem.* Such scholars have been fooled by the myth of stockholder control. Stockholders are no longer in control, are no longer the effective principals, in large corporations. As is now well understood, top management hires itself and its successors, sets its own level of compensation, and names the board of directors that ostensibly represents the stockholders. When the agents work for the agents, or more precisely, the principals work for themselves, the so-called agency problem disappears.

57. Nussbaum and Dobrzynski, "The Battle," 76.

58. Galbraith, *Annals of an Abiding Liberal,* 79.

59. John Braithwaite, *Corporate Crime in the Pharmaceutical Industry* (London: Routledge & Kegan Paul, 1984), 2.

60. J. Scott Armstrong, "Social Irresponsibility in Management," *Journal of Business Research*, 5 (1977): 185-213.

61. Quoted in Herman, *Corporate Control, Corporate Power*, 259.

# 4

# The Dominion of the Corpocracy

The institution that most changes our lives we least understand
or, more correctly, seek most elaborately to misunderstand.
That is the modern corporation. Week by week, month by
month, year by year, it exercises a greater influence on our livelihood and the way we live than unions, universities, politicians,
the government.

John Kenneth Galbraith, *The Age of Uncertainty*[1]

CITIZENS IN DEMOCRATIC societies are prone to guard against
government encroachment on their liberty. But what about *corporate*
encroachment?

More concerned about the government's possible abuse of power,
most of us give little attention to the power of the corporation. But this
is a power that has grown virtually without restraint. The potential of
big business to affect the lives of individuals is now, in many domains,
greater even than that of government.

The public is beginning to sense this. By a margin of 73 percent to
21 percent, people think large corporations have too much power for
the good of the country.[2]

Since we know, as was shown in Chapter 2, that the corporation has been diverted from its original public purpose to today's accepted goal of maximizing the stockholders' bottom line, we should seriously examine the extent of that power and consider what effects it can have on us. Although we are generally concerned with the power of all business entities and especially with corporations, our emphasis here will often be on the largest corporations, that relatively small number of enterprises that dominate, in size and influence, all the rest.

## "A Day in the Life . . ."

A good way to start is to return to the day in the life of an average person, an office secretary, introduced in Chapter 3.

Our hypothetical person has a lot of freedom in a democracy. We place great value on that freedom and are quick to draw contrasts with other systems where the government controls much of the citizens' daily life.

But our hypothetical citizen's life is also dominated in many ways through power exercised by large corporations and other businesses. This influence is so pervasive that it is often taken for granted, no longer noticed.

Begin with the morning alarm. As the song says, she awakes and looks around her.

> She sees the inside of her house. The selling price of the house was negotiated with a *corporation* (or possibly a partnership) if she bought the house new, probably an individual if she bought it used. The quality was determined by the builder (probably a small *corporation*), along with previous owners and herself.
>
> Quality, safety, and cost of bed, linens, bedclothes: *corporations.*
>
> Lights on: *corporation* for power (regulated, but not owned or operated, by *government*).
>
> Shower: *corporation* for water (again regulated, but often not owned or operated, by *government*).

Furniture:  mostly *corporations.*

Quality, safety, cost, and choices available for breakfast food (also lunch, dinner, breaks, snacks):  *corporations,* mainly food store chains and food packagers/processors (noncorporate farmers have little effect on final quality, safety, cost, or availability of choice), with some regulation from *government.*

Quality, safety, and cost of automobile driven to work: *corporations;* some regulation by *government.*

Fuel for automobile:  *corporations.*

Streets driven to work:  *government.*

Quality and safety of construction and layout of office building:  *corporations* most likely; possibly a partnership or proprietorship.

Safety and quality of work equipment:  *corporations,* with extremely limited regulation by *government.*

Safety and quality of job:  *corporations,* with extremely limited regulation by *government.*

Salary for day:  depends on the employer; *corporations* for 65 percent of us, *government* for 21 percent, unincorporated businesses or self-employment for 14 percent.

Income taxes on salary, Social Security withheld:  *government.*

Police and fire protection:  *government.*

For the evening's entertainment she is free to choose from among several possibilities including television, movies, theater, nightclubs—and in virtually every case the availability, quality, content, and cost will be determined by *corporations.*

Many details are omitted from our citizen's day, but the overall picture is accurate: unless she breaks the law, she is much more affected day in and day out by the power of corporations than by that of government (with some trend toward increasing the relative power of corporations through privatization of government services).

So it is with most of us. The corporation has a significant and continuing degree of influence, of power, over our lives, from our first wakening sight until we close our eyes in sleep.

Numbers can be numbing, but they are sometimes better than words in helping us to understand reality. This is especially true when we are dealing with money. So now a few numbers to illuminate this social force.

## How Big is the Corpocracy?

In terms of the raw number of business enterprises, simple one-owner unincorporated businesses—sole proprietorships— predominate. They make up about 72 percent of all the businesses filing income tax returns; 9 percent are partnerships, and the other 19 percent are corporations.[3]

Despite their large numbers, sole proprietorships and partnerships are generally smaller (usually much smaller) than corporations, and in the aggregate have considerably less *power* than corporations. Corporations account for most of the nation's employment—far more than government—and control the lion's share of business revenue, assets, and income.

We spend nearly half our waking hours at work. Our income and the comfort or pain of our retirement depend on our job. For most of us our sense of significance, of making a meaningful contribution with our lives, depends mainly on our job. The job can be a source of danger; many workers are killed, injured, or sickened on the job. Certainly our overall happiness, our stress level, and sometimes our mental health are tied to our work. Since work is so important in our society, the number of a corporation's employees is a significant indicator of its potential impact. But its reach extends well beyond the number of employees since each employed worker in the U.S. supports an average of 2.13 additional persons.[4]

Just seven corporate giants account for a payroll equal to that of the entire United States government.

Besides the number of employees, the power of the corporation can be understood by considering the resources it controls. How much does it take in (and spend), and how much wealth does it control?

Receipts by corporations run to nearly nine times the total for partnerships and proprietorships taken together.[5] This reflects the growing dominance of business by corporations, which, as illustrated in Figure 1,[6] now account for virtually all of our national output (not quite 100 percent, of course, but so close as to almost look like that on the chart).

In today's economy corporations receive and spend more than *10 trillion* dollars *every year*.[7] How this money is spent largely determines who gets what in our society. Which smaller, supporting companies will survive, which will fail. What kind of jobs we will have, where they will be, who will get them. Which communities will thrive, which will stagnate and deteriorate. What we will eat, wear, drive, watch, read. And to a substantial degree, what we will think, because corporate advertising and promotion enormously influence our attitudes, our opinions, and our personal and even political preferences.

Now corporations don't come together in collusion to control our society. It is true that some of their expenditures are made with conscious intent to influence—activities of their lobbyists and their

**Figure 1.  Output Value Produced by Corporations
vs. Other Business Forms**

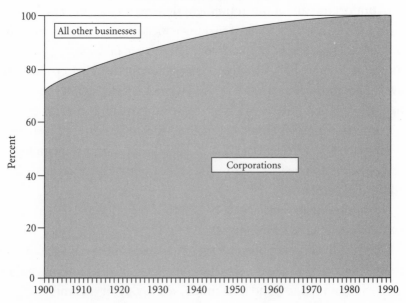

political action committees (PACs), efforts to sway public opinion and legislative action by corporate officers, so-called institutional advertising, pressure brought on cities and states for tax exemptions and similar favors, and opposition to unions. But many expenditures are made in what corporate managers consider to be the normal course of business, with neither specific intent to control nor knowledge of the aggregate effects.

These casual, even accidental, effects may be a cause for greater concern than the more deliberate efforts, since there is little thought of anyone taking responsibility. For example, a simple decision to stop buying a component from a supplier and to produce it internally instead could mean bankruptcy for the supplier, unemployment for the supplier's workers, death to smaller companies supporting that supplier, and hardship for the supplier's community—hardship that may be reflected in a smaller tax base, less police and fire protection, deteriorating streets, accumulation of trash, and poorer quality education for the community's children. The corporate manager who makes that decision may have little idea of the real effects on suppliers.

Harry Braverman put it clearly in his *Labor and Monopoly Capital*: "The fact that ... government activities are highly visible, in comparison with those of the corporation, has led to the notion that the prime exercise of social control is done by government. On the contrary, so long as investment decisions are made by the corporations, the locus of social control and coordination must be sought among them; government fills the interstices left by these prime decisions."[8]

How does the spending power of corporations compare with the spending power of the United States government? Who has the greater power to stimulate or depress a region or a sector of our economy? The federal government's total receipts, including Social Security collections, are running around $1.25 trillion a year,[9] while corporations are taking in and spending more than *eight times* that much—more than $10 trillion. When we recognize that every dollar spent, whether intentionally or unintentionally, has an effect and is a manifestation of power, we cannot escape the conclusion that, collectively, Corporate America has considerably more real, day-to-day power than that of the

> Concentration of economic power in all-embracing corporations
> . . . represents private enterprise become a kind of private gov-
> ernment which is a power unto itself—a regimentation of other
> people's money and other people's lives.
>
> Franklin D. Roosevelt, acceptance speech,
> Democratic National Convention, June 27, 1936

United States government. (In fact, much of the money spent by the government is in support or regulation of the corporate system; there is thus an ironic reciprocity in money spent by Corporate America to influence the government.)

The gross domestic product (GDP) is the measure of final goods and services produced and sold. For 1993 the United States GDP was $6.4 trillion.[10] *Corporate receipts are nearly twice as great as our total gross domestic product.* This apparent impossibility is explained by the fact that most corporate expenditures—for labor, materials, supplies, utilities, etc.—are passed through many corporate treasuries and turned over many times before coming to rest in "final" goods and services. But there is no escaping the significance of corporate spending power; it is greater than the total output of our economy!

A similar picture develops when large corporations are compared to sovereign nations. While the size of nations and corporations is constantly changing, a ranking by revenues places our larger corporations snugly among the larger countries of the world (see Figure 2). Several multinational corporations command resources greater than the tax revenues of developed nations such as Switzerland, Denmark, and Austria,[11] not to mention the scores of smaller countries. In their ability to affect lives through expenditure of funds, the largest corporations are more powerful than most countries.

As Lester Brown, president of Worldwatch Institute, wryly observed:

It was once said that the sun never set on the British Empire.
Today the sun does set on the British Empire, but not on the

### Figure 2. Government and Corporate Spending (Excluding U.S. and Nonmarket Economies)

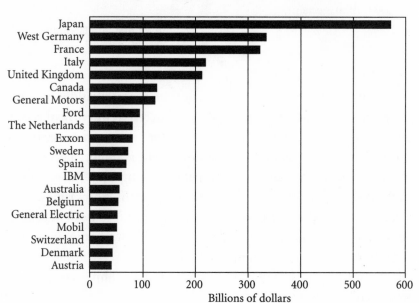

Billions of dollars

scores of global corporate empires including those of IBM, Unilever, Volkswagen and Hitachi.[12]

Of course corporations like General Motors, Ford, and Exxon will usually be spread out over several states and countries. All their spending doesn't take place in one area. Nevertheless, the ultimate power to spend is concentrated at the top of the corporation and can be moved around practically at will (albeit with some possible delay). A facility in California can be moved to Idaho; dealerships in Arkansas can be sold to a competitor and the proceeds reinvested in Argentina; and computer operations that had been decentralized can be combined in one center in Switzerland, using satellite communication. And so it goes.

## The Reach of Corporate Power

With this kind of power, a corporation has substantial leverage with a state or a host country. That is not to say that a corporation can readily

> The truly giant corporations . . . are independent republics of their own management.
>
> John Kenneth Galbraith[13]

run roughshod over a government, or even that it would if it could. Cases of such abusive behavior have occurred frequently in recent enough history and will occur again, but they are not necessarily the norm. Corporate influence is both more subtle and more pervasive. It works its ways in the halls of government, in its impact on an economy, in the molding of the public's taste and opinions. Sometimes, if we examined this influence closely, we would judge it to be beneficial to society, sometimes neutral—and sometimes negative, iniquitous. But the influence is there; it is unquestionably extensive, continuous, and cumulative. As early as 1897 it had grown to where John P. Davis would write in his *Corporations*:

> When the workman finds his wages determined by the corporation that controls the business employing his labor, and seeks refuge in a trade union that deprives him of his individuality, when the farmer finds his connection with a market dependent on the regulations of a railway company, when the businessman finds the volume of credit and currency subject to the curtailment or expansion of banking, trust and investment companies, when the small investor finds his only avenue of investment in savings banks and trust and investment companies . . . they all begin to realize that they are governed more by corporations than by the state, that [corporations] are the major part of the mechanism of government under which they live.[14]

In the final analysis, government has the power of life and death. It can make war, and it can administer the death penalty. But corporations can kill us too—in the workplace, as we consume adulterated or inadequately tested products, or as our lungs metastasize from years of absorbing industrial carcinogens.

Think about this: from 1973 through 1991, the latest year for which comparable data are available, 173 people were killed by the government by execution for serious crimes. Another 1,354 died in military action, primarily from the Vietnam conflict before we got out in 1975. That is a total of 1,527 deaths attributable directly to federal and state government.

During that same period 156 times as many workers, a total of 239,300, died on the job at the hands of industry (see Figure 3). An additional untold number of people died from industrial pollution, poisonous food and medicine, and dangerous appliances, equipment, and vehicles. (The 239,300 industrial deaths even dwarf the 48,000 American battle deaths during the entire Vietnam War. Our worst year for casualties in Vietnam—1968—resulted in 14,623 battle deaths— just a bit more than the number killed back in the United States on the job.)[15]

**Figure 3. Deaths at the Hands of Government and of Industry, 1973–1991**

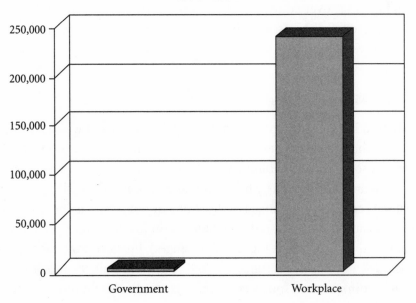

Fifteen hundred deaths occurred in eighteen years at the hands of government, many of them met by massive citizen resistance. The demonstrations and public mobilization against the war in Vietnam were of such a magnitude that they actually define an era of our history. Implementation of the death penalty often evokes an outpouring of feeling and editorial expression; it has been a major issue in gubernatorial campaigns.

But a hundred or a hundred thousand deaths at the hands of private corporations evokes no public outcry, no national demonstrations, no political pontificating. We have been desensitized to a point that we accept this carnage as a necessary product of business. Power over life and death has passed, to an extraordinary extent, into the hands of unseen and unaccountable corporate bureaucrats whose decisions are driven by the tyranny of the bottom line.

## Corporate Control of Our Culture

Power accrues to the corporation through its money, property, armies of employees, access to the media, and influence on politicians. Corporations influence us through their advertising, their connection with and leverage over education, the standards they set for morality and interpersonal relations, and ultimately in their dominant presence—an omnipresence—in our daily lives.

### At the Mercy of Madison Avenue

We couldn't escape corporate advertising if we tried, not without moving to the proverbial desert island or to a mountain cave. It is everywhere, sometimes at subliminal levels we don't even see.

We are bombarded by business and corporate advertising. It pursues us constantly, as long as at least one of our senses is "on." Newspapers and magazines, radio and television (even "public" television now displays corporate logos and messages), buses and taxicabs, billboards and commercial signs, handbills, and junk mail. It's also on athletes' uniforms and sports equipment and intrudes on our personal telephone and FAX lines. Advertising has even invaded public restrooms.

No one has counted, no one could count, the number of times we are hit by advertising in a day or a year or a lifetime. But some effort has been made to research exposure to advertising, mainly in the narrow area of children and television commercials. Liebert says a typical child sees 22,000 commercials a year, an average of over *400* a week. That works out to some 350,000 commercials by age eighteen.[16]

And no one can tell what cumulative effect advertising has. But we can be dead certain that it does affect us—that it changes our behavior and our decisions. Corporations would not spend nearly $138 billion[17] a year on advertising if their research didn't show that it was effective.

We do have some knowledge of advertising's effects, although it's pretty spotty. In a comprehensive study Pollay reviewed the work of "all North American authors known to have written on the cultural character of advertising."[18] These were some of the conclusions:

+ Advertising wields a social influence comparable to that of religion and education. (citing David M. Potter)

+ Advertising employs techniques of intensive persuasion that amount to manipulation. (citing UNESCO)

+ Its intent is to preoccupy society with material concerns.

+ Advertising promotes self-doubt, makes the consumer acutely unhappy with his or her lot, and in the process fosters self-contempt. It teaches that the simple cure for the spiritual desolation of modern life is consumption. (citing Christopher Lasch)

+ Reverence for nature has been replaced by a determination to process it. Thrift has been replaced by the duty to buy. The work ethic has been replaced by the consumption ethic. Modesty has been exorcised with help from the sexual sell. Advertising has fostered a consumption binge that has been fouling our air, water, roads, streets, fields, and forests. (citing Erik Barnouw)

+ In portraying the desirable woman as beautiful, slender, sexy, with a brilliant smile (and, needless to say, perfectly straight teeth), mysterious and seductive eyes, luminescent skin, and almost or barely out of her teens, corporate advertisers "bear a large part of the responsibility for the deep feelings of inadequacy that drive women to psychiatrists, pills, or the bottle." (citing Marya Mannes)

◆ Advertising reaches beyond our taste in manners, dress, and food to affect the basic patterns of society: the structure of authority in the family, the pattern of morals, the meanings of achievement in society. (citing Daniel Bell)

Many adults believe they can resist the effects of advertising—although research indicates that our ability to do so is considerably more limited than we might like to think. But virtually no one would claim that children have the degree of sophistication and experience necessary to resist advertising—or even to always recognize it as advertising. In fact children, especially those of preschool age, often confuse advertising with regular programming. It is no exaggeration to say that, given sufficient exposure, Corporate America could exert more control over the developing morals and character of children than their parents, churches, or schools.

Think about that. Are you willing to turn your child's development over to a corporation whose measure of morality is the bottom line—a business enterprise with neither a conscience nor a particular interest in your child's well-being?

Advertising is not a benign, neutral entertainment medium for the kiddies. Corporate advertisers are dead serious. Our children are grow-

---

If I were asked to name the deadliest subversive force within capitalism, the single greatest source of its waning morality—I would without hesitation name advertising. How else should one identify a force that debases language, drains thought, and undoes dignity?

Robert L. Heilbroner[19]

ing up viewing 350,000 carefully crafted, psychologically tested, expensive, imaginative, artistic efforts to persuade them to want, to beg and plead, to be jealous of the possessions of others, and to covet material goods.

Through advertising large commercial enterprises can have their own massive propaganda vehicle. The $138 billion they spend annually is more than the total salaries we pay for all of our public elementary and secondary school teachers and administrators.[20] It is one-and-a-half times as much as we spend—from federal, state, and local government funding, tuition, and all other sources—on public institutions of higher learning.[21] Enormous power, incalculable influence.

And without accountability. Corporations exercise this influence on schoolchildren with no requirement for accountability, no reporting on message content or effects, no need to explain their actions before a skeptical public, never even a requirement to go before the citizens and stand for reelection.

Of course advertising not only impels women and men—and children—to pursue an appearance and a persona that nature never intended; it demeans women by using their nearly nude forms as attractive bait for wholly irrelevant products—beer, motorcycles, lawn mowers, even computers. This tendency, so pronounced in the 1950s, was resisted to some degree in the 1960s and 1970s as both women and men became more conscious of the exploitation of women in society. But it has been returning with renewed vigor. Prove it for yourself: this week count the beer and car ads that feature largely unclothed, youthful women—not using the product, but adorning it, pure lure, with the implied promise that she's yours when you buy. Ever see a man, in a bikini or a G-string, wrapped around a beer bottle or across the hood of a car as a come-on?

Corporate and business advertising makes us want things and encourages us to be dissatisfied or uncomfortable or insecure without them. It creates needs that had not previously existed. It goads us to outdo our neighbors, to dress more expensively (although not necessarily more tastefully) than our co-workers, to drive a flashier, faster, and above all more costly automobile (or pickup truck, camper, boat, motorcycle, even lawnmower). It tells us that, with a particular model of car or brand of jeans or perfume, we will be more attractive, more desirable sexually, or appear to be more prosperous and successful.

We learn through advertising to judge ourselves and to judge each other in terms of the brand names on our cars, clothes, beverages, wristwatches, cosmetics. Personal qualities are displaced by these "commercial" qualities. We are taught to focus on products over people. We become preoccupied with material concerns.

To the extent that we respond to this materialistic advertising, we will eat out more, and when we don't eat out we will eat out of packages. Corporations sell more and make more profit this way, but we get more fat and cholesterol and sugar and salt, more chemical additives, more caffeine, and certainly spend more money than if we prepared our own meals. We will suffer more diabetes, more heart attacks, more cancer, more obesity.

Advertising, and especially television advertising, also conditions us to accept lying.

> ... perhaps one of the most powerful effects of television has been to teach a national tolerance of falsehood, exaggeration, and distortion. Parents who ask their children to tell the truth must explain that of course a certain cereal will not transform them into great athletes, as the highly-paid announcer says, nor will the drug mentioned really cure hemorrhoids, or cancer, or arthritis. The announcer is really lying.[22]

Of course corporate advertising can have beneficial effects as well. Pollay cites the facilitation of marketplace efficiencies, and others commend some advertising for providing useful, if not always reliable or truthful, information. Advertising could help us get along better with each other and create a better society—for example, it could condition us to be less prejudiced toward other races. Advertising could do this and more, but what we usually get from business/corporate advertising is much less.

> Advertisements are now so numerous that they are very negligently perused, and it is therefore become necessary to gain attention by magnificence of promises and by eloquence sometimes sublime and sometimes pathetick [sic]. Promise—large promise—is the soul of advertising.
>
> Samuel Johnson, 1758[23]

Even when doing good, advertising is still an instrument of the far-reaching power of the corporation, power over our wants, our thoughts, our relations with each other, our standards of behavior and morality—power over our culture and our lives.

It is a power that has grown dramatically in the last few years of the human experience: we have only had printing since the fifteenth century, radio since the nineteenth, and television some fifty years. We can be sure that the advertising industry is perfectly aware of the potential of technologies like subliminal persuasion and virtual reality. Can there be any doubt that new means of sensory intrusion are even now being developed that will broaden advertising's reach and corporate power far beyond what we can even imagine today?

## The Corporate Academy

As noted earlier, corporate television advertising reaches preschoolers some 22,000 times a year. Each message is intended to induce children to plead for the advertised products. Advertising continues to pursue them through their school years and then throughout the rest of their lives.

But corporations also influence children in less overt and perhaps less deliberate ways. This influence helps shape their ethical standards, their life goals, their view of the world, and the way they value other persons. It occurs substantially through the educational system, especially in our colleges and universities.

We once thought of secondary and vocational schools as preparing people for jobs, while college was to give them a well-rounded, liberal education in the arts, humanities, history, social science, psychology, philosophy, and the like. While this may once have been so, it is no longer, thanks substantially to corporate influence. In 1971 over two-and-a-half times as many graduate degrees were awarded in the liberal arts as in business and management studies. This huge lead was practically erased in just twenty years; by 1991 only 13 percent *more degrees were awarded in the liberal arts than in business.*[24]

Why have college students turned from the pursuit of a broad, well-rounded education to a much narrower, vocationally oriented degree in business? There were no doubt many contributing factors, but the hand of Corporate America is unmistakably in evidence. The fingers of this hand reach to all areas of the university—from initial advising and counseling through course offerings and content, the majors students select and the careers they seek, university and student financial resources, and ultimately the policymaking bodies at the highest levels of the university.

Corporate recruiters, despite lip service to liberal arts, seek mainly business school graduates. Of course there are other recruiters, but the great majority of job interviews on any campus are with large corporations (and with the accounting, consulting, and law firms that serve them). Students take note of the majors the recruiters want to interview, see where the jobs are, and head straight for the business school.

There, in their rather tender years, they are taught the lesson that the purpose of the corporation is to maximize the bottom line.

Corporate foundations and philanthropy favor the business schools. Gifts of art, or contributions to the athletic program, may help a university in a general sense, but they do little for academic programs. Academic aid, in the form of scholarships, endowed professorships, research grants, and contributions of equipment, is what really counts; it is heavily concentrated on the business and engineering schools.

Corporations naturally enough support their own. They support teaching the religion and philosophy of the bottom line. The unsur-

prising consequence is that the business schools have grown vigorously and were less affected by the tight budgets experienced in recent
years at institutions of higher learning.

Corporations leverage their campus recruiting and financial
support by placing their executives in critical policymaking positions
within the university's top management. Look at the highest levels. In
most states a statewide board, variously called the board of regents, the
university coordinating board, or the like, is appointed by the governor
and oversees the public universities and colleges. In virtually every state
a majority or at the minimum a sizable minority of its members come
from business—mostly from big business.

Individual campuses may also have separate governing boards,
where again we find the same dominance by corporate executives.
Some universities have nongoverning but highly influential advisory,
foundation, or endowment boards—again dominated by corporate
executives. There will often be one or more advisory boards for the
business and engineering schools, composed almost entirely of representatives of corporations and their accounting firms.

Usually the corporate representatives will have the numbers to simply outvote opposition to their ideas for higher education—but this will
not often be necessary. University administrators want to be loved and
respected, just like the rest of us. They especially want to be respected
by the hard-nosed professionals they think of as leading their community's great corporations. Thus university presidents, vice presidents,
and deans seek the advice and counsel of the corporate representatives.
And they show great reticence in taking any action that might be con-
strued by business people as "ivory tower" or in some way not "real-
world." Not infrequently the corporate representatives find they do
not even need to press their views—their mere presence, and their
image among university administrators as holders of the keys of power,
may be sufficient.

This attitude was exemplified by the executive vice president at
a large midwestern university, a person who above all appeared to seek
approval as a peer among the community's business leaders. Expressing

herself on the role of the university, she declared that, "Our job is to find out what IBM wants from our graduates and then give it to them."[25]

The corporate influence is strongest, and most obvious, in higher education, but it extends increasingly into the secondary and elementary schools. Many corporations now prepare materials for free distribution in the public schools—a seductive offer most funds-strapped schools find difficult to resist.

In this environment we should not be surprised to see Corporate America exploiting the power of television. A for-profit venture, Channel One, entices public, tax-supported schools into regularly and repeatedly exposing the nation's children to corporate commercials with the promise of "free" programs and video equipment. Channel One reportedly generates $100 million a year in ad sales,[26] while beaming commercials to eight million students in 12,000 schools.[27]

In a similar program Star Broadcasting plans to broadcast music and commercials in school cafeterias; over 1,000 schools in twenty-four states have reportedly signed up to give Corporate America access to these captive and impressionable audiences.[28] And the Telephone Advertising Corporation of America is reportedly busy installing pay telephones with video kiosks that flash product messages over and over throughout the school day.[29]

Corporations have offered schools "educational" videotapes that are, for the corporation, essentially advertising vehicles. *Dollars & Sense* reports on one such tape accepted by seven urban school districts that was designed to replace an hour of instruction a day—an hour removed from teacher instruction and turned over to material provided by enterprises motivated first by the bottom line and not necessarily by educational excellence. One-sixth of the tape was devoted to commercials![30]

---

Maybelline cosmetic ads stare down from the walls of Wichita's Southeast High School.

"Business Goes to School Looking to Give Some, Gain a Lot,"
*The Wichita Eagle*[31]

Meanwhile giant enterprises like Dow Chemical, Exxon, Proctor & Gamble, and Burger King are flooding schools with printed materials, games, posters, and other exhibits that bombard students with product logos and propaganda.[32] Corporate America has learned well how to exploit the schools' reduced budgets and the yearnings of teachers and administrators for snazzy materials to supplement the often-meager materials their institutions can afford to buy.

## The Church of the Holy Corpocracy

The power of the corporation is not limited to advertising and education; it has unmeasured and usually unnoted sway over our personal relationships and attitudes. The corporation and its accountants teach us to value each other in terms of our income and wealth—after all, that is how the corporation is valued, by the bottom line. It is not what we do, what we create, or the lasting contribution we might make to society that the bottom-line philosophy teaches us to value; it is how much money we make.

So the wheeling and dealing Wall Street operative and the corporate executive, whose annual incomes may run to millions of dollars, are esteemed far above the person who teaches high school civics, the police officer who patrols our mean streets, the emergency medical technician who saves a life or two every Saturday night, the ministers, artists, poets, social workers, nurses, and so many others who contribute great value to our society.

Because this furthers its self-interest, the corporation teaches us to place obligation to the company and to the job over obligation to family, friends, and community. Virtually all corporations, or more precisely their "public affairs officers," will deny this, but it is self-evident to the manager who aspires to get ahead. Work late to get the report out, or attend the daughter's school play? Those who have been there know it is not even a choice. Sure, you can attend the play, put family above the corporation—and be permanently marked for the slow track, or more accurately the sidetrack.

Ulcers? Burnout? Kids into drugs? Spouse finding affection someplace else? Stress? Alcohol? Heart attack? If you want to succeed in most corporations, you don't mention them. This ethos from the corporation is then brought home and at least by example taught to our children. They grow up, then go and do likewise. And so the system produces generations of "successful" but unhappy, unfulfilled, over-stressed managers.

We have a long tradition of individualism in America. From Jamestown to space pioneers, the Daniel Boones, Kit Carsons, Wyatt Earps, Calamity Janes, Geronimos, trappers and traders, explorers, and entre-preneurs—they all stir in us the spirit of individual self-sufficiency. This may not always be good, but it is a part of our character and heritage. The large corporation is changing that character. Individualism in thought, behavior, and attire is neither welcomed nor rewarded. All is by committee, by group. Americans may still pride themselves on their individualism, but this is a diminishing trait and a diminishing pride, exercised almost exclusively outside the corporation.

The most dangerous and insidious effect of corporate collec-tivism is its replacement of personal responsibility with collective responsibility. In this ethos no individual is seen as responsible for the corporation's actions. When decisions, however abhorrent they may be, are made by committee or are run through a round-robin approval cycle, no one person feels or accepts responsibility. Not only is respon-sibility thus avoided, but the individual manager can reason that the action must not really be bad because it has been sanctioned by pro-fessional colleagues. Inflated billings, shortcutting workplace safety, tax evasion, secret dumping of toxic waste, even deadly products—appar-ently all can seem acceptable when the decision is made by a group.

This is how good people end up making harmful decisions in cor-porations. This is how corporate managers, whose personal morality, conscience, or religion would prevent them as individuals from ever willingly placing others' lives in jeopardy for a few dollars of profit, will do exactly that in the corporation. Good people end up taking such harmful actions because, when they enter the corporate environment, they come under great pressure to accept the corporate morality, to allow it to dominate their personal morality. And the corporate moral-ity, as we have seen, is a soulless morality defined by the single com-mandment: "Maximize the bottom line!"

> Even the most upright people are apt to become dishonest and
> unmindful of their civic responsibilities when placed in a typical
> corporate environment. . . . The culprit is not personal value but
> corporate culture. . . . People's personal values are getting blocked
> by the needs of the company.
>
> *The Wall Street Journal*[33]

## The Corporation and Crime

The corporation has had a profound effect on our attitudes about
crime. If you or I were to be caught robbing a liquor store of, say, $500,
we would surely pay, very likely with a term in jail. But if a corporation steals $10 million from its customers through price fixing, or
from its neighbors by discharging toxic pollution into the air, it will
get off with a slap on the wrist, a fine that is a fraction of the bottom
line gain.

The corporate advocate will say that a corporation may occasionally slip up, perhaps due to placing unwarranted trust in dishonest
employees, but that at most a handful are guilty of anything even
approximating criminal activity.

*Fortune* magazine, no enemy of Corporate America, took a look
at corporate crime.[34] Counting only major crimes and even excluding
cases of foreign bribery, kickbacks, and other improper payments, *Fortune*'s investigators found that *at least* 11 percent of the 1,043 corporations studied had been involved in one or more major crime in the
previous ten years.

*Fortune* included only cases that had resulted in conviction on federal criminal charges or in consent decrees (where companies don't
admit guilt—but promise not to do it again). They omitted minor cases
of corruption far down the chain of command; "the standard throughout was corporate responsibility at a high level."

One out of every ten! Who are these rogue corporations, these
felons? They include Allied Chemical, American Airlines, American
Brands, American Can, American Cyanamid, Anheuser-Busch, Ashland

Oil, Beatrice Foods, Bethlehem Steel, Boise Cascade, Borden, Borg-Warner, Braniff International—and those are just the As and Bs.

Suppose the police came to your door and told you that one out of every ten of your neighbors was a convicted felon. What kind of neighborhood would you think you were living in? Well, that appears to be the sort of neighborhood—or more precisely, the sort of nation—that these corporate scofflaws have given us.

Seeking to explain this rampant corporate lawlessness, Stanley Sporkin, then the SEC's chief of enforcement, blamed what he called the *bottom-line philosophy*: "In many instances where people are not lining their own pockets you can only explain corporate crime in terms of 'produce or perish.'"[35]

Part of the cultural contribution of large corporations is white collar crime. Another contribution is to desensitize the nation to this corporate crime; we have practically learned to take it for granted. Many people are not nearly as outraged when a General Electric commits a multi-million dollar fraud[36] as they are when a lone burglar steals goods worth a couple of thousand dollars. And, relative to their respective assets, we have come to accept the burglar's disproportionate fine and prison sentence against a fine for the corporation that doesn't even equal the amount stolen.

So now we have to think of crime in two categories: individual and corporate. We might as well say little crime and big crime. Little crime gets pursued and prosecuted with vigor. Big crime often gets excused; when it is prosecuted the penalty is barely felt. And as a society, we teach our children the morality that wealth and power excuse corruption, while poverty makes it more sinful.

## Power Over Public Policy

When the CEO of a large corporation calls, virtually any member of Congress is ready to listen. When you or I call, we get a busy signal.

That's called "access." It's guaranteed for the large corporation. Partly that's because they control political action committees that can drop thousands of dollars into a politician's campaign chest. Partly it's because CEOs know and talk with each other, so the influence and resources of one are magnified. And partly it's because large companies have many employees who vote, contribute, write letters, and campaign.

Once this was subtle. Now it has become blatant. IBM, for example, recently sent an internal, electronic mail memo urging its 110,000 employees to fight for the defeat of two Democratic health-care bills in Congress (whether the IRS will review the tax deductibility of depreciation and other costs associated with IBM's internal electronic communication system remains to be seen). Employees were asked to send a personal message to Congress—a message written by IBM's Vice Chairman Paul Rizzo.

In an internal letter Mobil Corporation's Chairman Lucio Noto opposed the health-care bills and "invited" Mobil employees to contact Congress. So did DuPont Chairman Edgar Woolard. General Mills held meetings in which employees were shown a company-made video that urged them to contact Congress and oppose any health-care bill that would require employers to pay for coverage.[37] As we know, the health-care bills were indeed defeated.

> ...a friend of business [points out] that it has fought every progressive piece of American legislation of this century, from child labor laws on up.[38]

A comprehensive and current study of business influence over legislation and public policy has not been done. However, this influence is apparently so extensive that it warrants introduction of a new dictionary term: "corpocracy," to take its place alongside terms like democracy, autocracy, plutocracy, and bureaucracy. But whatever it is called, business influence over our government, our society, and our lives is great and growing.

This discussion has dealt with the power and influence of larger business enterprises, especially in the aggregate. Sometimes the mind is benumbed by large numbers; it may be helpful to consider the reach of a single corporation.

## The Power of One Company

So for perspective, let's take a look at the power of just one of the larger corporations. We'll choose General Motors, one of the largest companies in the world, but the story would be about the same with dozens of other companies. While this company is very large, it may or may not be very successful during any given period of time. Size does not necessarily equal quality or success, but it does equal power.

By any measure General Motors is one of the largest multinational corporations, with nearly 700,000 employees around the world.[39] Earlier in this chapter, I noted that each employed worker in the U.S. supports an average of 2.13 additional persons. Worldwide the ratio is probably higher; this would mean that decisions by the head of General Motors directly affect the well-being, the livelihood, and the future of a population of more than 1.5 million people.

This one corporate CEO has influence over more people than the governor of Alaska, Delaware, Hawaii, Idaho, Maine, Montana, Nevada, New Hampshire, North or South Dakota, Rhode Island, Vermont, or Wyoming. Power over a greater mass of people than those concentrated in cities like Atlanta, Boston, Cleveland, Dallas, Detroit, Kansas City, New Orleans, St. Louis, San Francisco, Seattle, and Washington, D.C.

Companies the size of General Motors can dominate local communities. Their size, number of employees, and economic significance would all combine to produce influence, even if the corporate managers had no interest in such influence (although such a disinterest would be exceptional). From Ford in Dearborn to Boeing in Seattle, Caterpillar in Peoria to RJR in Winston-Salem, communities are usually no match for large resident corporations.

Even states are not always powerful enough to buck the larger corporation. Mark Dowie and Theodore Brown described one case: "The Du Pont family, majority owners of the company, virtually control the entire state of Delaware, from the governor to the attorney general to the state's two biggest newspapers. The company's dominance results in a tax structure favorable to the family and the company and an almost absolute say in land use decisions."[40]

> Most men are servants of corporations.
>
> **Woodrow Wilson**

The number of General Motors employees is greater than the populations of several sovereign countries—more, even, than the populations of eleven countries put together. Like some of those countries, General Motors, in common with other corporate giants, is run by a government that the voting public did not elect and cannot recall, impeach, or even petition effectively.

General Motors is larger than the U.S. Army, larger than the Air Force, larger than the Navy and Marines Corps combined.[41]

For 1994 GM had revenues of $155 billion.[42] That would make its budget about the size of the governments of Sweden or The Netherlands—or of Norway, New Zealand, Finland, Greece, and Ireland combined. General Motors controlled funds *four times* as great as the budget for the entire U.S. Department of Transportation, five times the budget for the Department of Education, and fourteen times the budget of the Department of Justice.[43]

How has General Motors used this tremendous power? What kind of corporation is this?

It is a company that has pleased many customers with its products. General Motors' stockholders may think it is fine. It won the Malcolm Baldrige Award for quality (although corporations apparently promote themselves for this award with massive campaigns like those for Hollywood's Oscars). And as already noted, it employs hundreds of thousands of workers.

But it is a corporation that on too many occasions has seriously abused its power.

It has harmed its customers:

- GM and thirty-four Northern California dealerships were charged by the California Department of Motor Vehicles with fraudulently reselling vehicles with serious mechanical problems, without telling the buyers. GM agreed to a settlement.[44]

♦ General Motors rejected a $15 stabilizing bar for its rear-engine Corvairs while car owners were being killed and dealers were complaining about its instability. U.S. Representative John L. Burton charged that, "GM manufactured and marketed 1.2 million unsafe Corvairs for the 1960–1963 model years, knew about the inherent safety defects, yet did nothing to correct them. . . . GM acted in reckless disregard for human life."[45]

♦ Ralph Nader charged GM with using "accident prone wheels" on earlier trucks as a cost-cutting measure, and also with marketing defective school buses that showed repeated problems with brake failures, transmissions, steering, and tires.[46]

♦ GM's pickup trucks with "sidesaddle" gas tanks have been charged by critics with being responsible for more than 300 deaths (see Chapter 7 for fuller discussion).[47]

♦ General Motors Acceptance Corporation, a GM subsidiary, required its customers to pay more into escrow accounts than the amounts that were legally allowed. The company then profited from interest from investing the excess funds. It settled for $100 million.[48]

It has unnecessarily risked the health and safety of its employees:

♦ In Oklahoma City the Occupational Safety and Health Administration fined GM $2.8 million for fifty-seven violations, including one that cost the life of a maintenance worker at the plant there. OSHA said GM was ignoring safety regulations.[49]

It has taken advantage of the communities in which it operates:

♦ The company whose abuse of Flint, Michigan, was chronicled in the movie Roger and Me mounted what appeared to be a coordinated "blitzkrieg" raid on twenty Michigan communities, suddenly demanding over $50 million in tax abatements. These demands were on top of substantial tax breaks, usually 50 percent, previously given. If GM had been successful this move would have reduced local government budgets by as much as 45 percent. Speaking of the GM CEO, the Genesee Township assessor said he "just wants to stomp us into the ground. All he wants to do is make more money."[50]

◆ In return for tax abatements—more than $1.3 billion over a twenty-year period—GM promised to retain 8,000 jobs in Ypsilanti, Michigan. Then the company arbitrarily announced that it was closing the plant there and moving production to Arlington,

---

... Every large corporation should be thought of as a political system, that is, an entity whose leaders exercise great power, influence, and control over other human beings ... by its decisions the large corporation may

◆ cause death, injury, disease, and severe physical pain, e.g., by decisions resulting in pollution, poor design, inadequate quality control, plant safety, and working conditions.

◆ impose severe deprivations of income, well-being, and effective personal freedom, e.g., by decisions on hiring and firing, employment, discrimination, and plant location.

◆ exercise influence, power, control, and even coercion over employees, consumers, suppliers, and others, e.g., by manipulating expectations of rewards and deprivations, by advertising, propaganda, promotions, and demotions, not to mention possible illegal practices.

Robert A. Dahl, "Governing the Giant Corporation"[51]

Texas. In court GM admitted that the move was not for economic necessity; observers speculated that it was for a more pliant labor environment.[52]

It has cost the nation:

♦ Citizen Action reports that General Motors is one of the ten biggest corporate polluters in America.[53]

♦ General Motors was convicted in 1949 of criminally conspiring (with Standard Oil of California and Firestone) to eliminate the electric rail system, so it could be replaced with their buses; GM then sought to monopolize the sale of those buses.[54]

This is how one large company uses its power. Unfortunately, the same story could be told for many others.

As we've seen in this chapter, corporations—especially the larger corporations—have great power without accountability. If they were driven by concern for the public interest, that might not be such a problem. But when their moral yardstick is the mandate of the bottom line, abuse, sooner or later, becomes virtually inevitable.

In the next chapter we move to a broader examination of the ways in which the great power of corporations is abused and how it costs the communities and societies in which they operate, as well as their employees, customers, suppliers, and neighbors.

## Notes

1. John Kenneth Galbraith, *The Age of Uncertainty* (Boston: Houghton Mifflin, 1977), 257.
2. *Washington Post*–ABC News nationwide poll, July 1992.
3. Bureau of the Census, *Statistical Abstract of the United States 1992*, Table 827, "Number of Returns, Receipts, and Net Income, by Type of Business, 1970 to 1988, and by Industry, 1988."
4. Ibid., Table 608, "Employment Status of the Noninstitutional Population 16 Years Old and Over: 1950 to 1991," and Table 2, "Population: 1900 to 1991."

5. Ibid., Table 826, "Number of Returns and Business Receipts, by Size of Receipts and Type of Business: 1970 to 1988."

6. Derived from F. M. Scherer, "Corporate Ownership and Control," In *The U.S. Business Corporation: An Institution in Transition*, ed. John R. Meyer and James M. Gustafson (Cambridge, Mass.: Ballinger Publishing, 1988), 43–66.

7. Bureau of the Census, *Statistical Abstract of the United States 1994*, Table 832, "Number of Returns and Business Receipts . . ."

8. Harry Braverman, *Labor and Monopoly Capital: The Degradation of Work in the Twentieth Century* (New York: Monthly Review Press, 1974), 268–69.

9. Bureau of Census, *Statistical Abstract of the United States 1992*, Table 492, "Federal Receipts, by Source: 1980 to 1992."

10. *Economic Report of the President* (Washington, D.C.: U.S. Government Printing Office, February 1994), Table B-1, "Gross Domestic Product, 1959–93."

11. Bureau of the Census, *Statistical Abstract of the United States 1990*, Table 1456 (1987 tax revenues), and "Fortune 500," *Fortune*, 24 April 1989, 354.

12. Lester R. Brown, *World Without Borders* (New York: Random House, 1972), 214–16.

13. John Kenneth Galbraith, *Almost Everyone's Guide to Economics* (Boston: Houghton Mifflin, 1978), 57.

14. John P. Davis, *Corporations: A Study of the Origin and Development of Great Business Combinations and of Their Relation to the Authority of the State* (New York: Capricorn Books, 1961), II: 267–68.

15. Bureau of the Census, *Statistical Abstract of the United States 1985*, Table 712; *Statistical Abstract of the United States 1989*, Tables 326, 547, 680; *Statistical Abstract of the United States 1992*, Table 665.

16. Robert M. Liebert, "Effects of Television on Children and Adolescents," *Developmental and Behavioral Pediatrics* (February 1986): 43–48.

17. Bureau of the Census, *Statistical Abstract of the United States 1992*, Table 913, "Advertising—Estimated Expenditures, by Medium: 1980 to 1993."

18. Richard W. Pollay, "The Distorted Mirror: Reflections on the Unintended Consequences of Advertising," *Journal of Marketing* (April 1986): 18–36.
19. In *Business Civilization in Decline*, cited in Pollay. "The Distorted Mirror," 18–36.
20. Bureau of the Census, *Statistical Abstract of the United States 1994*, Table 250, "Finances of Public Elementary and Secondary School Systems . . ."
21. Ibid., Table 277, "Institutions of Higher Education—Finances: 1980 to 1991."
22. Harry J. Skornia, *Television and Society* (New York: McGraw-Hill, 1965), 158.
23. Samuel Johnson, *The Idler*, 1758; cited in *The Great Quotations*, comp. George Seldes (New York: Pocket Books, 1967), 5.
24. Bureau of the Census, *Statistical Abstract of the United States 1994*, Table 294, "Masters and Doctorate Degrees Earned, by Field: 1971–1991."
25. Lecture by the university's then-executive vice president to the Wichita State University Women's Opportunity Resource Center, Spring 1988.
26. "Is Disney Ready To Go To School?" *Business Week*, 2 August 1993, 22.
27. "Clifton Teenager Hits the Big Time: Broadcast News in L. A.," *The Bergen Record*, 21 February 1995.
28. "Ads Could Hit School Halls," *USA Today*, 30 July 1993.
29. "Video Ads by Phones Ring Up School Funds," *USA Today*, 3 December 1991; "Atlanta Firm Plans to Launch 'Video Kiosk' Advertising At High School Pay Phones," *Education Hotline (Teacher Magazine Education Week)* (October 1990): 2.
30. Dave Corbett and Thea Lee, "Learning for Sale: Will Business Set the Agenda for School Reform?" *Dollars & Sense* (October 1989): 13–15.
31. "Business Goes to School Looking to Give Some, Gain a Lot," *The Wichita Eagle*, 20 November 1989.
32. "Corporate Dumping," *Washington City Paper*, 11 December 1992, 21–22, 24.
33. "Nature or Nurture? Study Blames Ethical Lapses on Corporate Goals," *The Wall Street Journal*, 9 October 1987.

34. "How Lawless Are Big Companies?" *Fortune*, 1 December 1980, 56–64.
35. Ibid.
36. "GE Is Fined $10 Million in Criminal Case," *The Wall Street Journal*, 27 July 1990; "Israeli Military Aid Scandal Jolts GE; Company to Settle Fraud Charges, Defends Ethics Program," *The Washington Post*, 20 July 1992; *Infact Brings GE to Light* (Boston: INFACT, 1988), 28.
37. "Some Firms Urging Workers to Oppose Health Care Bills," *The Washington Post*, 20 August 1994; " 'Office Politics' is Taking On a New Wrinkle," *The Washington Post*, 11 September 1994.
38. Henry Mintzberg, *Power In and Around Corporations* (Englewood Cliffs, N.J.: Prentice-Hall, 1983), 527.
39. General Motors Media Relations Office, Washington, D.C., 14 November 1990 (data for third quarter 1990, worldwide, including all subsidiaries).
40. Mark Dowie and Theodore A. Brown, "Taking Stock: The Best and Worst of American Business," *Mother Jones*, June 1985, 25.
41. *Statistical Abstract of the United States 1994*, Table 553, "Department of Defense Manpower: 1950 to 1993."
42. "G.M.'s Profits a Record in Quarter and Year," *The New York Times*, 1 February 1995.
43. *Statistical Abstract of the United States 1994*, Table 509, "Federal Outlays, by Detailed Function: 1980 to 1994."
44. "General Motors: Reckless Homicide?" *Multinational Monitor* (December 1994): 10–11.
45. Russell Mokhiber, *Corporate Crime and Violence* (San Francisco: Sierra Club Books, 1988), 130–38.
46. Ralph Nader, ed., *The Consumer and Corporate Accountability* (New York: Harcourt Brace Jovanovich, 1973), 81–83.
47. "Data Show G.M. Knew for Years of Risk in Pickup Trucks' Design," *The New York Times*, 17 November 1993.
48. "G.M. Unit Settles Mortgage Escrow Suit," *The New York Times*, 28 January 1992.
49. *USA Today*, (national roundup), 27 September 1991.
50. Louis Nemeth, "Mendacity in Michigan," *Multinational Monitor* (31 March 1986): 3–7, 12.

51. Robert A. Dahl, "Governing the Giant Corporation," in *Corporate Power in America*, ed. Ralph Nader and Mark J. Green (New York: Grossman Publishers, 1973), 10–24.
52. "Stop Capital Flight: A Strategy for Corporate Accountability," *Multinational Monitor* (June 1993): 12–15.
53. "Neighbors of Texas Plant Felt No Threat from Its Pollutants," *USA Today*, 11 July 1991.
54. Mokhiber, *Corporate Crime and Violence*, 221–28.

# Part Two
# Consequences of Unaccountability

# 5

# The Harm to Our Communities and Our Nation

CORPORATE MANAGERS ARE not, by and large, mean or thought-less persons. They do not set out purposely to do harm. But when their every action, every decision is driven by the tyranny of the bottom line, harm is often the result.

The harm corporations do is borne by their stakeholders. It is borne by those who give the corporation life, provide the means for its success, patronize its products, and nurture it by providing an essential infrastructure at public expense.

In a market economy transactions are supposed to represent a fair exchange. Customers pay the price to get goods and services. Employees give their time and labor, and receive compensation in exchange. Communities grant special favors and benefits, and expect jobs, contributions to the economy, and, eventually, tax revenues in return. This is how most of us think of the social contract with corporations.

But too often that is not how it works. Our relationship with large corporations is unbalanced, with the far greater power on the corporations' side. As we've seen in Chapter 3—and contrary to protests we sometimes hear from corporate executives—this power is exercised with substantial latitude and no real accountability. As a consequence, stakeholders suffer.

Although the stories have often been told, we need to consider some examples of how corporations, driven by the tyranny of the bottom line, harm us. This is not intended as an exercise in "corporate bashing," nor is it an attack on corporate management; neither would be constructive. This and the following three chapters are meant instead to provide a perspective on just how much the tyranny of the bottom line costs us all. Then we can constructively develop a prescription for change.

We begin in this chapter with a look at the effects on local communities and our broader society.

Communities invest in corporations, often substantially. These investments are made in expectation of a fair return to the community. Although the record is replete with exaggeration and hype, many times the benefits to the community are indeed substantial. We will not have a fair picture of the impact of the corporation, however, if we concentrate solely on the benefits and ignore the costs.

Communities give corporations tax breaks, zoning exemptions, and special services. Communities provide a vehicle for corporations to obtain capital at low interest rates by issuing industrial revenue bonds for the corporation. (Interest earned on industrial-revenue bonds is not subject to federal income tax, so the interest rate paid by the corporate borrower is lower.)

Citizens of communities make up for business tax breaks out of their own pockets and bear the brunt of corporate air, water, noise, and aesthetic pollution. Communities bear the cost of congestion and provide the roads, sewer, police, and education infrastructure that is so very important to corporations. Communities pay for the education of the corporation's workers, providing it with an educated and skilled workforce, largely at taxpayer expense.

And sometimes the community investment on the corporation's behalf is far greater than even all this, as it was at Love Canal, Bhopal, Times Beach, Stringfellow Pits, Idaho's Silver Valley—and how many others not yet discovered?

## Love Thy Neighbor

Corporations can be good neighbors. Some erect architecturally appealing facilities, install attractive landscaping, and control their pollution and waste. But many don't. At Love Canal, Hooker Chemical didn't.

Niagara Falls is a beautiful, romantic place, a place of enchantment for honeymooners and vacationers. But for the residents in the area around Love Canal, it became a hellhole, a fiendish presence that silently attacked their homes, their bodies, their children—with a poison that invaded their nervous systems, their blood cells, their brains.

At first, it just looked like a public-spirited offer by a socially responsible corporation—giving a parcel of land to the Niagara Falls Board of Education for one dollar. Of course there *was* that provision in the deed that said the company would not be responsible if anyone incurred physical harm or died because of the buried wastes on the site, so the company could claim that the school board *had* been warned.

But the board went ahead and constructed an elementary school and a playground. And people bought homes and started families and planned their futures.

Then things began to go wrong. First there were the phosphorous rocks that exploded when kids threw them against concrete. Then trees and gardens began to wilt and die; some were scorched, like they had been hit by a brush fire. Groundwater ate away redwood posts. Sometimes fires and explosions just erupted spontaneously. Black gunk seeped up into yards; basements started emitting a noxious, threatening odor.[1]

A dog's nose was burned as it sniffed the ground. Pets lost fur, produced skin lesions, and developed severe nasal problems and internal tumors.[2]

And then the human sickness began. Headaches, asthma, breathing problems. Erupting sores, hair loss, dizziness, nosebleeds, nausea, fainting. Epilepsy, nervous breakdowns, attempted suicide. Tests by the Environmental Protection Agency revealed that eleven persons out of thirty-six tested—30 percent—had developed a rare type of chromosome breakage, indicating a greater risk of cancer, genetic damage, miscarriages, stillbirths, and birth defects.[3]

Couples were terrified. A baby girl was born with an irregular heartbeat: her heart had a hole in it. She also had a cleft palate, bone blockage in her nose, partial deafness, and deformed ears. Her teeth came in with a double row on the bottom. She was mentally retarded and later developed an enlarged liver.[4] A boy was born with his diaphragm and intestines outside his body.[5]

In one age group a third of the women had miscarriages; the odds against a rate that high are 250 to 1.[6] Over a five-year period, *more than half* the babies were born with birth defects[7] (in only one block, four were born mentally retarded).[8] Five crib deaths were discovered within an area of a few blocks.[9] Out of one group of fifteen pregnancies there were only two normal births![10]

A little boy had been playing baseball and football, with no sign of problems. Then suddenly his body swelled up, and he died.[11]

How do parents feel when they learn that the school playground, where their children play every school day, could be killing them? What do you do when you discover your home may be a death trap?

The state health department had helpful advice: "Don't eat out of your gardens. Don't go in your backyards. Stay out of your basement—just throw the laundry in there and come right back up. Have the children walk on the sidewalk; make sure they don't cut across the canal or walk on the canal itself."[12] A state biophysicist analyzed the air in one basement and determined that the safe exposure time there was 2.4 minutes.[13]

The mayor was little help. He blamed a neighborhood group, accused it of hurting tourism.[14]

But the problem wasn't caused by a neighborhood group. It was not caused by the individual citizens of Niagara Falls or by the residents of the Love Canal area. And the problem wasn't caused by the school board or other public officials, although they made it worse.

The problem was caused by a *corporate* citizen of Niagara Falls—Hooker Chemical (now Occidental Chemical Corporation). It was caused by the disposal of toxic wastes in an old dry channel that had originally been intended as a canal to connect the upper and lower Niagara River. Hooker covered the wastes in the canal, then sold the land to the Board of Education.

What was buried in Love Canal that percolated to the surface for elementary school children to play on and in?

+ Hexachlorocyclopentadiene, a chemical "capable of causing damage to every organ in the body."[15]

+ Polychlorinated biphenyls, the infamous PCBs.[16]

+ Carbon tetrachloride and chlorobenzene, both of which can readily cause narcosia or anesthesia.[17]

+ Dioxin, which has been characterized as "the most deadly of all chemicals," as "the most toxic substance ever synthesized by man." Dioxin is found as a contaminant in triclorophenol, and there were over 200 tons of triclorophenol buried in Love Canal.[18]

+ Benzene, well known for causing leukemia in humans.[19]

+ Chloroform, toluene, lindane[20]—and over 200 other compounds.[21] Some 22,000 tons of stuff,[22] including at least twelve cancer-producing carcinogens.

By February of 1981, more than 400 families had moved from Love Canal, taking their illness, their pain, and their heartbreak with them. Hundreds more were trying to move, if they could find a way to afford it.

Love Canal was a hideous experience for these families (one can imagine that it became hideous for Occidental Chemical Corporation as well, when a federal judge ruled that the company was liable for more

---

**Reassurance on Dioxin**

There is absolutely no evidence of dioxin doing any damage to humans, except something called chloracne. It's a rash.

President of Dow Chemical Company[23]

than $250 million in cleanup costs[24]). But Love Canal is history; it happened several years ago. We don't have to worry about those kinds of problems any more—do we?

Unfortunately we do—now even more than in the past. According to Dr. Clark Heath, medical epidemiologist at the U.S. Centers for Disease Control, "The Love Canal situation is just the tip of the iceberg. There are thousands of these dumps all over the country."[25] The Environmental Protection Agency thinks it can locate *thirty* to *fifty thousand*.[26] Many are a present threat: the U.S. Office of Technology Assessment says that more than ten thousand of these sites require cleanup *now* to protect public health.[27] The cost of dealing with these may run as high as $100 billion.[28]

Love Canal was unique, just as every community is unique. But many other communities—in developed countries and less developed ones in the United States, Mexico, Japan, Italy, Brazil, Ghana, India, France, in every area of the globe—have been harmed by business's pollution and waste. A few examples are listed below.

+ Bhopal, India, made famous by Union Carbide's methyl isocyanate gas leak in 1984 that killed at least 2,500 people and injured 200,000 more. The company was charged with designing the plant negligently and with misrepresenting its safety.[29]

+ Institute, West Virginia—also made famous less than a year later by Union Carbide. This time it was a leak of toxic methylene chloride that sent 134 people to hospitals and another 300 to emergency aid stations. This factory had been promoted by Union Carbide as a model of chemical-industry safety, but the Occupational Safety and Health Administration still levied the largest fine it had ever imposed for "conscious, overt and willful" safety violations. OSHA's investigation found deliberate underreporting of worker injuries, along with sloppy maintenance of safety devices and other "very serious" safety lapses at the plant.[30] These are not new experiences for Union Carbide. In the 1930s some 750 Union Carbide workers died, and hundreds more were injured, from exposure to silica dust during construction of a

**Legal Notice**

Court of Shri Gulab Sharma, Chief Judicial Magistrate, Bhopal, Madhya Pradesh, India; Docket R.T. No. 2792 of 1987 (Arising Out of Case - RC 3/84-ACU(I) CBI SPE New Delhi State Through Central Bureau of Investigation, New Delhi, India

vs.

Mr. Warren Anderson, Former Chairman, Union Carbide Corporation, U.S.A., and eleven others–Accused

Whereas complaint has been made before me that Mr. Warren Anderson, S/O late J.M. Anderson, Former Chairman, Union Carbide Corporation, U.S.A., R/O 54, Greenwich Hill Drive, Greenwich CT 06831 U.S.A. has committed the offence of culpable homicide not amounting to murder, voluntarily causing grievous hurt by dangerous weapons or means, mischief by killing of animals and the commission of such offences with criminal intention of knowledge etc., . . . and it has been returned to a warrant of arrest thereupon issued that the said Mr. Warren Anderson cannot be found, and whereas it has been shown to my satisfaction that the said Mr. Warren Anderson has absconded or is concealing himself to avoid the service of the said warrant;

Proclamation is hereby made that the said Mr. Warren Anderson . . . is required to appear at Bhopal, Madhya Pradesh, India before this Court to answer the said complaint on the 1st Day of February, 1992.

(Gulab Sharma)
Chief Judicial Magistrate,
Bhopal, Madhya Pradesh, India

Classified advertisement,
*The Washington Post*, 1 January 1992

tunnel in West Virginia. Union Carbide was alleged to have exposed these workers to unsafe working conditions that made the problem even worse.[31]

♦ Chicago, where it was discovered that an eight-acre site donated to Goodwill Industries by a corporate executive contained more than seventy storage tanks containing hazardous solvents and lead. Goodwill, as the current owner, finds itself faced with potential cleanup costs running to many millions of dollars. Paying even a portion of these costs could bankrupt the charity.[32]

♦ Mexico City, where the tragic explosion of liquefied natural gas tanks claimed 452 lives, with hundreds more never accounted for.[33]

♦ The Tidewater area of Virginia, with seventy victims of Kepone poisoning.[34]

♦ Seveso, Italy, with a 41 percent jump in birth defects following a Hoffman-La Roche Givaudan chemical plant leak of dioxin into the atmosphere.[35] Ten million cubic feet of contaminated earth had to be "buried" in large pits,[36] where it patiently awaits unsuspecting future generations—Italy's own Love Canal.

♦ Texas City, Texas, where two freighters loaded with nitrates exploded on consecutive days, killing 576 and injuring 2,000.[37]

♦ Yusho, Japan, which saw a sixteenfold increase in the rate of liver cancer caused by exposure to polychlorinated biphenyl (PCB).[38]

♦ Times Beach, Missouri, now a ghost town after 2,000 residents fled to escape the dioxin-contaminated groundwater and soil. The flight from Times Beach was wise; 86 percent of those tested showed abnormalities in blood, liver, or kidney functions.[39]

♦ Oklahoma's Illinois River, where Kerr-McGee's Sequoyah Fuels plant routinely discharged 11,000 pounds of uranium annually. This plant's history of spills and leaks of radioactive materials into ground and surface waters led the local druggist to observe, "They're there for the bucks and a town of 600 is not a high price to pay."[40]

A Guided Tour by the Mayor of Times Beach, Missouri

"The man who lived in that home has had a lung removed. I remember the minister's wife who lived next door there had a miscarriage. The lady who lived here, she had two miscarriages. Kidney cancer over there, and the home here, the wife died in childbirth. This next family, the dog had a seizure disorder, and their little girl had terrible stomach and bladder problems. One of my daughters has a seizure disorder; she tried to commit suicide in 1983. Another daughter, she's hyperthyroid; we almost lost her to cancer of the cervix at twenty-one. My former husband has a liver impairment."[41]

◆ Cubatão, Brazil, where a pipeline explosion killed at least 500 and seriously injured many others.[42]

Bhopal, Institute, Times Beach, Seveso, Texas City, Yusho, Cubatão. Faraway places—not in *my* back yard. But maybe not far enough away, either. The Congressional Research Service says that *75 percent of all the people in the United States* live in proximity to a chemical plant.[43]

Our potential risk is enormous. If these dangerous materials were under the control of people and organizations whose performance standards placed our safety first, we might rest assured. But when the performance standard effectively tells the manager, "Do what you have to do to maximize the bottom line," when it leaves our community out of the equation, we have good reason to be concerned.

## Take the Profits and Run

We have seen how plant closings cost workers their jobs, their security, often their marriages and health. These are the obvious and most direct costs. But there are other costs, costs that spread throughout the community and may be felt for years.

The direct job losses from plant closings are always followed by spillover effects that echo throughout the community. When

Youngstown Sheet and Tube closed, 4,100 jobs were lost directly, but another 12,000 were estimated to have disappeared as suppliers, retailers, and service industries cut back and cut back again, in response to the economic shrinking of the community.[44] Haas figures that GE's closing in Ontario, California cost 2,000 jobs beyond the 1,000 lost directly by GE workers.[45]

> Old-timers will remember the GE slogan, "Progress is our most important product." Hogwash! Profits are their most important product.
>
> Boris Block, secretary-treasurer, United Electrical Workers[46]

As jobs are lost and the unemployment rolls grow, tax collections drop at the very time that greater demands are being placed on social service budgets. The invariable result is that services are cut and life in the community becomes meaner. In Detroit, for example, the auto industry crisis required the city to furlough hundreds of police officers, dismiss over 700 teachers, and cut time out of the school day.[47]

If we go back a few years before a major plant closing, we will often find a record of special benefits granted to that corporation at community expense. These may include industrial development bonds, tax rebates and remissions, zoning exemptions, friendly legislation, access roads, utility line extensions, or special utility rates—all granted without a reciprocal commitment from the corporation.

For example, when Derby Refinery mothballed two refineries in El Dorado and Augusta, Kansas, a county commissioner lamented, "The county just gave them $1.9 million in IRBs [industrial revenue bonds], and they talked like it was really going to go and be in business a long time."[48]

Greenville, Mississippi, put over $22 million into renovations for a Boeing plant. Four years later Boeing left, leaving Greenville taxpayers—not Boeing stockholders—holding the bag, or, in this case, the debt.[49] Greenville taxpayers invested in Boeing, but they had no say when Boeing decided to leave.

Driven by the bottom-line mentality, corporations and their executives often make promises that are never kept. Lee Iacocca promised Kenosha, Wisconsin, that Chrysler would keep its plant there open for at least five years—then closed it the next year.[50]

This is not why we created corporations and gave them charters—and why we grant them special privileges. To restore corporations to their public purpose, to bring them to take community costs into account as much as they consider stockholder costs, we need a different scorecard—one that accounts for the effects of corporations on all their investors, all their stakeholders, and not solely their stockholders.

## What's Good for General Motors . . .

Charlie Wilson, who had been a General Motors executive before becoming secretary of defense, achieved a sort of fame by asserting, "What is good for the country is good for General Motors, and what is good for General Motors is good for the country."[51]

Secretary Wilson was partly right. If it's good for General Motors, it can also be good for this nation. But what is good for General Motors can also be quite costly and harmful to the rest of the nation. The same is true, of course, for all the other giant corporations.

It is fine for corporations to make a profit for stockholders, but that is not why they were created through publicly granted charters in the first place. We charter corporations and endow them with near-human rights and special privileges; this is—or was earlier—done in expectation of corporate service to society. We are justified in expecting a fair return and a fair accounting from corporations to the nation, on whose facilities and services corporations so heavily depend.

Nowhere is this more obvious than in defense contracting. This is special business that is critical to our nation's well-being. It could be performed in the public sector, as it is in some other countries. In the United States this business is largely contracted out to private corporations. Whose interests should come first here—the corporation's or the nation's?

## "To Hell With the National Interest"

Government has assumed many of the functions that we earlier assigned to corporations—building and maintaining roads and bridges, public transportation, fire protection, water systems, education. But in the United States government still assigns a major public purpose to private corporations: the production, and often the development, of military weapons.

So at least in this domain, we can expect corporations to attend to their public purpose. Surely they would not exploit the taxpayers solely for selfish gain? Surely they would not put their balance sheet above the nation's defense?

Surely they would. As sad as it seems, the nation's defense is mainly, to corporations, a cash cow, to be milked for all it is worth.

Citizens recoil at this assessment. "Maybe there are one or two bad apples in the military-industrial-complex barrel, but surely most of the contractors are honest and honorable, and deliver fair value for the dollar." An appealing, but regrettably unjustified, notion. Crooked dealings on defense contracts appear to be the norm, not the exception. Recent headlines tell the tale:

"Firm Put Jet Pilots At Risk, Navy Says Spring Valley Plant Is Accused of Fraud," *The San Diego Union-Tribune*, 1 March 1995.

"Fastener Supplier Admits Defrauding the Pentagon," *The Philadelphia Inquirer*, 24 January 1995.

"General Instrument Fined $10M for Fraud," *Newsday*, 26 October 1994.

"Ex-Contractor Pleads Guilty; Falsified Results on Missile-launch System," *Newsday*, 14 September 1994.

"Boeing Facing 21 Pentagon Probes: U.S. Congressman Dingell," *AFX News*, 27 July 1994.

"Undercover at G.E.—A Special Report; F.B.I. Inquiry on Jet Engines: New Jolt to Company Image," *The New York Times*, 18 July 1994.

"Litton Unit Enters Guilty Plea in Finale of Corruption Probe," *Wall Street Journal,* 17 January 1994.

"Rohr Is Said to Agree to Plead Guilty in $7 Million Settlement of U.S. Charges," *Wall Street Journal,* 5 January 1994.

"Grumman Agrees to Pay U.S. $20 Million," *The New York Times,* 24 November 1993.

"Federal Probe Finds California Firms Allegedly Traded Bogus Airline Parts," *Wall Street Journal,* 21 October 1993.

"Teledyne to Plead Guilty Second Time in 10 Months to Charges of Lying to U.S.," *Wall Street Journal,* 24 August 1993.

"Goodyear to Pay $9.12 Million Settlement; N.C. Firm, Irvin Industries, to Get 20 Percent as a 'Whistleblower,'" *The Washington Post,* 5 January 1993.

"Distributor Accuses Medical Firm of Inflating Prices to Government," *The Washington Post,* 14 October 1992.

"GSA Suspends Citicorp Division From Bidding on Contracts," *The Washington Post,* 5 September 1992.

"U.S. to Investigate Makers of Military Bolts and Screws," *The Washington Post,* 5 September 1992.

"Md. Defense Contractor Faces Criminal Charges; Sale of Substandard Hardware Alleged," *The Washington Post,* 5 August 1992.

"Hughes Aircraft Accused of Lying About Tests on Weapons Systems," *The New York Times,* 13 December 1991.

"Rockwell Division Gets Suspension for U.S. Contracts," *Wall Street Journal,* 11 November 1991.

"Former Officers of Fairfax Firm Indicted; Cerceo, Simonson Charged With Bilking U.S. on Defense Contracts," *The Washington Post,* 25 October 1991.

"Unisys to Pay Record Fine in Defense Fraud," *The Washington Post,* 7 September 1991.

"Electronics Giant Agrees to Pay $3.7 Million in Fines," *United Press International,* 21 September 1990.

"E-Systems Pleads Guilty in Army Radio Fraud," *The New York Times*, 28 August 1990.

"Supplier of Parts for Shuttle Is Indicted on Fraud Charges," *The New York Times*, 9 August 1990.

"G.E. Agrees to Pay $16.1 Million Fine for Pentagon Fraud," *The New York Times*, 27 July 1990.

"Prosecutors Seek to Ban Contracts for Northrop," *The Washington Post*, 27 July 1990.

"Raytheon Pleads Guilty in Defense-Data Case; Contractor to Pay $1 Million Penalty," *The Washington Post*, 21 March 1990.

One or two bad apples? Looks more like a rotten barrel. In just one four-year period, "every one of the top 10 defense contractors has been challenged for overcharging, bill-padding or producing inferior weaponry."[52]

Well, accounting for things like bombers and missile systems is complicated, and an occasional mistake is bound to creep in, right? Humans do make mistakes.

Sure. So what kind of mistakes were these companies charged with?

♦ Litton Industries pleaded guilty to defrauding the government out of $6.3 million on defense contracts—300 counts of making false claims and twenty counts of mail fraud. Internally, the company jokingly referred to its inflated cost figures as "chicken fat."[53]

♦ General Electric pleaded guilty to defrauding the government on the Minuteman missile nuclear warhead system. The indictment charged company managers with altering employee time cards, having employees submit blank cards and filling them out themselves, and transferring nonreimbursable costs to other contracts. Company officials tried to pass it all off as "bookkeeping errors," but the Air Force demanded return of $168 million in spare parts profits.[54] Assistant U.S. Attorney Ewald Zittlau observed, "Higher management was blueprinting the intentional mischarging being done by lower-level managers."[55]

◆ General Dynamics was charged with billing the government for costs such as a $14,975 party at a suburban Washington, D.C. country club, babysitting expenses of a company officer, $491,840 for the company chairperson's personal flights on corporate jets (often to and from his farm in Albany, Georgia), $571.25 for a king-size Serta Perfect Sleeper mattress and box-spring (delivered to a motel in suburban St. Louis!), travel expenses for an executive's birthday party, and the cost of boarding an executive's dog. They were also charged with giving "gifts" (not bribes, of course) of some $67,000 to Admiral Hyman Rickover during the time he headed the Navy's nuclear submarine building program (including a pair of diamond earrings for his wife) and with bribing officials of foreign governments. General Dynamics tried to get the American taxpayers to pay for a disco dancer and "$10,713 for losses incurred at the executive barbershop." Total amount in question: "several hundred million dollars."

General Dynamics' executive vice president admitted, "We were out to make money and *to hell with the national interest*" (emphasis mine). And make money they did: *Business Week* labeled General Dynamics' profit level "stunning."[56] A Pentagon spokesperson was not so impressed; he called the overcharges "nauseating."[57]

◆ McDonnell Douglas charged taxpayers $62,071 to cover the costs of an "image-burnishing campaign" after one of the company's DC-10 aircraft crashed in Chicago killing 273.[58] It also tried to charge the government for $24 million in legal fees.[59]

◆ Newport News Shipbuilding was charged with billing Uncle Sam for the cost of settling a sexual harassment case.[60]

◆ Bell Helicopter allegedly "overcharged the Pentagon by $100 million through deliberate computer chicanery."[61]

◆ Lockheed was charging $640 apiece for toilet seat covers. They agreed to cut the price to $100 after this price was questioned.[62]

◆ Not to be outdone by Lockheed, Boeing's Military Aircraft subsidiary was charging taxpayers $748 for a pair of duckbill pliers.

After an engineer testified that a similar pair could be bought at a hardware store, Boeing cut the price to $90. But Boeing then tacked on other expenses so that the total bill to the Air Force didn't change.[63]

♦ Meanwhile Boeing was also charging the government $11,750 for the costs of the World Paper Airplane Championship, plus the costs of traffic fines, golf outings, political campaign contributions, and a dinner honoring its chief executive officer.[64]

The nation has been willing to invest heavily in national defense. But because the national security is at stake, quality and reliability in the systems purchased are critical. Unfortunately, the tyranny of the bottom line appears to place national security as much at risk as it does consumer safety or employees' jobs. The evaluation of auditors, engineers, and other experts that keeps coming up is "shoddy"—a description applied, for example, to McDonnell Douglas's FA-18 fighter plane tail assemblies, Raytheon's work on the Patriot missile, and Martin Marietta's work on the Pershing II missile.[65] The Defense Department was kinder to Hughes Aircraft; in that case the charge was not "shoddy" work; only "systematic deficiencies in workmanship and quality control on high-tech missiles."[66]

President Eisenhower warned us, over three decades ago: ". . . we must guard against the acquisition of unwarranted influence, whether sought or unsought, by the military-industrial complex. The potential for the disastrous rise of misplaced power exists and will persist."[67] As long as our national security relies on corporations driven not by the national interest but by the bottom line, we would do well to heed his warning.

THE HARM TO OUR COMMUNITIES AND OUR NATION    133

# Notes

1. Lois Marie Gibbs, *Love Canal: My Story* (Albany, N.Y.: State University of New York Press, 1982), 23. Michael H. Brown, *Laying Waste: The Poisoning of America by Toxic Chemicals* (New York: Pantheon Books, 1980), 5–6.
2. Gibbs, *Love Canal*, 17.
3. Brown, *Laying Waste*, 16–17. Gibbs, *Love Canal*, 143.
4. Brown, *Laying Waste*, 7.
5. Gibbs, *Love Canal*, 141.
6. Brown, *Laying Waste*, 23.
7. Gibbs, *Love Canal*, 5–6.
8. Edwin Chen, *PBB: An American Tragedy* (Englewood Cliffs, N.J.: Prentice-Hall, 1979), xv.
9. Gibbs, *Love Canal*, 16.
10. Ibid., 6.
11. Ibid., 70–71.
12. Ibid., 68.
13. Brown, *Laying Waste*, 22.
14. Gibbs, *Love Canal*, 41–42.
15. Brown, *Laying Waste*, 16.
16. Ibid., 15.
17. Ibid., 21–22.
18. Gibbs, *Love Canal*, 4. The U.S. Public Interest Research Group (U.S. PIRG) notes that, according to a new EPA report, dioxin may be even more dangerous than previously thought: "The report found that exposure to even small amounts of the chemical may cause cancer, birth defects, learning disabilities, reproductive disorders, immune system deficiencies and other health problems." *U.S. PIRG Citizen Agenda*, vol. 10, no. 3 (winter 1995): 1.
19. Gibbs, *Love Canal*, 4.
20. Brown, *Laying Waste*, 43.
21. Chen, *PBB*, xv.
22. Gibbs, *Love Canal*, 3–4.

23. "Dioxin Puts Dow on the Spot," *Time*, 2 May 1983, 62.

24. "Occidental Liable for Love Canal," *The Wichita Eagle-Beacon*, 24 February 1988.

25. Chen, *PBB*, xv.

26. Gibbs, *Love Canal*, 3–4.

27. "Toxic Waste Risk Rated Above EPA Estimates," *Austin American-Statesman*, 10 March 1985.

28. Ibid.

29. "India Sues Union Carbide," *The Wichita Eagle-Beacon*, 9 April 1985; David Weir, *The Bhopal Syndrome* (San Francisco: Sierra Club Books, 1987), 44.

30. "Carbide Violations Draw Fine," *The Wichita Eagle-Beacon*, 2 April 1986.

31. John Summa, "Union Carbide," *Multinational Monitor* (October 1988): 23–24.

32. "Donations Land Charities in Trouble," *The Wall Street Journal*, 27 October 1989, B1.

33. Weir, *The Bhopal Syndrome*, 193.

34. Chen, *PBB*, xv.

35. Chen, *PBB*, xiii.

36. "Hazards of a Toxic Wasteland," *Time*, 17 December 1984, 32–34.

37. Weir, *The Bhopal Syndrome*, 188–89.

38. Chen, *PBB*, xiv.

39. "Dioxin Puts Dow on the Spot," 62.

40. Dennis Bernstein and Connie Blitt, "Lethal Dose," *The Progressive*, March 1986, 22-25.

41. "Living Dangerously, with Toxic Wastes," *Time*, 14 October 1985, 86–90.

42. Weir, *The Bhopal Syndrome*, 193.

43. Ibid., 116.

44. David Moberg, "Shuttered Factories—Shattered Communities," *In These Times*, 27 June 1979, 11, cited in Barry Bluestone and Bennett Harrison, *The Deindustrialization of America: Plant Closings, Community Abandonment, and the Dismantling of Basic Industry* (New York: Basic Books, 1982), 69.

45. Gilda Haas & Plant Closures Project, *Plant Closures: Myths, Realities and Responses* (Boston: South End Press, 1985), 6.
46. Haas & Plant Closures Project, *Plant Closures,* 6.
47. Bluestone and Harrison, *The Deindustrialization of America,* 78.
48. "Derby Mothballing 2 Refineries," *The Wichita Eagle-Beacon,* 5 February 1987, 1D, 6D.
49. "Boeing to Close Mississippi Plant," *The Wichita Eagle-Beacon,* 30 November 1988.
50. "Last Car Rolls Off Line," *USA Today,* 22 December 1988.
51. Speaking to the U.S. Senate Armed Forces Committee, 1952 (cited in *Bartlett's Familiar Quotations,* 15th ed. (Boston: Little Brown, 1980), 817.
52. "Outcry Grows Over Defense Purchases," *The Wichita Eagle-Beacon,* 14 April 1985.
53. "Defense Contractor is Accused of Fraud," *Fort Worth Star-Telegram,* 16 July 1986.
54. "Outcry Grows Over Defense Purchases."
55. "GE Admits Defrauding Pentagon," *The Wichita Eagle-Beacon,* 14 May 1985; "GE Faces Charges of Fraud," *Dallas Times-Herald,* 27 March 1985; "Air Force Temporarily Suspends GE from Defense Contracts," *Waco Tribune-Herald,* 29 March 1985.
56. "The Fugitive Accuser," *Time,* 8 April 1985, 24; "General Dynamics Accused of Lying," *The Wichita Eagle-Beacon,* 1 March 1985; "General Dynamics Under Fire," *Business Week,* 25 March 1985, 70-76; "Navy Freezes Future Deals with Firm," *The Wichita Eagle-Beacon,* 22 May 1985; "Questionable Defense Bills Widespread, House Panel Says," *The Wichita Eagle-Beacon,* 16 May 1985.
57. "Overruns Unearthed in Contractor Audit," *The Wichita Eagle-Beacon,* 5 April 1985.
58. "Questionable Defense Bills Widespread, House Panel Says."
59. "Outcry Grows Over Defense Purchases."
60. "Questionable Defense Bills Widespread, House Panel Says."
61. "Pentagon to Probe Overbilling," *The Wichita Eagle-Beacon,* 3 May 1987.
62. "Outcry Grows Over Defense Purchases."

63. Ibid.
64. "Questionable Defense Bills Widespread, House Panel Says."
65. "Outcry Grows Over Defense Purchases."
66. Ibid.
67. Farewell radio and television address to the American people, 17 January 1961 (cited in *Bartlett's Familiar Quotations*, 15th ed., 815).

# 6

# Expendable Employees, Disposable Suppliers

ONE OF THE major contributions of corporations, and one reason communities support them, is the jobs they provide. Unfortunately, the payoff for a lot of these jobs isn't just in the form of a paycheck. Millions of workers risk injury, illness, and death from workplace hazards. As important and costly as employees are to industry, decisions driven by the bottom line often do not give adequate attention to the health and safety of workers.

Suppliers, like workers, sell services and goods to corporations. And like workers, suppliers often are treated shabbily by large corporations that are willing to use their greater power to bully smaller firms.

## "Obviously a Deathtrap"

Most workers think federal and state regulators, such as OSHA, keep a pretty close eye on plant safety. Workers—and the families of those who died—at the Imperial Food Products chicken processing plant in Hamlet, North Carolina, learned to their regret that this is false security.

When a fire broke out, workers were trapped, some in areas with no doors, others blocked by locked exits. Twenty-five workers died and another fifty-six were injured. Afterward investigators identified eighty-three safety violations, fifty-four of them "willful." They included locked exits, inadequate emergency lighting, work stations too far from escape doors, unmarked exits, no automatic sprinkler system, and no fire-evacuation plan.[1] Asked whether the plant was a deathtrap, a state investigator said, "Well, obviously it was."[2]

Why did Imperial Food violate safety standards to such a serious, dangerous degree? Its managers will probably never tell (the press couldn't reach them after the fire because they had disconnected the headquarters telephone), but the reported belief was that the company feared low-wage employees would steal chicken parts![3] So for the sake of some chicken wings, workers were sacrificed on the altar of the bottom line.

Just like the coal companies. Only this time instead of just one company, 500 mining companies—practically the entire industry—were charged with "flagrantly violating a major law governing mining safety."[4]

Coal mining companies are required to periodically submit dust samples in a monitoring program designed to measure miners' exposure to black lung disease. But instead of submitting actual samples taken from the mines, the companies were doctoring the supposed samples to be sure they were clean enough to pass inspection. Yes, the companies were caught in 1991, and many paid fines—this time— but these did little to help the miners. To avoid the costs of providing reasonable safety in a dangerous work environment, and for a little more in earnings per share for stockholders, employees' health and safety were once again put at risk.

## "The Greatest Corporate Mass Murderer in History"

It's a painful killer. It eats away at your lungs, takes your breath. At first you just have chest pains and tire quickly. Then you begin to lose weight and develop lesions. Your bones rot. Finally you die. Your family watches and tries to help—but they know.

It's asbestos. And it's everywhere. Even though corporations have stopped installing it, millions are exposed to asbestos flaking daily.

> Each day he ate less and lived for the hypos to kill the pain. . . .
> He died with carcinoma of the lungs and metastatic lesions all
> through his body caused by asbestosis of the lung, and the bones
> in his legs were as though they were moth-eaten. . . . The last
> words he said were to his brother; he jerked the oxygen out of
> his nose and said, "John, this is hell." . . . In the end he was chok-
> ing on the pills he had to take because he couldn't take in
> enough air to hold his breath while he took the pill. . . . The doc-
> tor came back from the operating room and told me his intestines
> were completely grown together with tumors and that it was just
> a matter of time. . . . He died the night he came home from the
> hospital. He came home and sat up. He even got on his feet. The
> doctors shook their heads. They couldn't believe it. He tried to get
> well. He loved life and he wanted to live for me and the kids. He
> laid down and when his last breath went out, he called me and
> said, "Honey, I'm dying." Then he died.
>
> **Excerpts from asbestos widows' letters[5]**

Asbestos may be in your electric blanket. It could be in your dish-
washer, your frying pan, popcorn popper, or curling iron. There's a
good chance that your home's insulation is silently but persistently
drifting invisible and lethal fibers into your family's lungs with every
breath. If you live in Boston, Philadelphia, Atlanta, San Francisco, or
Seattle, be especially cautious; it may be in your drinking water.[6]

The workplace is worse. If you're an auto mechanic, you're probably getting a full dose from the brake jobs in the shop. If you work in
building maintenance, repair, renovation, or demolition, you could be
inhaling fibers every day from asbestos insulation. In all, over *ten million* workers are directly or indirectly exposed to this killer.[7]

They're all at risk, and they're all expendable. Dr. Irving J. Selikoff,
former director of the Environmental Sciences Laboratory at the Mount

> The fibrosis of this disease is irreversible and permanent so that eventually compensation will be paid to each of these men. But as long as the man is not disabled, it is felt that he should not be told of his condition so that he can live and work in peace and *the Company can benefit by his many years of experience* [emphasis provided].
>
> Manville's medical director[8]

Sinai School of Medicine in New York and one of the world's leading experts on asbestos disease, estimates that twenty-four out of every one hundred of the presently living Americans who work or have worked with asbestos will die from asbestos-related cancer within the next thirty years unless a major breakthrough is made in early diagnosis and treatment.[9] Total deaths may number more than 400,000 by the year 2027.[10]

Manville (formerly Johns-Manville) was the leading producer of asbestos. It, as well as the other asbestos companies, knew about the danger from asbestos for years.[11] As far back as 1933, Manville settled several asbestos workers' compensation cases out of court, a common procedure used then and now to avoid a public record of guilt. In its own study in 1949, Manville found lung changes in an incredible *68 percent* of its asbestos workers.[12] Through those years and later, the record is one of distortion and suppression of data that could have saved workers' lives, of "studies" bought and paid for by the asbestos industry, of coverup and obfuscation. But the industry kept on producing and selling and installing asbestos, exposing a nation to asbestosis, cancer, and death.

And that is why one victim charged the asbestos industry with "mass reckless homicide."[13] That is why a lawyer called Manville "the greatest corporate mass murderer in history."[14]

Asbestos may take years to do its damage. As the toll at Manville began to mount, so did the damages—with punitive damages piling on

> Attorney: "Mr. Brown, do you mean to tell me you would let them work until they dropped dead?" Vandiver Brown, head of Manville's legal department: "Yes, we save a lot of money that way."[15]

top of actual damages. (Punitive damages are assessed for "outrageous and reckless misconduct."[16]) Hundreds of lawsuits portended millions, even billions, in damages.

Fearing the potential of inestimable losses, Manville took bankruptcy but finally agreed in 1985, after several years of wrangling, to set up a fund for the claimants. The victims—workers who had given their productive lives—were now left to fight among themselves for the money available.

Bankruptcy allowed Manville to wash its hands of further responsibility. The workers, and their survivors, were faced with the choice of accepting too little or receiving nothing. For those in whom asbestosis had not yet revealed its malignant presence, there was the prospect of being excluded from any damage recovery at all.

Manville was merely responding to its scorekeeping system, its profit and loss statement, the bottom line. If a different scorekeeping system had been in place, one that showed not only benefits to stockholders but also the costs to employees, customers, and communities, managers would have seen that the total costs, to *all* stakeholders, far outweighed the benefits.

Although we may be surrounded by asbestos, at least we aren't installing it anymore. But corporations are installing other insulating materials in buildings, spraying pesticides on crops, injecting cattle, pork, and chickens with "growth enhancers," and treating clothing with chemicals.

Some of these will turn out to be toxic, carcinogenic, or otherwise harmful to humans. We, the customers, don't know which ones today, so we can't protect ourselves. We probably won't know until we've been exposed for several years, because the effects, as with asbestos,

> The reasons why the caution labels were not implemented immediately—it was a business decision as far as I could understand. . . . if the applications of a caution label identifying a product as hazardous would cut into sales, there would be serious financial implications.
>
> Manville's medical director[17]

may take years to become evident. But somewhere today a *company* and its managers know. Yet they continue because a corporation does not have the conscience of a human; its moral standard is defined by the bottom line.

## So You Think You've Got a Pension Plan

Consider the case of Gertrude:

"Joe, I've been thinking about moving from Ajax over to your company. I'm not getting any younger, you know. I think I'd better be paying some attention to my retirement, and I'm just kinda getting worried about the Ajax pension plan. It's not insured by the government, and I don't know if Ajax is really all that strong. If something happened, I could end up an old woman on the dole."

"Yeah, Gertrude, I know what you mean. We're in good shape here at Titan Industries. The whole pension fund is insured by some government deal—I think it's called the Pension Benefit Guaranty Corporation. So we're set no matter what happens. Titan can go down the tubes and I know I'll still have my retirement."

Poor Gertrude. Her pension fund is one of the 763,000 private plans not insured by the Pension Benefit Guaranty Corporation (PBGC). She has good cause to be concerned.

And poor Joe. His fund is insured by the PBGC, but he may not be much better off. After audits indicated that one out of every four insured funds was violating the law, federal officials warned that "fraud and mismanagement could wipe out the retirement nest eggs of millions of working Americans in private pension funds and saddle taxpayers with a multibillion-dollar bailout."[18]

Investigations of pension plans by the U.S. Labor Department found that pension administrators had siphoned off millions of dollars by underreporting earnings; employers had never made required contributions; and substantial fraud and abuse had occurred. "There's an insidious and steady siphoning off," the department's inspector general concluded.[19]

Mismanaged, misused, and underfunded corporate pension funds will cost not only the workers who think they're covered but also taxpayers nationally as the PBGC has to come to the rescue. For example, when Allis-Chalmers Corporation terminated its pension plan in 1985, it added $165 million to the PBGC's burden.[20] But this pales beside the bailout for LTV Steel; when LTV's failure to comply with minimum pension funding standards forced the PBGC in 1986 to take over LTV's liabilities, this one company kicked up PBGC's deficit by nearly *two billion dollars.*[21]

It could be even worse. Even if your employer has a solvent pension fund, you could work for years earning the right to retire with a decent annuity and then find yourself on the street with no job and no pension—while the company goes on to higher and higher profits.

That's what employees—now former employees—of Continental Can discovered, according to an exposé by ABC's "20/20." The reporter is 20/20's Lynn Sherr:

> This is a story about trust and the American worker, specifically, workers in the canning industry who believed, like most of us, that years of work on the production line would earn them pensions at retirement. But this is also a story about the violation of that trust for men and women who made cans for these familiar products, because when their employer, Continental Can, realized the cost of those pensions, they came up with a shocking scheme, a secret plan to avoid paying for them. . . .

It was here at this Pittsburgh plant that Continental first put its plan into effect on a large scale. This was one of Continental Can's oldest factories, so hundreds of workers here were growing close to being eligible for their pensions. But, starting in the mid-1970s, Continental systematically started getting rid of those older workers, firing them for a reason they would not discover until much later.

[Sherr then asks a worker how close he was to vesting in his pension plan when he was laid off. He tells her he needed only one more day. Another says he needed sixteen days. . . . ]

What Continental called its "BELL manual" contained the corporate plans to "shrink" and then "cap" the work force at its plants to prevent any employees from getting their pensions. And just what did the code word "BELL" stand for? Well, spell it backwards, and you get—

[Attorney Dan McIntyre responds: "Lowest level of employee benefits," or "Let's limit employee benefits," depending on which of the BELL jargoneers you want to listen to. . . .]

Continental's plan to deprive workers of their benefits by firing them in large numbers was run out of the company's Chicago headquarters. Inside this building, a huge computer . . . generated complex electronic pictures that warned corporate executives exactly when large waves of workers would approach the twenty-year mark. That way, they'd know the best time to get rid of them. . . .

In June of 1989, Judge Lee Sarokin ruled, in effect, that . . . documents relating to Continental's policy were more than a smoking gun; they were a fusillade, and he said for a corporation of Continental's magnitude to engage in a secret and deliberate scheme raises questions of corporate morality, ethics and decency.[22]

True enough. But above all, the Continental episode raises questions of corporate accountability to the employees who invest the best years of their lives so the corporation can earn profits. It highlights a scorekeeping system that counts only effects on stockholders and makes it extremely difficult for a humane manager to act in the interest of all stakeholders.

## The Plant Will Close Today at 5 . . .

Leviathan Industries closes its plant in Smallburg, Pennsylvania, and moves production to a new plant just over the Mexican border. Leviathan's president announces that the Smallburg shutdown was unavoidable because labor costs are lower in Mexico. When questioned by the press, he doesn't deny that the Smallburg plant was earning a good profit, but says "we can get more in Mexico." Workers and community leaders in Smallburg bemoan the shutdown but accept it as a business necessity. Leviathan is, after all, in business to make a profit.

But how does Leviathan measure profit? Costs to stakeholders— Leviathan's workers and the community of Smallburg—are not calculated or recognized (except, perhaps, with a public statement that "it's too bad, but . . ."). No one questions the legitimacy of this involuntary economic transfer, this transfer from the taxpayers and workers of Smallburg to a corporation and its stockholders. The trail left behind— unemployment, broken families, reductions in social services, empty factories, shuttered stores, poorer schools, higher taxes, suicides—is taken as simply a recurring cost of our business system. The bottom-line mentality teaches us to accept an unjust redistribution of wealth.

That mentality was at work at Levi Strauss. This company's public statements talk about empowerment, honesty, and teamwork. Its success with products like Dockers jeans is little short of phenomenal; operating earnings were reported as "higher than ever" in 1988 and 1989,[23] and up again sharply in 1990.[24] But in pursuit of the bottom line, this company shut down plants during those three years in Elizabethton and Maryville, Tennessee, and in San Antonio, moving the work offshore to the Caribbean for cheaper labor.[26] Yes, higher profits for stockholders may have resulted. But what about the losses to employees and communities? Should they figure into an evaluation of Levi Strauss's performance?

> The power to start and stop a plant at will is relatively harmless in the hands of the small business man, but to give this same right to our huge impersonal corporations which employ millions of people is quite another matter. The time has certainly come to set up some social safeguards; there is enough dynamite in the exercise of this power to wreck our whole economic structure, including the corporations themselves.
>
> **Henry A. Wallace, founder of the Pioneer Hi-Bred Corporation and former U.S. vice president, 1936**[25]

A study by the Plant Closures Project concluded, "Virtually all studies of workers who lose their jobs as the result of a plant closing show that a large proportion of the unemployed take years to recover their lost earnings and many never find comparable work at all."[27] Nearly three out of every five older workers—those between the ages of fifty-five and sixty-four—who lost their jobs between 1979 and 1984 had not found new jobs by the end of that period.[28]

What are the costs of this unemployment? In a study covering more than thirty years, Harvey Brenner found that a 1-percent increase in the aggregate unemployment rate was associated with:

- 37,000 total deaths, including 20,000 cardiovascular deaths
- 920 suicides
- 650 homicides
- 4,000 state mental hospital admissions
- 3,300 state prison admissions
- plus billions of dollars in foregone income, mental hospital outlays, unemployment and welfare payments, and lost tax revenues[29]

These are not just cold statistics. They represent human beings, families, working people whose lives have been disrupted or destroyed. The

*It is July 1988.* You're Mike. You're forty-five fine years old, healthy and robust . . . You have a family you're very proud of, five kids ranging in age from toddler to teenager . . . And after all these years—it's been twenty since you got your degree in business administration—you still feel enthused about climbing out of bed every morning and driving off to work. You're operations and purchasing manager for a local business where you've worked your entire career. What you are, essentially, is the No. 3 man on the company totem pole. Your life is a good one.

*It is August 1988, just one month later.* You can't believe it. You just got the ax. Your company changed hands, and, unexpectedly, you were canned. "The new people called me in on a Friday," you remember, "and thirty minutes later, that was it. They said they eliminated my position. . . I wasn't worried too much. I had a lot of confidence in myself. I have a resume that's pretty impressive." So your wife finds a job to keep some money coming in while you throw yourself into looking for something else, maybe something better.

*It is July 1989.* Almost a year after you lost your job, you're still looking. . . . You have responded to dozens and dozens of ads. And got no offers. And what's most frustrating is that only a handful of employers even talked to you. Most either didn't answer your letters or sent form rejections to the resume you consider "pretty impressive" . . .

"I tell you what," Mike said. "It's getting scary now. This is just something I never thought I'd have to go through. The only thing I can conclude is I'm forty-five, and they all think I'm over the hill. But I'm not—not by any means."

Column by Bob Getz,<br>
The Wichita Eagle-Beacon[30]

emotional strain that comes from losing your job when a plant is closed, or even from an extended layoff, can lead to mental and physical illness, alcoholism, family crises, child and spouse abuse and other violence, divorce, crime, and suicide. For example, the suicide rate among workers who have lost their jobs to a plant closing increases to an astounding *thirty times normal*.[31]

Corporations sometimes tell us there is nothing wrong with moving a plant. They will say that this just moves the jobs from one area to another, "spreads the wealth around." One area loses, but this is offset by the other area's gain. An appealing, but unfortunately inaccurate, argument. It suggests that what typically turns out to be no more than a nominal improvement in average wages, even in Third-World countries, and a gain of a fraction of a percentage point in the new area's employment rate, is a fair tradeoff for the misery and devastation left behind. In the old location, lives may be destroyed. Can the gains in the new location offset that cost?

Plant closures and runaway mills have become virtually a national epidemic. A study by Gilda Haas found that between 1978 and 1982 6.8 million manufacturing jobs were lost as a direct result of plant shutdowns in the United States; one out of every three manufacturing jobs had disappeared in just four years.[32] The U.S. Bureau of Labor Statistics estimates that 10.8 million workers lost their jobs between 1981 and 1986 because of business closures and permanent layoffs.[33] And the carnage continues: In the first six months of 1993, according to *Business Week*, "Corporate America unveiled plans to do away with close to 255,000 jobs, 23 percent more than in the same period last year [which in turn was more than the year before], and the largest first-half tally ever."[34]

As former Vice President Henry Wallace put it: "Under the rules of the game when volume falls off, a continuous dividend policy takes precedence over a continuous employment policy."[35]

Sometimes a plant or a company is so marginal that the only way for it to stay in business is to get costs down, and this may require moving. But more often it's a matter of simply trying to ratchet an already decent return on investment up a little higher. Sort of like in the old

Clint Eastwood movie, workers and communities are sacrificed "for a few dollars more."

This is basically a question of how the total corporate profit pie is to be divided up. Should workers, suppliers, and supporting communities get a reasonable share, or should all the gains go to top management and stockholders?

If corporations were accountable to their workers and communities, if they recognized the substantial investments of all their stakeholders, they would not move or close a profitable plant for just a few cents more in earnings per share. Not when the cost is so great to workers and their families and neighbors. And especially not to free up funds merely for speculative acquisitions.

Plants would still be moved, and truly outdated ones might be closed. But many more businesses would stay put if we had true corporate accountability.

When plants *must* be closed, it can be done harshly or it can be done humanely. With Youngstown Sheet and Tube, Lykes Corporation showed one way: no advance notice, no assistance, no evident concern.[36] Lykes, unfortunately, is not unique; it may in fact be close to the norm. The General Accounting Office found that, in a third of plant closings, *no advance notice at all*, not even one day, was given. The median length of notice was only seven days.[37]

This reality finally forced Congress to pass a bill requiring sixty days' notice for plant closings or massive layoffs.[38] The law doesn't require severance pay. It does not require the company to provide help to workers in finding new jobs. It doesn't say a company has to have a good reason to close a plant. It doesn't require repayment of monies spent by the community on the corporation's behalf or repayment of tax breaks that may have been granted. It does not ask the company to take the workers' and the community's loss into account. It only requires notice. It is simply an application of the concept that workers and communities must have *information* in order to protect themselves in the marketplace—the same concept that led to the creation of the Securities and Exchange Commission and to standards of disclosure to stockholders.

## Let the Supplier Beware, Too

Individual workers are no match for the power of the large corporation. Neither are smaller suppliers. Their experience with the corporate giants is sometimes economically fatal.

The pattern may look like this: A small company is working to create a niche and grow to be a larger company. The company is still run by its founder, perhaps assisted by family members. A deal comes along with a large corporation that will increase revenue by 25 percent, 50 percent, even 100 percent or 500 percent. But the corporation makes demands—product design changes, faster delivery, goods strictly on consignment (so the supplier finances the buyer's inventory), different packaging, even a whole new product. The supplier knows there's a risk, but "after all, this is the kind of deal we've been working toward." So they go out on the limb—and then the large corporate customer just walks away. "Sorry, changed our mind. Don't need it anymore."

Of course the supplier tries to get commitments in writing, but the big customer balks. "This is our standard arrangement. Corporate policy allows no exceptions."

This is how it looked to Winchester Foods in Kansas. It thought it had a commitment from Doskocil Companies to buy 70,000 pounds of sliced meat every week, so Winchester borrowed over $3 million for the necessary plant expansion. After $600,000 of the plant improvements had been made, Doskocil stopped ordering. And Winchester went bankrupt.[39]

And it is what happened to Air Midwest. This small airline had an arrangement with much larger Braniff Airlines to provide feeder flights into Braniff's Kansas City hub. Since 25 percent of Air Midwest's passengers connected to Braniff flights, Air Midwest had a substantial and legitimate interest in Braniff's schedules, performance, and future. Air Midwest was a significant Braniff stakeholder.

But Braniff wasn't accountable to its stakeholders. When Braniff cancelled flights out of the Kansas City hub amid widespread speculation it would file for bankruptcy, Air Midwest was one of the last to know. Air Midwest's president said he had no contact from Braniff about the cancellations. "I'm just flabbergasted that Braniff hasn't contacted me," Robert Priddy said.[40] Priddy learned, the hard way, that Braniff's scorecard had no place to count Air Midwest's loss.

The tyranny of the bottom line leads corporations to take actions that hurt their employees and suppliers, as well as our communities and our society. And of course, as we see in the next chapter, they also harm their customers, who may pay twice for corporate products.

## Notes

1. "N.C. Plant Fined $808,150 After Fatal Fire," *The Washington Post,* 31 December 1991; also 7 September 1991.
2. "N.C. Plant Fined $808,150 After Fatal Fire," *The Washington Post,* 31 December 1991.
3. "25 Die As Fire Hits N.C. Poultry Plant," *The Washington Post,* 4 September 1991.
4. "Big Business Is Plagued by Greed and Stupidity," *The Atlanta Journal and Constitution,* 29 April 1991.
5. Paul Brodeur, *Outrageous Misconduct: The Asbestos Industry on Trial* (New York: Pantheon Books, 1985), 355–57.
6. Russell Mokhiber, *Corporate Crime and Violence* (San Francisco: Sierra Club Books, 1988), 284.
7. Ibid.
8. Ibid., 283.
9. Ibid., 284.
10. "Asbestos Pact: Legal Model or Monster?" *The Washington Post,* 11 May 1994, citing *The American Journal of Industrial Medicine.*
11. See, for example, "Bankruptcy Can Make Survival Costly," *The Wichita Eagle-Beacon,* 13 November 1988.
12. Mokhiber, *Corporate Crime and Violence,* 278.
13. Ibid., 287.
14. Brodeur, *Outrageous Misconduct,* 231.
15. Ibid., 276–77.
16. Ibid., 5.
17. Mokhiber, *Corporate Crime and Violence,* 279.

18. "Pensions May be Built on Illusions," *The Wichita Eagle,* 14 November 1989.
19. Ibid.
20. Samuel F. Hankin, "PBGC Cracks Down on Funding Waivers," *Pension World* (January 1986): 10.
21. Steven Grostoff, "LTV Pension Funds Double PBGC Deficit," *National Underwriter* (19 January 1987): 3, 50.
22. ABC News, "20/20," 20 September 1991.
23. "Jeans Fade But Levi Strauss Glows," *The New York Times,* 26 June 1989.
24. Floyd Norris, "Market Place," *The New York Times,* 7 June 1989.
25. Henry A. Wallace, *Whose Constitution—An Inquiry Into The General Welfare* (New York: Reynal & Hitchcock, 1936), 160.
26. "Jeans Plant to Be Closed; 835 Workers to Lose Jobs," *The Wall Street Journal,* 12 September 1988; "Levi Strauss," *The New York Times,* 2 February 1989; "Levi Strauss Closing Plant," *The New York Times,* 18 January 1990.
27. Barry Bluestone and Bennett Harrison, *The Deindustrialization of America: Plant Closings, Community Abandonment, and the Dismantling of Basic Industry* (New York: Basic Books, 1982), 10.
28. Gilda Haas and Plant Closures Project, *Plant Closures: Myths, Realities and Responses* (Boston: South End Press, 1985), 9.
29. Harvey Brenner, "Estimating the Social Costs of National Economic Policy: Implications for Mental and Physical Health and Clinical Aggression," A report prepared for the Joint Economic Committee, U.S. Congress. (Washington, D.C.: U.S. Government Printing Office, 1976). Cited by Barry Bluestone and Bennett Harrison, *The Deindustrialization of America,* 65.
30. Bob Getz, "Would You Hire This Man? Even If He's 45 Years Old!" *The Wichita Eagle-Beacon,* 2 July 1989.
31. Sidney Cobb and Stanislaw Kasl, "Termination: The Consequences of Job Loss," Public Health Service, Center for Disease Control, National Institute for Occupational Safety and Health, U.S. Department of Health, Education, and Welfare (Washington, D.C.: U.S. Government Printing Office, June 1977), 179. Cited in Bluestone and Harrison, *The Deindustrialization of America,* 65.

32. Haas and Plant Closures Project, *Plant Closures,* 12.
33. "GAO Study on Plant Closings," *DH&S Review,* 14 September 1987, 3.
34. "Downsizers Chalk Up a Record First Half," *Business Week,* 25 July 1993, 20.
35. Wallace, *Whose Constitution,* 161.
36. Terry E. Buss and F. Stevens Redburn, *Shutdown at Youngstown* (Albany: State University of New York Press, 1983), 22.
37. "GAO Study on Plant Closings," 3.
38. The law requires employers of 100 or more employees to give 60 days' advance notice of plant or unit closings or layoffs of 50 or more workers. Community and state officials must also be notified.
39. "Winchester Foods Wins Ruling," *The Wichita Eagle-Beacon,* 22 March 1989.
40. "Money Woes Ground Braniff," *The Wichita Eagle,* 28 September 1989; also see "Air Midwest Grounds Planes, Lays Off 30," *The Wichita Eagle,* 3 October 1989.

# 7

## Customers Pay Twice

FEW CORPORATIONS COULD exist without customers. As much as stockholders, they are investors in the corporation. Of course customers invest money in their purchases. But they can risk much more.

### The Tobacco Industry Speaks

Customers of tobacco companies risk their lungs, their lives, and the health of those around them. How does the bottom line mandate of the corporate system teach executives to feel about profiteering in their customers' health? Stanley Rosenblatt, a Florida lawyer, had an opportunity to ask during a recent trial in Miami. Mr. Rosenblatt is questioning Bennett S. Le Bow, chairman of the Brooke Group Ltd. that owns the Liggett Group:

Q: Is it fair to say, then, that since you're satisfied that you have a legal right to sell cigarettes, you have never really explored or studied the issue of whether or not cigarettes cause disease?

A: That is absolutely correct.

Q: If I asked you, does smoking cause lung cancer?

A: I don't know.

Q: O.K., and you really don't care because you're selling a legal product?

A: Correct....

Q: If there was not this lawsuit, and if—if—you know, you and I were friends, and we were just talking, and I said, you know, "You're in this business, and I'm very anti-smoking. I can get together for you, any time you ask, twenty leading authorities in the world on the issue of whether or not cigarette smoke causes lung cancer, heart disease, emphysema and other diseases, and you can have as long as you want to question them because I would really like you to be convinced that cigarettes are dangerous, would you avail yourself of that opportunity?"

A: No.

Q: Why not?

A: I have no interest....

Q: If I mention to you a report that got a lot of attention, of the Environmental Protection Agency, relating to smoke and health, does that ring a bell to you?

A: I read something about it in the newspapers, yes.

Q: Do you remember even generally what you read?

A: There was some claim about second-hand smoke, you know, causing various diseases.

Q: All right.

A: That was the claim.

Q: You never read it?

A: Never read it.

Q: And I assume you don't have any knowledge on the subject?

A: I have no knowledge.

Q: No knowledge.

A: No.

Q: And basically, no interest in acquiring any knowledge?

A: That is correct.

Q: As I understand your position, generally, that kind of issue is somebody else's battle, and you're going to do your thing, as long as it is legal to do it?

A: That is correct.

Q: And make as much money as you can while you're doing it?

A: I'm a businessman.[1]

Victor Crawford would not have been surprised by Mr. Le Bow's views. Mr. Crawford contracted a severe case of cancer, called by his doctor a "textbook case caused by smoking," which Mr. Crawford had begun at the age of thirteen. A former lobbyist for the Tobacco Institute, Mr. Crawford now sees things from the customer's perspective. He says that the people he worked for "couldn't care less about public health":

> They're in it for the money. I was in it for the money, and I was never concerned if people were dying. I knew what I was doing—my job was to kill bills that would discourage smoking, and encourage bills that would encourage smoking and make them money. I did whatever it would take to win, and a lot of times, I won.[2]

## Prescription Drugs: What You Don't Know . . .

Prescription drugs are supposed to help, not harm, us. We know, of course, that development of new drugs is an uncertain process and that, even with the best controls, unforeseen problems can develop. We can handle that. What we don't want is for the corporation to falsify its tests, cover up deleterious research results, and ignore warning signals. Such corporate abuse makes all of Corporate America look bad and fuels public demands for more regulation and stronger punishment.

A single drug, the sleeping pill Halcion, has brought in almost $2 billion for the Upjohn Company. This is the kind of revenue potential that corporate managers dream of. Could it also make them doctor the research?

That's what plaintiffs claim in lawsuits filed against Upjohn. Take a recent suit filed on behalf of three Halcion users who committed suicide, one who attempted suicide, and a fifth who clubbed his father into a coma. The suit alleges that Upjohn relied on falsified clinical studies and payoffs to researchers to disguise Halcion's psychotic side effects—depression, rage, paranoia, delusions, hallucinations, anxiety, amnesia, and suicidal thoughts.[3]

Additional suits assert that Halcion provoked acts of violence against others, as well as injury to the user of the medication. A recent petition even alleges a conspiracy between the company, researchers, regulators, and lawyers in violation of RICO—the Racketeer Influenced and Corrupt Organizations Act.[4]

Remember when President Bush went to Japan and passed out at a state dinner? He had taken Halcion a day or so before. Upjohn now lists fainting on the Halcion package as one of its side effects.[5]

Let's put this in perspective. Here is a company charged with getting a product on the market by lying—purposefully and knowingly—about the research results. Lives were placed at risk. Some Halcion users apparently committed murder or suicide, allegedly influenced by the drug. People died, others suffered in traumatic ways, families experienced immeasurable loss—and the corporation made millions of dollars.

## "A Deadly Depth Charge in the Womb"

You're excited about a new product for your company: an intrauterine device (IUD) with enormous sales potential. You've just bought the rights for $750,000 and trained a force of several hundred salespersons. You haven't actually tested it on humans, or even on animals, but the doctor who developed it makes impressive claims for its effectiveness in preventing pregnancy.

Right off things start to go sour. Your staff is warning that the effectiveness has been exaggerated; a polyfilament string creates a "wicking" effect that literally draws bacteria into the uterus. They say you need to do further testing.

But hey, sales are great. In the first year you've captured 56 percent of the market. And Wall Street has boosted your stock's price by 40 percent!

Still, the bad reports keep flowing in. One doctor tells of patients suffering life-threatening, spontaneous infected abortions. Then the FDA asks you to halt distribution. You decline, reasoning that this would be tantamount to a confession of liability. Reports continue to come in of high rates of pregnancy with complications, as well as pelvic and other infections. The FDA advises that your device produces a greater risk of septic abortion, septicemia, and death than other devices.

What to do? Hire public relations experts. Put out misleading information. Publicize only the tests that show the device in a good light.

But now the lawsuits start. Quickly, locate any incriminating documents and burn them. If you're asked about the documents at trial, claim you don't remember, didn't know, never saw them. At trial, try to intimidate the women into dropping their claims by asking detailed questions about their sex lives.

It's not enough. You're losing the lawsuits and losing big. Your company is charged with engaging in an ongoing fraud by "knowingly misrepresenting the nature, quality, safety, and efficacy" of the intrauterine device.

Run to Congress. Contribute half a million dollars to members of the Senate Commerce Committee. Pick a new member of the committee from your company's home state and give him a $100,000 contribution. Great—he introduces your bail-out bill. But then, alas—the reaction from women's groups, trial lawyers, consumer advocates, unions, and newspapers creates too much heat, and he backs off.

What now? Time for "The Manville Solution"—Chapter 11 bankruptcy. Johns-Manville took bankruptcy in the face of billions of dollars of personal injury claims from its workers, so why not you? First

---

I told [my supervisor] that I couldn't, in good conscience, not say something about something I felt could cause infections. And he said that my conscience did not pay my salary.

A. H. Robins quality control supervisor[6]

you'll take care of your stockholders with a plan that gives them $700 million and also takes care of all the creditors (other than the device's victims, of course). Then you can create a fund for the victims to fight over. And with a little help from your friends, you'll get a healthy tax deduction, so the public will get to share the cost. Now you can wash your hands of all this and get on with the business of making money.

That, of course, is exactly what the A. H. Robins Company, maker of the infamous and tragically fatal Dalkon Shield intrauterine device, did.

Tens of thousands of women who relied on the Dalkon Shield suffered sterility, spontaneous abortions, and pelvic infections (pelvic inflammatory disease, or PID). Over a hundred thousand bought the Dalkon Shield for protection from pregnancy, but got pregnant anyway. Hundreds gave birth prematurely to children with blindness, cerebral palsy, mental retardation, and other grave congenital defects. Other babies were stillborn. Cases filed were eventually reduced by the court to a pool of 196,000 "active claimants"[7]—196,000 women, 196,000 human beings, nearly four out of every 1,000 women of child-bearing age in the United States.

Every $1 million in profit A. H. Robins' stockholders made on the Dalkon Shield cost women who used it *$20 million* for medical care.[8]

And at least twenty women died.[9]

> There is not a damn thing wrong with the Dalkon Shield. Ninety percent of these gals, Christ, you ought to read their histories . . . It's unreal. The number of men they screw would knock you off your seat.
>
> A. H. Robins lawyer[10]

"A deadly depth charge in the womb, ready to explode at any time." That's what Judge Miles Lord called the Dalkon Shield. Judge Lord then gave the company officers a "Dutch uncle" talk:

It is not enough to say, "I did not know," "It was not me," "Look elsewhere." Time and again, each of you has used this kind of argument in refusing to acknowledge your responsibility and in pretending to the world that the chief officers and directors of your gigantic multinational corporation have no responsibility for its acts and omissions.

Today as you sit here attempting once more to extricate yourselves from the legal consequences of your acts, none of you has faced up to the fact that more than nine thousand women have made claims that they gave up part of their womanhood so that your company might prosper.

The only conceivable reasons that you have not recalled this product are that it would hurt your balance sheet and alert women who have already been harmed that you may be liable for their injuries. You have taken the bottom line as your guiding beacon and the low road as your route.[11]

## "Take That Damnable Product Off the Market!"

There may be no good way to die, but toxic shock syndrome—TSS—is surely one of the worst. The victim's suffering is almost indescribable, as her body is wracked with successive waves of ever more violent, wrenching pain.

The culprit is superabsorbent tampons, like Playtex's Super-Absorbent Deodorant Tampon and Proctor & Gamble's Rely. But when Rely was linked to a large number of TSS cases, P&G pulled it off the market. If Playtex had withdrawn its Super-Absorbent Deodorant Tampon at that time, then Betty O'Gilvie, and how many other women, would have lived.

The superabsorbent tampon is associated with the production of a highly toxic substance, Toxic Shock Syndrome Toxin-1 (TSST-1). "As TSST-1 builds up and invades the blood stream, it weakens the walls of blood vessels so that they begin leaking. The rapid seepage of blood and plasma out of the circulatory system can lower the blood pressure enough to impair brain, liver, and kidney function, often with lightning speed—and that's where shock comes in."[12] Death is the result in one case out of every twenty.

In Betty O'Gilvie's case, the jury said that Playtex officials knew their tampons increased the risk of TSS and that they recklessly disregarded the danger by not warning customers. The jury was so disturbed by Playtex's crass willingness to endanger its customers, to risk their lives for profit, that they awarded Ms. O'Gilvie's husband and children $11 million in actual and punitive damages. According to Judge Patrick Kelly, the jury was telling Playtex: "Take that damnable product off the market."[13]

Which Playtex finally did, in response to Judge Kelly's offer to reduce the damages by $8.5 million if they would do so[14]—too late, of course, for Betty O'Gilvie and the other women who were living sacrifices to the corporation's bottom line.

## A Child's Life

Millions of children have received the DPT—diphtheria, pertussis (whooping cough), and tetanus—vaccine. Sometimes "hot" batches contain unusually large amounts of harmful organisms that can produce permanent brain damage. Lawyers have argued that the vaccine's manufacturer, Wyeth Laboratories, was negligent in producing an unreasonably dangerous vaccine, one that could be made safer for just a few pennies a dose.

As one lawyer testified to Congress:

> There can be no doubt that these manufacturers were aware of the reactogenicity of their products, the reasons for the reactions and the technology to substantially reduce these reactions some 20–30 years ago. There can be no doubt that the same companies, for reasons which yet remain unknown, conducted inadequate studies, ignored laboratory findings, disregarded clinical reports and continued to manufacture a vaccine which knowingly caused injury rather than produce a safer product or warn an unsuspecting public and the medical profession of the nature and rate of reactions and possible alternatives.[15]

For reasons which yet remain unknown? Where's the mystery? Weren't these corporations simply doing what the bottom line requires—maximizing profit, regardless of the cost to customers?

A jury in Wichita, Kansas, agreed, to the tune of $15 million in damages against Wyeth Laboratories for Michelle Graham, a young girl who suffered severe, permanent brain damage.[16] The award may not erase the parents' grief or make Michelle whole, but it will force Wyeth to pay the cost of her lifetime care.

These damage awards may appear large, but they never adequately compensate the victims and their families. I know because I did the economic loss analysis and testimony in some of these cases. And to the companies, such awards may appear as simply a cost of doing business, the result of an analytical calculation that compares the probability and discounted present value of damage costs against much greater profits to be made. The corporate performance scorecard only records the costs and profits to the company; it never counts the lives lost and the pain customers suffer.

## Angels of Mercy, Angels of Death?

Birth control devices and sanitary tampons as well as children's vaccines are some of the most personal products in our lives. Must we fear for our lives with each exposure? As long as corporate managers are driven by the tyranny of the bottom line, such fear may be well justified.

In these highly personal areas, we as consumers are practically blind. We cannot test each product—except on ourselves. We cannot, each of us, have the medical and scientific knowledge required to critically evaluate ingredients and construction and potential unintended side effects. We have little choice but to rely on the judgment, the competence, the honesty, and the honor of our doctors, our pharmacists, and the corporations that produce the products they dispense.

Federal regulations provide some protection, but federal regulators will never be able to monitor every producing corporation and every batch of every product.

Our need to trust is especially great with pharmaceutical companies. We rely on their products to alter our bodies—our systemic functions—and this intrusion can expose us to enormous risk. These products have to be potent to be effective, which means they will carry dangerous possibilities for harm. We are left with little choice but to give the pharmaceutical companies our blind trust.

What do they give in return?

Many excellent products—products that save lives, cure ills, relieve misery. Surely some managers are motivated by such goals, but when they are, and when they act on them rather than simply seeking to maximize profits, they are rowing upstream against the goal to which the corporate scorekeeping system holds them accountable. Managers risk their own career success when they place customer and patient benefits above the bottom line.

So sometimes, how often we can never know, pharmaceutical companies willingly, even knowingly, risk our safety for an extra dollar. Whenever you take a Bayer aspirin, you might keep this in mind.

Corporations periodically go through name changes and reorganizations, usually to improve customer receptivity; Bayer was once I. G. Farben.[17] According to Joseph Borkin in *The Crime and Punishment of I. G. Farben*, this company ran a concentration camp for Hitler (and evidently for its own experimental purposes) at Auschwitz. At one point Farben headquarters requisitioned 150 women from the concentration camp for experiments with a "new soporific drug." Letters from headquarters to the camp reveal the corporate conscience:

> ". . . Received the order of 150 women. Despite their emaciated condition, they were found satisfactory. We shall keep you posted on developments concerning this experiment."

And then:

> ". . . The tests were made. All subjects died. We shall contact you shortly on the subject of a new load."[18]

Today we thank the current version of I. G. Farben for easing our headaches, but back then the company "brutalised its slave labour force in their quest to build an industrial empire to match Hitler's political empire," and further supported Hitler's goals by "producing Zyklon B, the extermination gas used at Auschwitz."[19]

Ciba-Geigy may have learned its morality from Bayer/Farben. According to Mark Shapiro writing in *Mother Jones*, internal company memos show that this company conducted experiments with Galecron, a carcinogenic pesticide, in which "six Egyptian children were paid $10 each to stand in a field while an airplane sprayed them from an altitude of fifteen feet."[20]

These are pharmaceutical companies on which we rely for our health. Are they angels of mercy? Or angels of death?


## "Pencil Whipping"

Passengers and crew members on troubled Eastern Airlines didn't know whether to be angry or grateful. A federal grand jury had just charged Eastern with criminal conspiracy to falsify its maintenance records and lie about maintenance not performed.[21] Should they be angry that their safety had been placed in jeopardy for Eastern's bottom line—or grateful that the maintenance not performed had not cost their lives?

The indictment accused Eastern, among other failures, of putting planes in the air without inspecting for engine cracks; without checking to see whether components like wing flaps and flight controls had been lubricated; and without testing critical electronic modules— sometimes sending aircraft up with defective electronics.

Eastern could not blame this on out-of-control workers: the indictment said it was all directed by the vice president for maintenance! And it was hidden from the FAA through record falsification and forgery, a practice the industry, presumably with a snicker, calls "pencil whipping." Eastern eventually pleaded guilty and was fined $3.5 million.[22]

In December 1988, an Eastern plane had to be grounded when a three-inch crack was discovered in its fuselage.[23] Days before an Eastern jet was forced to make an emergency landing when it blew a fourteen-inch hole in its fuselage—at 31,000 feet.[24] That August an overloaded Eastern plane allegedly blew two tires on landing at Washington

National Airport.[25] And earlier the same year, the FAA ordered forty-three of Eastern's planes taken out of service to correct safety problems.[26]

The power of the bottom line to overwhelm basic human morality is strikingly evident when it can lead a large airline to risk the safety of its passengers and crews to save maintenance costs. Like other corporations—or a chameleon—an Eastern Airlines may change its name, sell parts of its business, take bankruptcy, go through a corporate restructuring, or have its executives move to other airlines. But the corporate morality continues, controlled by a harmful scorekeeping system that drives managers to actions like "pencil whipping."

## Up in Flames

An automobile represents a substantial investment. Today a car costs half or more of a reasonable annual income—much more than the average stockholder's investment in a company. In making these investments, customers risk their purchase price, but they also risk their lives.

Cars, pickups, and vans should be able to safely carry a tank of volatile fuel along with several humans, negotiate turns and emergency maneuvers at legal highway speeds, absorb minor impacts with minimal cost from the damage, and perform dependably and effectively for several years. That is the minimum we should get for the $10,000 to $30,000 we shell out.

Most vehicles meet these minimal standards fairly well. Some won't, and sometimes the auto executives have solid reasons to know that they won't.

So it appears in the case of the GM pickup trucks with sidesaddle gas tanks. These tanks were mounted outside the protection of the body frame. Without this protection, side collisions were liable to rupture the tanks. Sparks could then ignite the spilled fuel, and the tank would explode, engulfing the vehicle in flames.

GM produced trucks like this from 1973 to 1987; by 1993 there were an estimated 5–6 million still on the road.[27] But as early as 1983, an internal GM document recognized that the sidesaddle tanks were in a much more vulnerable location than they would be if relocated inside the frame rails and ahead of the rear axle.[28]

Critics say fires resulting from gas tank ruptures during collisions in these trucks have killed more than 300 people.[29] According to the Center for Auto Safety's Clarence Ditlow, "GM knew about this deadly defect for twenty years and rejected a $10 fix recommended by its own top fuel tank experts."[30] Yet GM never got around to moving the tanks to a safer location until 1988, and even then the company claimed it was making the change for "design" reasons.[31]

GM recently settled dozens of class action lawsuits that claimed design deficiencies in these vehicles by offering certificates good for $1,000 off the price of a new GM pickup! A GM official conceded that this was a "marketing device," since litigants will have to buy a new truck to get the discount.[32]

It is appropriate for General Motors to try to produce and sell trucks to make a profit. It is not appropriate for General Motors to knowingly sell dangerous vehicles to unsuspecting consumers. This is even less defensible than knowingly selling worthless common stock to unsuspecting financial investors. Both types of investors know there is some risk that they will not recover the full value invested, but no one should be asked to risk his or her life for a corporation's bottom line.

The GM pickups take their position at the head of an evergrowing line of vehicles charged by critics with being dangerously unsafe, a list that includes models of the Ford Bronco II, Jeep Cherokee, Audi 5000, Ford station wagons, and Chevrolet Corvair.

And of course the infamous Ford Pinto. Most buyers of Pintos that were produced from 1971 to 1976 did not know that the gas tank, located only six inches from the rear bumper, was liable to be punctured in even a minor rear collision by bolts protruding from the differential housing. And then, any "spark from a cigarette, ignition, or scraping metal, and both cars would be engulfed in flames."[33] They did not know that "Ford management chose the bottom line over customers' lives."[34]

When Ford designed the Pinto, they wanted it light and they wanted it cheap. Ford president Lee Iacocca decreed "the limits of 2,000"—

weight under 2,000 pounds, cost under $2,000. And it had to be done fast, in less than 60 percent of the time normally taken to plan and produce a new car. This put tremendous pressure on the engineers.

But when early crash tests showed that in minor rear-end collisions the Pinto was a firetrap, the bottom line won out over customer safety. A one-dollar plastic baffle could have prevented many crash fires by protecting the gas tank from protruding bolts on the differential housing. But a dollar was too much for Ford to pay, and this protection was rejected.

A rubber bladder inside the gas tank could have kept fuel from spilling when the tank was ruptured. Crash tests showed the bladder worked well. But its cost would have been $5.08, and it was rejected.

Another change would have prevented gas tanks from breaking up so easily in rear-end collisions and in rollover accidents. It would have cost $11. It was rejected.

Ford's reasoning on this $11 safety improvement is particularly revealing. They produced a "cost-benefit analysis" showing that the deaths and injuries avoided would not justify a cost of $11 per car. Evidently they didn't ask their customers.

Eventually Ford's chickens came home to roost. After suffering millions in losses from liability suits, and even suffering the unprecedented ignominy of being the first *company* charged with murder, Ford was finally forced to recall the offending Pintos.

Ford did not set out intentionally to cause these deaths. It was only obeying its scorekeeping system, putting the bottom line above customer safety. As Yale law professor Peter Schuck observed, "Here, as in other such cases, nothing more malicious or reckless on the manufacturer's part was shown than a calculated, conventional decision to design a product in a way that traded safety off against cost and other marketing and engineering considerations."[36]

"Safety don't sell."

Lee Iacocca[35]

A calculated, conventional decision? A scorecard that makes such decisions merely "conventional" needs to be replaced by a more rational performance report, one that makes managers accountable to all stakeholders and not only the stockholders.

We'll see how to do this in the last section of this book. But first we need to pull together the costs of corporate actions on all stakeholders, "the public cost of private corporations."

## Notes

1. "On Cigarettes, Health and Lawyers," *The New York Times*, 6 December 1993.
2. "No More Smoke Screens," *The Washington Post*, 4 March 1995.
3. "$1 Billion Lawsuit Filed Against Maker of Halcion," *The Houston Chronicle*, 30 December 1993.
4. "Halcion Lawsuit Alleges FDA, Upjohn Conspiracy," *The Houston Chronicle*, 7 January 1994.
5. "Finding a Bad Night's Sleep with Halcion," *The New York Times*, 20 January 1992.
6. Russell Mokhiber, *Corporate Crime and Violence* (San Francisco: Sierra Club Books, 1988), 157.
7. Catherine Breslin, "Day of Reckoning," *Ms. Magazine*, June 1989, 46–52.
8. Mark Dowie, "The Corporate Crime of the Century," *Mother Jones*, November 1979, 23–25, 37–38, 49.
9. Material on the Dalkon Shield taken from: Morton Mintz, "A Crime Against Women: A. H. Robins and the Dalkon Shield," *Multinational Monitor* (15 January 1986): 1–7; "For Many Dalkon Shield Claimants Settlement Won't End the Trauma," *The Wall Street Journal*, 9 March 1988; "Judge Ready to Approve Robins Plan," *The New York Times*, 19 July 1988; Mokhiber, *Corporate Crime and Violence;* Morton Mintz, *At Any Cost: Corporate Greed, Women, and the Dalkon Shield* (New York: Pantheon Books, 1985).
10. "Piercing the Dalkon Shield," *National Law Journal* (16 June 1980): 13.
11. Mintz, *At Any Cost*, 264–67.

12. "Are Tampons Safer Now?" *Consumer Reports* (May 1986): 332–34.

13. Dara Lynn Trum, "Civil Procedure—Remittitur of Punitive Damages in Exchange for Product Recall—O'Gilvie v. International Playtex," *The University of Kansas Law Review*, vol. 34, no. 4 (summer 1986): 823-39. The case is found at 609 F. Supp. 817, 818 (D. Kan. 1985).

14. Judge Kelly's reduction of punitive damages was later overruled by a three-judge panel of the Tenth U.S. Circuit Court of Appeals.

15. Harris L. Coulter and Barbara Loe Fisher, *DPT: A Shot in the Dark* (New York: Warner Books, 1985), 435.

16. "Jury Awards $15 Million in DPT Case," *The Wichita Eagle-Beacon*, 15 October 1987.

17. Joseph Borkin, *The Crime and Punishment of I. G. Farben* (New York: The Free Press, 1978), 160-63.

18. John Braithwaite, *Corporate Crime in the Pharmaceutical Industry* (London: Routledge & Kegan Paul, 1984), 5, citing Jonathan Glover, *Causing Death and Saving Lives* (Harmondsworth, Eng.: Penguin, 1977), 58.

19. Joseph Borkin, *The Crime and Punishment of I. G. Farben*, pp. 160-63.

20. Mark Shapiro, "William Tell's New Targets," *Mother Jones*, August 1983, p. 50.

21. "Eastern Air Indicted on Inspections," *The Washington Post*, 26 July 1990.

22. "DOT Rejects Lorenzo's ATX Bid; Cites Safety, Compliance Problems," *Air Safety Week* (11 April 1994).

23. "Rupture Discovered in Another Boeing 727," *Washington Times*, 29 December 1988.

24. "Hole in Fuselage Forces Plane to Make Landing," *Christian Science Monitor*, 27 December 1988.

25. "Eastern Denies It Has Weight Problem," *Washington Times*, 24 August 1988.

26. "Probe Grounds 43 Eastern Airlines Jets," *San Francisco Chronicle*, 20 April 1988.

27. "GM Settles Truck Suits With Coupon," *USA Today*, 20 July 1993.

28. "Data Show G.M. Knew for Years of Risk in Pickup Trucks' Designs," *The New York Times*, 17 November 1992.

29. Ibid.

30. "General Motors: Exploding Gas Tanks," *Multinational Monitor* (December 1992): 13.

31. "Data Show G.M. Knew for Years of Risk in Pickup Trucks' Designs."

32. "GM Hopes Suit Settlement Translates to Truck Sales," *The Washington Post,* 21 July 1993.

33. Mark Dowie, "How Ford Put Two Million Firetraps on Wheels," *Business & Society Review* (Fall 1977): 46–55.

34. Lee Patrick Strobel, *Reckless Homicide: Ford's Pinto Trial* (South Bend, Ind.: And Books, 1980), 117.

35. Dowie, "Two Million Firetraps on Wheels," 46–55.

36. Russell Mokhiber, "Corporate Crime and Violence (editorial)," *Multinational Monitor* (April 1987): 4.

# 8

# The Public Cost
# of Private Corporations

CORPORATE FINANCIAL REPORTS purport to measure a firm's profit and loss. Nowhere in this accounting calculus, however, is there an allowance for the external diseconomies[1] or social costs, costs inflicted on society that are not incurred by the corporation itself and for which the corporation makes no sacrifice.

Of course corporations affect much more than their stockholders. Their impact on the environment, on the health and safety of employees and customers, on neighborhoods and communities, and on the national interest has provoked a growing concern over this broader corporate social impact. Those affected by corporate externalities—citizens, customers, workers—rarely have any say about them. The costs imposed on these stakeholders are effectively coerced assessments, forced taxation without representation.

Since corporations do not report their social costs, citizens have little knowledge of such costs, except when they are affected directly, as when a family member suffers exposure to toxic materials in the workplace. Local governments, frequently pressured for special benefits to business, have essentially no information on corporate social costs.

171

Congress and federal agencies frequently consider special benefits to Corporate America, such as protective tariffs, special tax deductions, foreign tax credits, defense contracts that may be designed to keep a particular company afloat, direct bailouts, or evisceration of regulatory requirements. In the debates over these issues, corporations and their media representatives understandably seek to present an impressive image of the benefits they provide: jobs, taxes paid, foreign trade, economic development, beneficial goods and services. But the issue of the public costs imposed on society is rarely mentioned, except as a generalization. That is partly because no one knows what corporations cost society. Congress has never funded a study of the aggregate cost of corporations. The accounting profession, while it has spent millions of dollars assessing such issues as the cost of regulation on corporations, has never evaluated the cost of corporations on society. Research foundations have not sponsored studies of the public costs of Corporate America.

Specific corporate social costs have been estimated in a variety of contexts, although no one has undertaken to bring these together into an aggregate estimate. These estimates are consolidated here with original research to develop a perspective on the total social costs of business enterprise in the United States.[2]

Government statistics, and therefore many research studies on business, usually do not differentiate between corporations and unincorporated partnerships and proprietorships. Since incorporated enterprises account for nearly all business receipts (see Figure 1 in Chapter 4), references to business firms and to corporations are used interchangeably in this chapter except where a clear distinction is possible and necessary. And while this book's concern is predominantly with larger business enterprises, it is usually not possible to separate the societal effects of smaller and larger firms. Hence, this analysis generally encompasses all business enterprise in the United States, corporate and noncorporate, large and small. And while it would be appealing to isolate costs created by defined categories of business, this is usually not practical; polluted air, for example, doesn't come color-coded to tell us which kind of business produced which pollution.

## The Problem With Costs

The definition of social cost can be controversial, since whether a phenomenon is a "cost" is to a degree in the eye of the beholder. For this study the Social Impact Statement framework presented in my *Corporate Social Accounting*[3] has been adopted, but for the aggregate of all corporations instead of for a single corporation. The costs considered here are those that have a "detrimental effect on society."[4]

The estimates used in this analysis are based primarily on costs that have been measured in some form by researchers. Some social costs have thus inevitably been either omitted or severely underestimated, perhaps most notably the cost of corporate crime, which in many cases simply goes unrecognized. Omission of a cost in this analysis does not mean that the cost is insignificant. It more likely indicates that the cost is especially difficult and expensive to estimate. For example, the annual cost of "corporate welfare," the direct government subsidies and tax breaks given to corporations, is not listed, although this cost has been estimated by Gregory Fossedal of *The Wall Street Journal* at $140 billion per year.[5]

Estimates for the present study are drawn from public and private sources as well as from original analysis. The several studies were necessarily undertaken at different times in different organizations by different researchers using differing methodologies. Dollar amounts can be adjusted for price-level changes to a common purchasing power, but adequate adjustments cannot be made for changes in the underlying social and economic structures that have occurred over time. The aggregate costs here developed cannot, therefore, be interpreted literally as the current social cost of corporations. The intent instead is to afford a perspective, to suggest a range of magnitude.

Some of these estimates represent first efforts and will certainly be refined through later research. A degree of double-counting is probably inevitable, but the estimates presented will be conservative since, in most cases, only those costs that are directly identifiable have been estimated. And other social costs, as well as secondary and multiplier effects, have generally been omitted.

These problems were recognized earlier by Kapp:

> It should be emphasized that the statistical data and esti-
> mates used in this book to illustrate the magnitude of the
> social costs are not only out of date but inadequate. They
> should be understood in terms of what they were intended
> to do—to illustrate the nature and kind of losses and to
> show the reader that even these far-from-satisfactory esti-
> mates are of such a magnitude as to make it imperative to
> bring them into the open.[6]

Even when cost estimates are available from prior or ongoing studies, they are problematical. A "cost" amount, like all "reality," is a construct.[7] Whether a phenomenon is a cost is a function of individual
preferences, temporal conditions, and social structure. The measurement of a cost's value may be biased by the measuring instrument or
methodology as well as by the experience, knowledge, and attitude—
not to mention the mere presence—of the measurer.[8]

While no approach can ever yield a completely reliable measure
of the full cost of corporate externalities,[9] the aggregate estimate developed here should be useful for considering economic, regulatory, and
tax policies. How does the total cost compare, for example, to the
amount of taxes paid by business, the cost of government regulatory
agencies, the national deficit, or total corporate profits?

Without such an aggregate estimate, policymakers and citizens
may be liable to dismiss the public costs of private corporations as not
significant. But with a total cost estimate available, the need for corporations to fully account for their social costs becomes more evident.
Legislators and policymakers should be able to make more informed
policy decisions about such programs as investment tax credits,
zoning exemptions, industrial development bonds, capital gains tax
reductions, and local tax abatements. Corporate managers, tyrannized by the demanding bottom line, can see more clearly the consequences of marching only to that despotic scorekeeper's one-note
melody.

The range of corporate social costs is broad; a partial listing is presented in Table 1.

### Table 1. The Public Costs of Private Corporations
### (a partial listing)

A. **The cost in the workplace**
  1. Workplace injuries, illness, deaths
  2. Discrimination (racial, gender, age, other forms)
  3. Sexual harassment
  4. Physical and emotional stress
  5. Psychological abuse
B. **The cost to the customer**
  1. Unsafe or shoddy products
      a. Injuries, illness, cancer
      b. Economic loss
  2. Price fixing, overcharging, deceptive practices
C. **The cost of pollution**
  1. Air pollution
      a. Health effects
      b. Discomfort
      c. Visual impairment
      d. Residential soiling
      e. Acid rain
      f. Odor
  2. Water pollution (effluent emissions, sewage, thermal discharge from power plants)
      a. Effects on health, mortality
      b. Reduced recreation (e.g., fishing, boating, water skiing)
      c. Loss of food fishing
      d. Reduction of water resources (aqueous beds, reservoirs)
  3. Visual (aesthetic) pollution
      a. Billboards and signs
      b. Plants, other facilities
      c. Dirty air
      d. Dirty water
      e. Advertising—radio, TV, newspapers, magazines (discomfort and ugliness factor)
  4. Noise pollution
      a. Factories and plants
      b. Construction

      c. Airports; planes

      d. Trucks, autos; commuter traffic

D. **The cost of waste**

    1. Sewage, trash (burden on treatment plants, landfills)

    2. Hazardous and toxic waste

      a. Radiation exposure

      b. Transportation danger

      c. On-site disposal (long-term risk)

      d. Disposal at waste facility—cost to community, nation

      e. Burning (toxic emissions)

E. **The cost of congestion**

    1. Streets, traffic, parking

    2. Pressure on school system; overcrowding

    3. Pressure on housing system; higher prices

F. **The cost of commercial encroachment**

    1. Zoning commitments not kept

    2. Loss in home values

G. **The cost of site damage**

    1. Leaking or abandoned underground tanks

    2. Destruction of trees, plant life; erosion

    3. On-site disposal of hazardous waste (also see cost of waste, section D)

H. **The cost of consumption of natural resources**

    1. Depletion of energy resources

    2. Consumption of other mineral resources

    3. Depletion of wildlife resources (animals, fish, fowl)

I. **The cost of manipulation of public opinion**

    1. Lobbying

    2. Advertising and promotion

      a. Gender stereotyping

      b. Encouragement/inducement of unhealthy behavior

        1. Smoking

        2. Drinking

        3. Fatty foods, other unhealthy dietary habits

J. **The cost of crime and fraud**

K. **The burden on government services:** police, fire protection, water supply, regulation, inspection, legislation, national defense

L. **The cost to the national economy**

    1. Balance of trade/balance of payments

    2. Productivity (lack of training, modernization, maintenance, competitiveness)

In Table 2 estimates are presented for only those costs that have been previously analyzed; a number of important costs, for which no estimates have been attempted, are omitted from Table 2. Public costs are grouped separately for customers, workers, communities, and the nation. For comparability all costs were first adjusted to 1991 dollars, and the total was then adjusted to 1994 dollars.[10]

**Table 2.  The Public Costs of Private Corporations**
**(Annual costs in billions; adjusted to 1991 dollars)**

| | |
|---|---:|
| **Costs to workers** | |
| Discrimination | $   165.1 |
| Workplace injuries and accidents | 141.6 |
| Deaths from workplace cancer | 274.7 |
| Other workplace illness and disease | ? |
| Other workplace costs (sexual harassment, abuse, etc.) | ? |
| Costs to workers: over | $   581.4 |
| **Costs to customers** | |
| Cost of price-fixing conspiracies, monopolies, deceptive advertising | $1,166.1 |
| Cost of unsafe vehicles | 135.8 |
| Cost of cigarettes | 53.9 |
| Other product injuries | 18.4 |
| Health/injury costs of personal, health, and food products | ? |
| Costs to customers: over | $1,374.2 |
| **Costs to communities** | |
| Stationary source air pollution | |
| Health costs | 225.9 |
| Architectural damage | 13.3 |
| Household soiling | 17.3 |
| Vegetation damage from acid rain | 5.9 |
| Mobile source air pollution | |
| Health costs | 1.7 |
| Crop losses | 3.1 |
| Corrosion and other material damage | 1.1 |
| Additional impairment in property values | 2.6 |
| Water pollution | |
| Impairment of recreational activities (fishing, boating, swimming, and water fowl hunting) | 10.9 |

| | |
|---|---:|
| Loss to commercial fisheries | 2.4 |
| Damage to health (morbidity and mortality) | 1.1 |
| Damage to fixtures and appliances | 0.3 |
| Aesthetic cost | 2.2 |
| Hazardous waste | |
|     Cleaning up existing sites | 20.0 |
|     Cost of waste generated currently | ? |
| Noise pollution | ? |
| Aesthetic pollution | ? |
| Costs to communities: over | $ 307.8 |
| **Costs to the nation** | |
| Defense contract overcharges | $ 25.9 |
| Other corporate crime | |
|     Income tax fraud | 2.9 |
|     Violation of federal regulations | 39.1 |
|     Bribery, extortion, and kickbacks | 14.6 |
|     Other crime costs not evaluated separately | 82.5 |
| Costs to the nation: over | $ 165.0 |
| Total (1991 dollars) | $2,428.4 |
| **Total of costs estimated (adjusted to 1994 dollars): in excess of** | **$2,618.1** |

The total of the social costs imposed by corporations on their stakeholders and the nation, and for which data are available, is estimated to be approximately $2,618 billion in 1994 dollars. Let us now examine the components of this estimate.

## The Public Cost to Workers

Employees of corporations receive salaries, wages, and fringe benefits; they pay for these with their work. Whether they receive fair compensation may depend on the relative bargaining strength of the two sides, employer and employee. These strengths depend in turn on such factors as the unemployment rate, worker mobility, local supply of labor and competitive demand for labor services, barriers to job entry (many jobs, from welding to nursing to accounting, require special training and/or certification), and the extent of unionization.

This is the obvious relationship between corporations and workers—work performed, wage paid. The amounts paid are recognized ("internalized") by both parties: income to the worker, cost to the corporation. But there are other relationships not recognized, at least not explicitly in dollars. These are the costs to workers from discrimination, layoffs, plant closings, and occupational injuries and illnesses. Such costs can significantly retard a worker's productivity and income for life, can damn a middle-aged person to a remaining life of unemployability, and can cripple and kill.

How much does all this cost workers?

> A corporate decision on the location of a plant may create a new city or destroy an old one.
>
> Dow Votaw, *Modern Corporations*[11]

## Discrimination

Discrimination costs the worker, in lost earnings, lost promotions, and lost opportunity. A study by Cotton concluded that the average black woman's wage was 21 percent lower and the average white woman's wage 15.5 percent lower than that of white males.[12] The white woman suffered economically because of sexual discrimination, and the black woman from both sexual and racial discrimination.

Cotton's study indicated that racial discrimination cost the black male, but, for those who were employed, this was more than offset by their gains from sexual discrimination against women; average earnings of the employed black male were about 1.6 percent higher than they would have been if neither racial nor sexual discrimination had occurred.[13]

The researcher took into account possible differences in factors such as education and training, and adjusted for these statistically to isolate the effect of discrimination.

Of course, differences in education and training are undoubtedly due, at least partially, to past discrimination, and this in turn contributes to the overall gap in male/female and white/black earnings. But this study focused on current, direct discrimination.

Assuming that the pattern of discrimination experienced by wage and salary earners is similar, we can apply Cotton's results to estimate the combined cost of sexual and racial discrimination. Based on aggregate national earnings (data from the *Statistical Abstract of the United States* and the *Economic Report of the President*) and adjusted to reflect business's share only, the cost of discrimination is estimated to be $165.1 billion.

This estimate may understate the cost. Andrew Brimmer, former member of the Federal Reserve Board, has estimated the cost to the U.S. economy of disparate treatment of blacks at $215 billion.[14]

Employment discrimination is a crime. Total federal outlays for administration of justice for 1991 were $12.3 billion[15]—less than 8 percent of the cost of this one national crime—and this is a crime that is borne by women and minorities, persons whose average economic circumstances are already severely depressed due to *past* discrimination.

### Workplace Illness and Injuries

At least partially due to the efforts of the Occupational Safety and Health Administration, the rate of workers killed on the job decreased from eighteen per 100,000 in 1970 when OSHA was created to seven per 100,000 in 1992 (the rate of disabling injuries only dropped from 2,860 to 2,717 per 100,000). But the 1992 totals of 8,500 deaths and 3,300,000 disabling injuries on the job still represent a dire social cost borne by workers and their families.[16]

An analysis of estimates made by the National Safety Council,[17] adjusted to 1991 dollars, indicates that these workplace injuries and illnesses cost workers approximately $141.6 billion per year.

### Deaths From Workplace Cancer

This estimate does not include the suffering and death from cancer contracted in the workplace. The National Safety Council has estimated that between 23 percent and 38 percent of all cancer deaths each year are due to workplace exposure.[18] This translates to roughly 151,646 lives lost annually from exposure to such dangers as radiation and chemical carcinogens on the job, and the number is increasing every year.[19] The total is undoubtedly understated, since diagnosis of cancer often occurs years after initial exposure. For example, the National Cancer Institute estimated that workplace inhalation of asbestos fiber, only one of a number of workplace carcinogens, would be responsible for 67,000 premature cancer deaths a year throughout the next thirty to thirty-five years.[20]

The 151,646 deaths from cancer contracted on the job can be costed based on the distribution of employment by gender and race, and applying standard techniques used in legal cases for valuing a premature or wrongful death. Civilian employment was distributed in 1991 as follows:[21]

|  | Number | Percent |
|---|---|---|
| White males | 55,557,000 | 47.5% |
| White females | 45,482,000 | 38.9 |
| Black males | 8,036,000 | 6.9 |
| Black females | 7,802,000 | 6.7 |
| Total | 116,877,000 | 100.0% |

The incidence of workplace cancer may be assumed to be distributed in proportion to participation in the workforce.[22] Assume that the average victim was thirty years old with some college education, but no degree.[23] Based on values for individual classifications from the *ESTES Economic Loss Tables*,[24] the annual cost of death from workplace cancer may be estimated as follows:

| | | |
|---|---|---|
| White males | .475 x 151,646 x $2,196,522 | $158.2 billion |
| White females | .389 x 151,646 x $1,425,379 | 84.1 |
| Black males | .069 x 151,646 x $1,720,968 | 18.0 |
| Black females | .067 x 151,646 x $1,419,103 | 14.4 |

Total annual cost of death
from workplace cancer                                      $274.7 billion[25]

## Other Workplace Death Costs

The estimates above are only for workplace costs that have been studied. Estimates are not available for other workplace injuries and illnesses, or for other costs. For example, no one has estimated the cost of serious poisonings of agricultural workers and consumers from pesticides, up to one million of them a year.[26] Nor has anyone estimated the costs of sexual harassment on the job, or of physical and emotional stress and psychological abuse.

Workers are paid for their efforts, their contributions, their time. Risk is an unavoidable part of some jobs, and workers generally take this into account. But there are also hidden and unnecessary workplace risks, risks that may be caused by cutting corners on safety, by using dangerous chemicals, or by treating workers as disposable goods.

These unrecognized costs to workers are partially offset by unrecorded costs to the corporation, such as malingering or sabotage. For many corporations, however, compensation levels have already been adjusted downward to allow for these costs. Thus the unrecognized costs to employees are a form of taxation, often without their knowledge or consent.

Actions that place workers at risk may be taken by managers for a variety of reasons, but mainly these actions are taken because managers feel they are compelled by the bottom line. If worker safety appears to cost more, in terms of the bottom line, than it can save in lost time and insurance premiums, then worker safety may become a costly luxury, inconsistent with the scorekeeper's tabulations. The same is true for customer safety, nondiscriminatory employment practices, pollution control, and all the other corporate social costs. We have all known a few managers who were mean or even evil, and yet the most humane, the most honorable managers may be driven by the corporation's bottom line morality to actions that harm workers.

## The Public Cost to Customers

Corporations benefit society by providing needed or desired goods and services. This benefit is substantial, although it is presumably compensated fully. That is, customers pay for the goods and services received; the corporation is not coerced to provide benefits at a loss.[27] But in the process of providing beneficial products, corporations sometimes sell dangerous goods and shoddy merchandise, engage in price fixing, and exploit customers, especially inner city residents, the elderly, and children, by overcharging. What do these practices cost customers?

## Cost of Price-Fixing and Deceptive Advertising

The cost of these consumer abuses is very difficult to research empirically and conclusively. An earlier projection was made by then U.S. Senator Philip Hart and was based on his investigation of monopolies and price-fixing conspiracies. He estimated that between 30 percent and 40 percent of all consumer spending is wasted.[28] Since Senator Hart's estimate, we have seen a vigorous corporate takeover movement accompanied by reduced government enforcement of antitrust laws (with some reversal of the latter trend under the current administration). Hence, although it is impossible to know with certainty how the cost estimated by Senator Hart has changed, these circumstances suggest that it has increased because of greater business concentration and thus less competition.

With personal consumption expenditures at $3,887 billion in 1991[29] and using Senator Hart's more conservative level of 30 percent, monopolies and price-fixing can be projected to produce an involuntary subsidy from consumers to business, a subsidy for which no corresponding value is received, of $1,166.1 billion.

## Cost of Unsafe Vehicles

Automobiles are a major consumer product. Most provide good service, but as discussed in Chapter 7, design or manufacturing defects sometime produce unsafe vehicles and customers pay the social cost with their lives. Many of these social costs are avoidable through better design and low-cost safety features.

Automobile manufacturers are prone to blame any higher-than-normal rate of accidents on "operator error" or road conditions. These charges are often accepted by a public aware of drunken drivers, reckless behavior, and their own faulty practices behind the wheel. Operator failings unquestionably cause many accidents, many injuries, and deaths. Better driver training and stronger traffic enforcement may be appropriate, and highways and streets may need better maintenance. But even if all accidents attributable to driver error and road conditions could be eliminated, there would still be dreadful carnage on our streets and highways due to poor vehicle design and manufacturing flaws.

Professor Murray Weidenbaum, chair of the Council of Economic Advisers under President Reagan, has estimated the cost that could be avoided through reduction of these flaws at $135.8 billion (1991 dollars).[30] Weidenbaum's estimate includes only costs attributable to design and manufacturing practices; he excluded from his estimate costs for accidents caused by operator error.

## Cost of Cigarettes

The danger from cigarettes has been well documented. The cost of this danger was estimated by the Bush administration at $53.9 billion per year (adjusted to 1991 dollars) in health expenses and time lost from work.[31] Most of this cost, but certainly not all, is borne by the direct customers of the tobacco companies. It all, however, represents an economic transfer from customers and the nation to private corporations. Some, presumably nonsmokers, might argue that this serves smokers right, but the costs to smokers are no less real.

## Other Product Injuries

Other products, although perhaps not as potentially harmful as automobiles or cigarettes, also injure their buyers. Customers cannot afford to be complacent about microwave ovens, electrical appliances, breast implants, highly flammable fabrics, heart monitors and pacemakers, lawnmowers, chain saws, hedge trimmers, and other products that can maim and mangle. Beyond the purchase price, what else do they cost?

The economic loss from the millions of these injuries suffered each year has been estimated by the Consumer Product Safety Commission at $18.4 billion a year in 1991 dollars.[32] This amount does not include the cost to consumers of product-related birth defects, cancers, and chronic illnesses, for which costs have not been estimated. Nor have dollar estimates been made for many other costs to customers, including the health and injury costs of personal, health, and food products. These unexamined costs, while potentially enormous, can only be identified, without quantification, at this time.

The magnitude of these unrecorded costs to consumers can give us a vision of the potential benefits if corporate decisions affecting product quality, pricing, safety, packaging, warranties, advertising, and service were to be made on the basis of the effects on all stakeholders, instead of being driven almost exclusively by the expected effect on the stockholders' bottom line.

## The Public Cost to Communities

Some of the more significant social costs created by corporations are imposed on neighboring communities. These include air and water pollution, waste generated, and congestion, as well as higher taxes (assessed on other taxpayers) for subsidies to corporations, tax abatements, and the burden on public facilities and services.

The present business scorecard has no place for effects on communities and neighbors. For example, once I was having lunch in Texas with three corporate executives. One was the chief financial officer of a public utility company, a company that talked a lot about being a good citizen and about its partnership with the communities it served. At that time this company negotiated utility rates with each city instead of dealing with a statewide utility commission. During lunch the utility executive was asked about how his company dealt with the various city councils throughout the state.

In response he snickered: "They're mostly a bunch of yokels. We go in and hit them with a pile of computer printouts full of numbers and lay on a lot of accounting jargon. Then they look solemn and try to sound responsible, before they give us everything we ask for." "Don't they ever balk?" he was asked. "No, they really don't," he replied. "If they ever did we would just start talking about deterioration of customer service, and they would fall right into line. It's great." The other executives at the table were greatly amused, and one observed, "Beats stealing."

## Air Pollution

When corporations pollute the air, they inflict costs on their neighbors and on society. These costs can even be exported to other countries, as with acid rain. The cost of pollution control is then avoided by the corporation and is imposed instead, through damage, on innocent persons. The damage is to lungs, vision, skin, crops, paint, property values, textiles, and aesthetics. Many cases of lung and skin cancer are attributed to air pollution, and corrosion damage to structures and electrical contacts is substantial.

Air pollution is generated from stationary sources and from mobile sources. Stationary source pollution includes suspended particulates and sulfur compounds. It is caused primarily by industry, and especially by coal-fired power plants.

Adjusting from a study for the Environmental Protection Agency, the health cost of stationary source air pollution is estimated at $225.9 billion per year in 1991 dollars.[33] The annual cost of architectural damage from sulfur dioxide is estimated very conservatively at $13.3 billion[34] and the additional cost of paint damage and other soiling at $17.3 billion.[35] These estimates at best capture only a part of the loss in property values.[36]

Acid rain is expected to kill all the fish and plantlife in 48,000 lakes in Ontario, Canada, and in 300 lakes in New York's Adirondack Mountains.[37] The cost for vegetation damage from acid rain due to sulfur dioxide, in the eastern United States alone, is estimated at $5.9 billion annually.[38]

The mobile sources of pollution are vehicles, trains, and aircraft. Business and industry are responsible for about 92 percent of this pollution, with the transportation industry accounting for almost two-thirds of this total.[39] Mobile source pollution consists primarily of carbon monoxide and oxidants, and causes aggravated heart and lung disease among the elderly, chest pain, coughs, headaches, and eye discomfort. It also damages crops and buildings and lowers property values. Costs of this form of pollution attributable to business are estimated at $1.7 billion in damage to health, $3.1 billion for crop losses, $1.1 billion for corrosion and other material damage, and $2.6 billion for additional impairment in property values.[40]

The combined cost of these categories of business-produced air pollution is approximately $270.9 billion a year.

## Water Pollution

Industrial effluent discharged into waterways kills fish, turns streams into sewers, and creates cancer and other risks for humans as polluted water recharges underground aquifers or otherwise finds its way into drinking water supplies. Citizens bear this cost through sickness and cancer, as well as with higher water processing costs required to make the water supplies potable.

In a study for the U. S. Environmental Protection Agency costs of water pollution were estimated, here adjusted to 1991 dollars, as follows:[41]

| | |
|---|---|
| Impairment of recreational activities (e.g., fishing, boating, swimming, and water fowl hunting) | $10.9 billion |
| Loss to commercial fisheries | 2.4 |
| Damage to health (morbidity and mortality) | 1.1 |
| Damage to fixtures and appliances | 0.3 |
| Aesthetic cost | 2.2 |
| Annual cost of water pollution | $16.9 billion |

These costs reflect the damages that regulators were not able to prevent. The total social cost of corporate water pollution would be considerably higher, because the government also spends over $12 billion for water pollution abatement and control, a substantial part of which would be devoted to industrial pollution.[42] For perspective, we might also note that the social cost of a single water pollution event, the Exxon Valdez oil spill, was estimated by government analysts at $3 billion.[43]

## Hazardous Waste

Toxic and hazardous wastes are a growing problem for cities and citizens. In 1979 the U.S. Environmental Protection Agency estimated that cleaning up what may be more than 32,000 hazardous waste sites would cost over $50 billion.[44] The Congressional Office of Technology Assessment has since raised the estimated number of sites to 50,000 and estimates that "the costs ... could easily be ... several hundred billion dollars."[45] With a minimum total cost of $200 billion and a discount rate of 10 percent, the annual cleanup cost would run to $20 billion every year, forever.

This estimate is certainly low—probably very low. The cost to clean up existing waste sites in California alone was recently estimated at $40 billion over the next decade.[46] Cleaning up just one illegal dumping by a spin-off company of Allied Chemical was estimated by the EPA to cost $8 billion,[47] and it may not be possible to restore the damaged river to its former state at any cost.

As conservative as it is, this is only the estimated cost of cleaning up existing sites. We continue to produce prodigious quantities of hazardous waste every year, and all the new waste will have to be dealt with at an unknown future cost.

## Noise Pollution

Noise pollution may be less tangible, more ephemeral than air or water pollution and hazardous waste, but its cost can nevertheless be substantial. Consequences of industrial noise include hearing loss, reduced property values, loss in work productivity, anxiety, stress, irritability, ulcers, spastic colons, and diminishment of the quality of life.

Individuals, governments, nonbusiness organizations, and the military also create noise, but the dominant share of noise pollution comes from business and industry—the noise of construction, delivery trucks, commercial aircraft, jackhammers, factories.[48]

The EPA's Office of Noise Abatement and Control has estimated that noise pollution is doubling in intensity every ten years, and that 15 percent of hearing loss among those age sixty-five or over comes from exposure to "the increasing deluge of noise."[49]

Current estimates of the cost of noise pollution are not available, but in the aggregate this cost would clearly be substantial. The EPA estimated the benefits of implementing an 85-dBa noise standard in industry, from reduced absenteeism alone, at $14.1 billion (adjusted to 1991 dollars).[50] And the cost of airport noise was emphasized by then U.S. Senator Alan Cranston, who observed that, "cities already are wasting *billions of dollars* that could be spent on legitimate needs because they are forced to buy up homes in aircraft flight paths."[51]

### Aesthetic Pollution

Some corporations do a good job of locating and landscaping their facilities. Others create eyesores that lower property values and make life less pleasant. While aesthetics may be in the eye of the beholder, most people would be willing to pay more for a home in a tree-shaded residential neighborhood than for one next to a cement plant, a foundry, a meat packing plant, or a lead smelter.

The total cost of corporate-created aesthetic pollution is unquestionably large, but the cost of this form of pollution is very difficult to assess and no estimates have yet been made of its aggregate national value.

## The Public Cost to the Nation

In addition to its effects on customers, workers, and communities, industry also inflicts social costs on the nation and even the world.

When corporate defense contractors overcharge on government work, they impose a cost on the nation that is paid by citizens.

## Defense Contract Overcharges

Sometimes overcharges on government contracts are discovered; some of these are rejected and some result in defense contractors being prosecuted. Many overcharges cannot be uncovered, however, without a government contract auditing function substantially greater than that which Congress has been willing to fund. While the full cost of undiscovered overcharges is therefore never likely to be known, Pentagon analyst Ernest Fitzgerald has estimated the Pentagon could save at least 24 percent of the value of prime military contract awards to business firms in the United States if it could eliminate contractor overcharges.[52] Applying the 24 percent to the 1991 budget, overcharges would amount to $25.9 billion per year.

## Other Corporate Crime

Beyond defense contract fraud and overcharges, corporations engage in other forms of illegal activity.[53] The national cost of these corporate crimes will always be difficult to estimate reliably, for obvious reasons. Criminals, including corporate criminals, prefer to keep their crimes secret. There is no admission in the corporate annual report of discrimination, income tax fraud, bribery, overbilling, off-the-books slush funds, falsification of defense contract charges, money laundering, mail and wire fraud, short-weighing, adulterated and padded shipments, price-fixing, illegal political contributions, bid-rigging, and "creative" accounting.

Except for the occasional outrageous case, corporate crime is not widely reported in the media and is not regularly tabulated by law enforcement agencies. The FBI keeps few statistics on the malfeasance of big business. In many cases victims are not even aware that they have been victimized.

Chapter 4 described research by *Fortune* magazine to assess the extent of corporate crime.[54] Its editors concluded that, by quite conservative standards, 11 percent of major corporations had been found to have been involved in corrupt practices.

In a later survey *U.S. News & World Report* concluded that 23 percent of America's 500 largest corporations had, in the prior decade, been convicted of at least one major crime or had been penalized for serious misbehavior ("serious misbehavior" was defined as a criminal conviction, or a penalty of more than $50,000).[55]

*Dollars & Sense* magazine, citing Russell Mokhiber, says that the overall picture is considerably worse: two-thirds of the 500 largest corporations would be included if all illegal behavior, whether or not it had been prosecuted, was counted.[56]

The cost of corporate criminal tax avoidance, based on estimates made by the Internal Revenue Service, is projected at $2.9 billion per year in tax liabilities not reported, while the Department of Justice assesses the annual loss to taxpayers from corporate violations of federal regulations at $39.1 billion, both adjusted to 1991 dollars (this amount may involve a degree of double-counting with some of the specific costs discussed earlier).[57]

Bribery, extortion, and kickbacks cost the nation, but these crimes also undermine our national standards of morality. According to the Chamber of Commerce of the United States, the cost of corporate bribery, extortion, and kickbacks, adjusted to 1991 dollars, runs to $14.6 billion every year.[58]

*Dollars & Sense* reports the cost of white collar crime as at least $100 billion every year.[59] By this estimate other corporate crimes cost the public $82.5 billion annually: $100 billion less the cost of income tax fraud ($2.9 billion), and less the cost of bribery, extortion, and kickbacks ($14.6 billion).

This additional cost is impossible to know with certainty, but the $82.5 billion estimate appears reasonable when the cost of even a few large corporate frauds is considered. In the Equity Funding fraud, policyholders, shareholders, and other insurance companies lost an amount equivalent to $7.7 billion in 1991 dollars.[60] This fraud has been described as involving more money "than the total losses of all street crimes in the United States for one year."[61] In another single incident, E. F. Hutton's mail and wire fraud cost the 1991 equivalent of $6.5 billion.[62] For insurance fraud alone, the Chamber of Commerce of the

United States estimates an annual cost of $5.2 billion.[63] In the most extreme corporate fraud to date, the looting of the savings and loan associations in the 1980s cost taxpayers, through the federal government's guarantee of depositor's accounts, some $150 billion.[64] Against these numbers the $82.5 billion calculation may be substantially understated.

## Summary: The Public Costs of Private Corporations

The history of the corporation is the history of a dramatic mutation of purpose, from serving the broad public interest to serving only the private interests represented by the bottom line. This change has, unfortunately, led to substantial social costs to stakeholders.

Corporate agents, through advertising and in other forums, assert great benefits from the corporate system, and they are not infrequently given to prophesying great loss to communities and society if business is made to pay higher taxes or is constrained by regulation.

Those who might challenge these claims do not usually have access to the same media or the same influential policymakers. In the public debate, as decisions are made by taxpayers and their representatives that may affect corporations—decisions on corporate tax provisions, industrial policy, corporate welfare, regulations and penalties for their violation, investment tax credits, zoning exemptions, tax abatements—no information has been available about the other side of the ledger: the aggregate costs to society of the corporations and business. No information has been available that would allow policymakers to better assess whether corporate activities that cost stakeholders are the public bargains so often claimed.

Estimates of social costs of corporations and other business that must be borne by customers, employees, communities, and society are consolidated and summarized in Table 2. The total of the annual costs estimated, in 1991 dollars, is $2,428 billion; adjusted to 1994 dollars, it is approximately $2,618 billion.

Although the individual costs will vary, this total should be fairly stable for several years. One can thus adjust to later years by applying the Gross Domestic Product Implicit Price Deflator.

The federal deficit is currently running between $150 billion and $200 billion per year. While there is not a direct correspondence, much of this deficit can be traced to government expenditures required to regulate and prosecute corporate misbehavior, and to undo the environmental and other damage caused by industry. Thus if industry could reduce its social costs by only 10 percent, the government could eliminate much of the deficit and our nation's economy would be considerably stronger.

Or viewed another way, the uncompensated social cost of business is over eight times the total expenditures on education in the United States; almost twice the whole federal budget; and equal to nearly half of the nation's gross domestic product ($6,374 billion in 1993).

Corporate social costs are a burden to the public and to the nation. They are real costs to those on whom they are imposed, but the corporate accounting system never recognizes them as such. In evaluating the contribution of corporations to society, these social costs should be related to the social benefits obtained. As Klein has noted, "If the social performance associated with business institutions and business decisions is to improve, that is, if the social costs of business are to be controlled within acceptable limits, business decision makers must include 'externalities' in their planning."[65]

The present business scorekeeping system, unfortunately, makes this difficult. While most people would surely include the social costs created by an enterprise among the components to be considered in fully assessing its performance, these costs are omitted from the business operating statement.

Corporate managers are thus forced to make their decisions substantially unaware of the magnitude of the effects of their actions on stakeholders. Managers are bound to the bottom line and kept in the dark about other effects; it is little wonder that they make decisions that may sometimes do substantial harm.

Full corporate accountability, as proposed in this book, can provide managers with the information they need to make responsible decisions that do the least possible harm. While some managers may at first resist, most will, after some experience, very likely conclude that they really prefer doing business this way. Their stakeholders, who stand to avoid many billions of dollars in externalized corporate costs, will never be in doubt.

## Notes

1. Occasionally there are beneficial externalities, or external economies, as well, but these are generally of limited consequence. The profit motive of business enterprise makes it little prone to give away much of value.

2. For other efforts at assessing corporate social costs, see K. William Kapp, *The Social Costs of Private Enterprise* (New York: Schocken Books, 1971). Also see Cheryl Lehman, *Accounting's Changing Roles in Social Conflict* (New York: Markus Wiener, 1992), 7–12, on costs of the international debt crises and of corporate mergers.

3. Ralph Estes, *Corporate Social Accounting* (New York: John Wiley, 1976), 96.

4. Ralph Estes, *Dictionary of Accounting*, 2nd ed. (Cambridge, Mass.: The MIT Press, 1985), 127.

5. Gregory Fossedal, "Corporate Welfare Out of Control," *The New Republic*, 25 February 1985, 17–19.

6. Kapp, *The Social Costs of Private Enterprise*, xii.

7. B. Holzner, *Reality Construction in Society*, rev. ed. (Cambridge, Mass.: Schenkman, 1972).

8. For a fuller discussion of these issues, see J. Becker, "Toward a 'Real' Value Accounting," *Advances in Public Interest Accounting*, 2 (1988) and T. Tinker, *Paper Prophets* (Westport, Conn.: Praeger, 1985).

9. A completely original study, assuming that the millions of dollars required could be obtained, would span years, during which social and economic structures would be continuously changing.

10. Cost estimates were adjusted using the ratio of relative Gross Domestic Product Implicit Price Deflators or Consumer Price Indexes, as appropriate. Other adjustments were made as necessary to make the resulting cost estimates comparable.

11. Dow Votaw, *Modern Corporations* (Englewood Cliffs, N.J.: Prentice-Hall, 1965), 2–3.

12. J. Cotton, "Discrimination and Favoritism in the U.S. Labor Market: The Cost to a Wage Earner of Being Female and Black and the Benefit of Being Male and White," *American Journal of Economics and Sociology* (January 1988):15–28.

13. More recently declining growth in real earnings for males appears to have altered this relationship, with black men now suffering substantial losses from racial discrimination that is partially, but not fully, made up from the effects of gender discrimination. It should be emphasized that unemployment hits African Americans, both men and women, much harder than it hits whites. The effects noted by Cotton for black males were experienced *only by those with earnings.*

14. "Racial Discrimination Has Become a Major Drain on the U.S. Economy," *The Washington Post,* 7 January 1993.

15. *Economic Report of the President* (Washington, D.C.: U.S. Government Printing Office, February 1992), 387.

16. U.S. Bureau of the Census, *Statistical Abstract of the U.S. 1994,* Table 676.

17. M. Green and N. Waitzman, *Business War on the Law,* rev. 2nd ed. (Washington, D.C.: Corporate Accountability Research Group, 1981), 94.

18. Ibid., 95.

19. U.S. Bureau of the Census, *Statistical Abstract of the U.S. 1991,* Table 116.

20. Green and Waitzman, *Business War on the Law,* 110.

21. *Economic Report of the President,* February 1992, Table B-32.

22. African Americans experience higher rates of cancer than whites, but their much smaller proportion in the population and workforce minimizes the distortion from this assumption.

23. Median years of school completed in 1989, for all persons age twenty-five and over, was 12.7; this has been increasing each year (*Statistical Abstract of the U.S. 1991,* Table 224).

24. Ralph Estes, *ESTES Economic Loss Tables,* 1991 Edition (Washington, D.C.: A.U. Publishing, 1991).

25. Studies of acceptance of risk indicate that "most middle-income Americans usually act as if their lives were worth $3 million to $5 million

based on what they demand in extra pay for dangerous jobs and what they spend for safety devices" ("How Much for A Life? Try $3 Million to $5 Million," *The New York Times*, 29 January 1995). The weighted average here of $1,833,217 per person is substantially more conservative than these estimates.

26. L. Regenstein, *America the Poisoned* (Washington, D.C.: Acropolis Books Ltd., 1982), 84–87.

27. Although corporations do not normally (and knowingly) sell below cost, customers do get bargains. This comes about especially through the interaction of the forces of demand and supply. With a downward sloping demand curve, customers other than those at the margin receive the benefit of "consumer surplus"—they would be willing to pay something more than the going price.

28. W. Proxmire, "Oligopoly Investigation," *Antitrust Law and Economics Review*, vol. 3, no. 1 (fall 1969): 7–19.

29. *Economic Report of the President*, 1992, 312.

30. Green and Waitzman, *Business War on the Law*, 34.

31. "Smokers' Health Toll Put at $52 Billion," *The New York Times*, 21 February 1990. The $53.9 billion for health and time costs may be understated; medical costs alone were estimated at $50 billion by the federal Centers for Disease Control and Prevention, while a survey of research by the New England Journal of Medicine concluded that the total for medical costs may have reached $65 billion in 1985 ("Smoking-Related Medical Care in '93 Estimated at $50 Billion," *The Washington Post*, 8 July 1994).

32. Green and Waitzman, *Business War on the Law*, 156.

33. Green and Waitzman, *Business War on the Law*, 115–16, and *Statistical Abstract of the U.S. 1992*, Table 354, "Air Pollutant Emissions, by Pollutant and Source: 1970 to 1990."

34. Green and Waitzman, *Business War on the Law*, p. 12.

35. A. Freeman, *Air and Water Pollution Control: A Benefit-Cost Assessment* (New York: John Wiley, 1982), 107; and U.S. Bureau of the Census, *Statistical Abstract of the U.S. 1991*, Table 359.

36. Freeman, *Air and Water Pollution Control*, 118.

37. Green and Waitzman, *Business War on the Law,* 12–13.

38. Freeman, *Air and Water Pollution Control,* 107.

39. Bureau of the Census, *Statistical Abstract of the U.S. 1988,* Table 909.

40. Freeman, *Air and Water Pollution Control,* 81, 91, 95, and 118.

41. Ibid., 159.

42. Bureau of the Census, *Statistical Abstract of the U.S. 1991,* Table 368.

43. "Value of Intangible Losses From Exxon Valdez Spill Put at $3 Billion," *The Washington Post,* 20 March 1991.

44. Green and Waitzman, *Business War on the Law,* p. 119.

45. "Toxic Time Bomb Ticks Away in Local Dumps," *Fort Worth Star-Telegram,* 21 October 1986.

46. *Environmental Health Issues Including Toxic Site Profiles* (Visalia, Calif.: Central California Health Systems Agency, February, 1986).

47. Green and Waitzman, *Air and Water Pollution Control,* 13.

48. The primary source of noise in society is transportation vehicles; business and industry generate an estimated 92 percent of all transportation activity. In addition, much of the use of personal vehicles, such as commuting, lunch trips, and travel, is business-induced and would not occur if the business organization did not exist.

49. Office of Noise Abatement and Control, U.S. Environmental Protection Agency, *Public Hearings on Noise Abatement and Control. Vol. VIII: Technology and Economics of Noise Control; National Programs and Their Relations with State and Local Programs* (Washington, D.C., 9–12 November 1971), 52, 328.

50. *Economic/Social Impact of Occupational Noise Exposure Regulations: Testimony Presented at the OSHA Hearings on the Economic Impact of Occupational Noise Exposure* (Washington, D.C.: U.S. Environmental Protection Agency, September 1976), 3–6.

51. *Public Hearings on Noise Abatement,* 329.

52. "Outcry Grows Over Defense Purchases," *The Wichita Eagle-Beacon,* 14 April 1985.

53. Employees and others commit crimes against corporations, including defalcations and fraud. When not redressed these crimes represent externalities improperly imposed on the corporation and its

stakeholders. There is no intention here to minimize these costs, but they are beyond the scope of this book.

54. "How Lawless Are Big Companies?" *Fortune,* 1 December 1980, 56-63.

55. Russell Mokhiber, *Corporate Crime and Violence* (San Francisco: Sierra Club Books, 1988), 19.

56. "Crime in the Suites," *Dollars & Sense* (November 1989): 5.

57. M. Clinard and P. Yeager, *Corporate Crime* (New York: The Free Press, 1980), 8.

58. N. Jacoby, P. Nehemkis, and R. Eells, *Bribery and Extortion in World Business* (New York: Macmillan Publishing, 1977), 42.

59. "Crime in the Suites," 5.

60. D. Simon and D. Eitzen, *Elite Deviance* (Boston: Allyn and Bacon, 1982), 91.

61. J. Johnson and J. Douglas, ed., *Crime at the Top: Deviance in Business and the Professions* (Philadelphia: J. B. Lippincott, 1978), 319–22.

62. "E. F. Hutton Co. Pleads Guilty to 2,000 Fraud Counts," *The San Diego Union,* 3 May 1985.

63. Chamber of Commerce of the U.S., *Handbook of White Collar Crime* (Washington, D.C.: Chamber of Commerce of the U.S., 1974), 42.

64. "Final Payments on the Bailout," *Business Week,* 27 February 1995, 34.

65. T. Klein, *Social Costs and Benefits of Business* (Englewood Cliffs, N.J.: Prentice-Hall, 1977), 5.

# Part Three
# A Practical Prescription

# 9

# *The Solution: A Better Scorecard*

Corporate accountability, in its broadest sense, includes the various ways in which corporations seek to justify their actions to all those affected by corporate activities, including employees, consumers, communities, federal, state and local governments and the public generally.

Securities and Exchange Commission, 1980[1]

CORPORATIONS HAVE ENORMOUS power; we have little power over corporations. In his 1956 book *American Capitalism*, John Kenneth Galbraith saw a system of countervailing power, with the strength of large corporations countered by that of labor unions and customers.[2] Today that system is tilted heavily toward the corporation. As Chapter 3 showed, none of the corporation's constituencies can effectively balance its great power.

The corporate system has grown into a colossus, unchecked and unaccountable. Its original public purpose has atrophied, replaced by the creed of the bottom line. And we have seen that, when the corporation is guided only by this goal of maximizing some narrowly defined "stockholder profit," great harm can result.

We need a different way of thinking about corporations—a paradigm shift—a return to the roots, to the original concept. When our cars or computers don't work right, we go back and read the instructions. Similarly, we need to return to the original concept of corporations: organizations that were granted charters to serve the public purpose.

To get there we can't simply tell the corporation to be responsible. And we can't effectively legislate responsible behavior. Legislation can help, but we're like the little Dutch boy who tried to plug the leaks in the dike with his fingers: new leaks keep springing up, and we can never have enough regulatory fingers to stop them all. Change must come instead at the source, in the *mechanism by which the corporation is operated.*

Corporate actions come from decisions made by corporate employees, mainly executives and managers. Some of these are far-reaching and obvious, but most are not. Taken together, though, they add up to countless effects that can be damaging and costly to stakeholders.

These decisions are always made with the performance measurement system, the scorecard, in mind. No matter what peripheral issues may command managers' attention, they are primarily concerned with the effect of every decision on bottom-line profit. And as we saw in Chapter 2, the measure of "profit" now in use does not reflect profit to workers or customers or the other stakeholders, nor does it even, in any logical sense, reflect profit to the corporation *as an entity.*

The present scorecard counts things as good (assets, revenues) and things as bad (liabilities, expenses) only when they *might* affect the interests of owners of common stock that way. (The emphasis on "might" is intentional; corporate management will sometimes give lip service to the notion of "profits for stockholders" but then use these profits with little apparent regard for stockholder interests.) Wages and benefits for employees, pollution-prevention measures, safety devices, warranties for customers, interest payments to lenders, taxes paid to communities—these obvious benefits to stakeholders appear only as expenses—as "bads"—in accounting's curious calculus.

/ So corporate managers make their decisions against the yardstick of the present narrow and deficient definition of profit. Although other standards may from time to time be announced, the bottom line is the only continuous and consistent performance standard to which managers are held accountable.

To restore corporations to their original, public interest function, this yardstick must be enlarged. It must be made to include the effects on *all* stakeholders. With an appropriate yardstick managers will become accountable to stakeholders, as their decisions are influenced by the probable effects on stakeholders.

How would this work? Today managers may be told to promote good corporate citizenship, to not discriminate or pollute or harm customers, but all managers know that ultimately they are judged primarily on a single dimension—the bottom line. If it is not high enough, all their good intentions and good deeds may be for naught. Indeed they may be out of a job. So in weighing day-to-day decisions, managers' internal, personal morality and good intentions will, too many times, give way to actions that may be harmful to stakeholders but promise to raise the bottom line. This doesn't mean they are evil people. It means they are in the clutches of a performance evaluation system, a scorekeeping system, that was never designed to account for the performance of the business.

Change the performance evaluation system and you change behavior. Introduce a valid, relevant system and you bring about actions and decisions more in line with the overall goals of the enterprise—which often are forceful enough in articulating responsible social goals, but are generally ignored because they aren't reflected in the profit and loss statement.

If the corporation, through its scorekeeping system, truly moves to evaluate managers not on a single dimension but on the balance they achieve among several dimensions, then managers will respond by seeking that balance. Tell managers, for example, that the company not only recognizes environmental responsibility in its corporate mission statement but will hold managers accountable for actual corporate performance on this dimension as they are now held accountable on the single dimension of financial profitability, and managers will much more carefully factor environmental effects into their everyday decisions.

Make the information public, and stakeholders as well as the media will respond. Top management may "talk the talk" today, but there is usually no way for the public to get inside the corporation to see whether they "walk the walk." So executives can sound great in public pronouncements but do nothing serious to ensure that the company acts on their lofty statements. But put it out for all the world to see, for stakeholders to act on, for the media to question, and executives are in a different ballgame. Those that speak, for example, of good working conditions had better be prepared to answer critics, perhaps on live television news, if their plant safety records are among the worst in the industry.

This is a systemic and cybernetic approach. It is self-directing and can modify itself, evolving as required to respond to environmental changes. It doesn't require government regulators to identify every corporate problem and then seek to control it.

Some would prefer a governmental "command and control" prescription. They would increase regulation over corporate behavior, even to explicitly regulating the decisions made at all levels in corporations. While the frustration of victims of corporate abuse—and their congressional representatives—is understandable, such regulation would be costly, restrictive, and intrusive—but, ultimately, not sufficiently effective. Although each new corporate abuse produces pressures for additional regulation, a purely regulatory approach alone cannot, in the long run, be a satisfactory or a sufficient solution.

Comprehensive regulation would be inordinately expensive. It would require regulatory, monitoring, policing, and enforcement efforts that would dramatically expand the federal bureaucracy. It could also unnecessarily limit the flexibility and responsiveness of corporate managers, applying a bureaucratic overlay to all business decisions.

In contrast, the approach proposed here would be simple, nonintrusive, and, in comparison to the benefits to be gained, inexpensive indeed. It is directly modeled after the prescription adopted in the United States in the 1930s to curb abuses in the securities markets.

Despite notorious securities shenanigans during the 1920s, Congress did not respond with laws to require that corporations present strong financial structures or that their securities be of high quality. The 1933 Securities Act and 1934 Securities Exchange Act focused on *information*. The intent was to require fair disclosure of relevant information so investors could make informed decisions.[3]

The theory behind these laws was that "shareholders would be better able to call a corporation's managers to account if they were given certain pieces of information about the corporation's business."[4] The financial regulatory function was left to investors, to the marketplace. With adequate information, investors would favor successful and reliable companies and discipline those that had pursued unsuccessful policies by withholding their investments.

This system of financial disclosure has worked fairly well, although not perfectly. Financial abuses still occur, but they appear to be exceptional rather than commonplace. An impressive "aftermarket" dealing in corporate financial information has developed over the years so that today corporate financial affairs are, to a substantial degree, transparent to the benefit of investors and potential investors. The financial marketplace is able to do a reasonably effective job of regulating corporate financial behavior through buy-and-sell decisions. This is not to say that financial investors are able to "control" the corporation; as shown in Chapter 3, stockholders have little effective control over the actions of management. But stockholders "voting with their feet" are able to impose a discipline on corporate financial behavior that was not possible prior to establishment of our corporate financial disclosure system.

## The Prescription

Congress's response to rampant financial fraud and abuse during the 1920s was to create the SEC to oversee financial information disclosure so that investors could regulate financial markets through better-informed decisions. The prescription for reining in corporate abuse

> Great corporations exist only because they are created and safe-guarded by our institutions; and it is our right and our duty to see that they work in harmony with these institutions. . . . The first requisite is knowledge, full and complete; knowledge which may be made public to the world.
>
> **Theodore Roosevelt, first annual message to Congress, 1901[5]**

in the 1990s is the same: require disclosure, but this time to *all* stake-holders.

What is needed is information that will allow stakeholders to make informed decisions concerning their relationships with corporations. By revealing the broad effects on stakeholders of corporate managers' decisions, full and fair disclosure will produce greater corporate responsiveness and accountability in much the same way that the securities acts brought about greater fairness and rationality in the securities markets.

Corporations use exactly this approach to control their divisions and subsidiaries; they require timely and comprehensive reporting of information to headquarters. In a similar manner, stakeholders acting as the marketplace will be able to better discipline corporations and other businesses if they have the information they need for rational resource allocation decisions. Comprehensive, periodic public reporting to stakeholders will contribute to restoring the corporation's public purpose and will substantially reduce the need for detailed regulation of specific corporate performance.

There have been some efforts, since the 1930s, to rely on information disclosure to protect the public and to encourage responsible corporate behavior. We now have on the books a number of laws that require corporate disclosure, sometimes in reports filed in Washington, in other cases in information posted at the corporation's facilities or filed with local or state agencies. Several examples are listed in the box.

**Some Laws and Regulations Mandating Corporate Disclosure**

Campaign finance reports required by the Federal Election Commission

Civil Rights Act of 1964 (establishing the Equal Employment Opportunity Commission)

Cost Accounting Standards Board

Emergency Planning and Community Right-to-Know Act

Employee Retirement Income Security Act

The Environmental Protection Agency's Environmental Impact Statements

Fair Credit Reporting Act

Magnuson-Moss Warranty Act

Occupational Safety and Health Act

Toxic Substances Control Act

Truth-in-Lending Act

Truth-in-Negotiations Act

Workers' Adjustment and Retraining Notification Act

As Russell Stevenson noted in *Corporations and Information: Secrecy, Access, and Disclosure,* "the interesting thing about these statutes . . . is that they constitute attempts to influence business behavior not by dictating what firms may and may not do but by changing the rules governing the availability of information about what they do." [6]

Unfortunately, this piecemeal, uncoordinated approach has required corporations to undergo considerable expense to provide information to regulatory agencies without ensuring that the information reaches the stakeholders who need to act on it. To correct the distortion of corporate purpose that accounting's too-narrow scorecard has wrought, we need a broader scorecard more relevant for the twenty-first century: a comprehensive *Corporate Report* to stakeholders.

## The Corporate Report

All large corporations should provide a single annual *Corporate Report* to stakeholders (smaller firms should do so as well, but our initial concern is with the corporate giants that dominate so much of the world's economies and cultures). A limited number of ad hoc or more frequent reports will also be necessary, such as reports on toxic leaks, but these can be held to an appropriate minimum. The *Corporate Report* should be freely accessible to any stakeholder, without fear or fee, just as corporations can obtain detailed information from customers, employees, communities, and other stakeholders who would do business with the corporation. As a minimum, copies should be available in corporate reception areas or other public facilities. Electronic access at no charge to the user, such as through the Internet, should be freely available.

By simply looking in the *Corporate Report*, you could see how many people had died from workplace injuries last year, what that brown stuff is pouring out of a company's smokestacks, and how the company has settled with customers over product problems, and how much top executives were making while they were "downsizing" your job.

Because companies seek transactions with stakeholders—purchases by customers, work from employees, police and fire protection and other infrastructure facilities from communities—it is appropriate that they voluntarily provide the information stakeholders require to participate fairly in these transactions. Responsible companies should begin to develop their stakeholder disclosure procedures forthwith.

To assist them in this voluntary progression, a full program to bring about corporate accountability is being developed through the Center for Advancement of Public Policy. This program is described in Chapter 11.

There will be some who will fear the *Corporate Report* will bear a high cost to industry. This should not be the case. The information needed by stakeholders, suggested in Chapter 10, is, to a substantial extent, already on file in most corporations. In fact, much of it is now included in a variety of disparate reports to the government. Consolidation and simplification of these reporting requirements may produce cost savings for industry that more than offset nominal costs of developing some additional data. Fold the annual report to stockholders into the *Corporate Report*, and printing costs will not be increased excessively. For some companies combining the stockholders' annual report, a multitude of government reports, and sometimes several reports to employees and other stakeholders (such as General Motors' roughly 100-page annual report touting its "social responsibility") into a single, nonduplicative document could produce net savings.

One would hope that responsible large corporations would provide leadership to the rest of the business community by moving expeditiously on the *Corporate Report*. In so doing, they will be able to influence the standards that will inevitably be developed voluntarily or through regulation. If sufficiently prompt voluntary action does not occur, however, it may become appropriate for Congress to consider a national "Corporate Accountability Act."

## The Corporate Accountability Act

After lobbyists and special interests finish working their will on Congress, well-intentioned statutory proposals too often emerge from the legislative process bearing little resemblance to the original idea and little relevance to the original goals. Similarly, regulations and regulatory agencies seem to often be captured by the very organizations they are supposed to be regulating. That's why a broader approach is proposed here, with legislation as a nearly last, instead of a first, resort. But if it becomes necessary, an act of Congress could be a useful part of an overall program to achieve corporate accountability.

A Corporate Accountability Act could be simple and succinct. A possible draft version is presented in Appendix 1.

Such an act could simply call for the Securities and Exchange Commission to be redesignated as the Corporate Accountability Commission, charged with establishing requirements for an annual, comprehensive, public *Corporate Report* to stakeholders. The commission would also be charged with bringing order and greater usefulness to corporate regulatory reporting by consolidating such reports into the *Corporate Report*.

In the Corporate Accountability Act, a *stakeholder* is defined as a person or other entity that has a significant interest in the performance, actions, and affairs of a corporation by virtue of an investment or potential investment (an investment is being considered) in the corporation (a fuller description of the stakeholder concept is provided in Chapter 1). Such an investment is defined as a commitment of tangible or intangible resources or services of value, including personal effort and risk.

### The Corporate Accountability Commission

With voluntary or regulated corporate reporting to stakeholders, it would probably be helpful to industry to have the guidance of a single government agency. While a new agency could be created to assist with and oversee consolidated corporate reporting to stakeholders, it seems to make more sense to assign this responsibility to the one agency that already has decades of experience in administering corporate regulatory reporting: the Securities and Exchange Commission, which could be renamed the Corporate Accountability Commission.

Some might argue that this role should be assigned to the Office of Management and Budget's Office of Information and Regulatory Affairs (OIRA). While OIRA reviews proposed government reporting regulations, it does not have the years of experience in regulating and overseeing corporate reporting, nor the auditing and enforcement capability and experience, of the SEC.

The Corporate Accountability Commission could be charged with assisting business to ensure full and fair reporting to all stakeholders. Since it is not now possible to lay out the disclosure details that will best serve all stakeholders, the Commission might hold hearings and conduct research to identify stakeholder information needs. For now, possible relevant information components are suggested in Chapter 10 and in Appendices 2–5.

A Corporate Accountability Commission could perform one step that would simultaneously help corporations, stakeholders, and government agencies. It could review the mass of federal reporting required of corporations, with a view toward bringing order and reducing redundancy in this reporting. Despite the intent of the Paperwork Reduction Act and the efforts of the federal Office of Information and Regulatory Affairs, corporate regulatory reporting requirements are uncoordinated and costly, while often not providing the information needed by the government and the public. Frequently one will seek out multiple reports only to discover that the needed information is still not available.

Most of the reports presently filed with the multitude of federal agencies could be consolidated into the *Corporate Report*. Corporations that now face duplication in report content, different reporting calendars, a range of administrative and audit procedures, and inconsistent requirements among agencies could be relieved of much of this burden and expense, while federal agencies could be spared the responsibility of administering reporting requirements and could concentrate on their original regulatory missions: protecting the public interest in such areas as health, safety, the environment, work conditions, and equal opportunity. This would require action by Congress, but a single agency such as the SEC, with the appropriate experience and administrative structure for dealing extensively with reporting, might more effectively assume this responsibility.

As we have seen, corporations collect and report a great deal of information, but it is scattered and fragmented. If most reporting requirements were consolidated into a single report filed with a single agency, everyone would win. Corporations could substantially reduce their regulatory reporting costs by replacing a multitude of reports with a single comprehensive report. Government would be able to reduce the cost of administration and oversight functions for corporate reporting in a host of agencies by consolidating that function in a single Corporate Accountability Commission. The public would win not only through tax savings but, most importantly, information that corporations must already prepare and stakeholders legitimately need would be readily available in the *Corporate Report*.

A massive new oversight bureaucracy would not be required. Compliance could be reasonably assured through the mechanism now used to obtain fair financial reporting—independent audits by certified public accountants. The scope of CPAs' audits would be expanded, but the nature of their responsibilities would not change significantly. In the process CPAs would have an opportunity to endow the word "public" in their titles with real meaning.

The proposed system is a cybernetic system. It can flexibly evolve in response to new stakeholder information needs while outdated requirements can be dropped. New laws would not be required to deal with every new corporate abuse; when full and relevant information is available, then customers, workers, and communities, comprising the marketplace, will regulate the corporation by their choices. And with true manager accountability to stakeholders, corporate abuses and misbehavior will be dramatically reduced, while managers and employees throughout the company respond more seriously to the stated goals of the enterprise.

## Objections to Corporate Accountability

Objections will be raised, of course, to this call for corporate accountability.

Some will say that the free market regulates the corporation and that if corporations do not provide good products at a fair price, they will not survive. Those who raise this objection reveal a confusion about the fundamental requirements for a free market system. Economists recognize that for such a system to work effectively, economic decision makers must have accurate and essentially complete information.

Sixty years ago Congress recognized that investors require reliable information if securities markets are to function in an orderly and effective manner (even though some argued then as well that mandating financial reporting would interfere with the free workings of financial markets). So it is with the market for goods and services. Customers cannot make informed economic decisions when they are faced with deception, hidden defects, or great scientific or technical complexity unless they have adequate information.

The same argument will be advanced with respect to workers: the labor market regulates the corporation, and that poor-paying, unrewarding, and unsafe or unhealthy jobs will go unfilled. This could be true if workers had adequate and reliable information, sufficient mobility to move to where the jobs are, and a reasonable array of job choices. But as with customers, the first requirement for informed choice is fair *information*. So corporate accountability to workers is essential if a system, which now too often abuses workers, is to function the way free market economic theory says it should function. In other words, corporate accountability, rather than *interfering* with the marketplace, is *necessary* for the market to function effectively.

Some will argue that corporate accountability constitutes an invasion of privacy or that the required disclosure will reveal proprietary information. This argument is certainly understandable: no one likes to reveal information that may make him or her look bad. A customer will not want to tell the seller about a bad credit record and a job applicant will not want to reveal a bad record on a previous job. But corporations insist on such disclosure to allow them to avoid bad economic decisions. Reciprocity, with the seller being equally revealing to customers and employers to employees, is not only a matter of equity but is essential for economic efficiency.

Corporations raised this privacy argument against the 1930s securities acts as well, but they have obviously learned to live with disclosure of their most intimate financial details—and even with outside auditors who virtually live in the company.

Concern will be expressed that development and reporting of the required information will be costly. But, as already noted, most of the information that should be reported will already have been accumulated within the corporation; additional "bookkeeping" will not, in most cases, be necessary. It is not so much the *creation* of new information as the *reporting of available information* that will be required. And consolidation and rationalization of present reporting requirements should serve to substantially reduce the costs presently incurred for regulatory compliance.

If the Securities and Exchange Commission is proposed as the agency to oversee a consolidation of corporate regulatory reporting and to assist corporations in providing full and fair disclosure to stakeholders, some SEC staff will welcome an expansion of authority, but some resistance would also be likely. With the complexity of financial reporting and securities markets seeming to offer manipulators standing invitations for abuse, SEC officials may fear additional responsibilities. But the additional responsibilities would of course be accompanied by a larger budget and additional personnel. As the SEC assumes responsibility for most government reporting to regulatory agencies, funds could be reallocated from budgets of other agencies (although this process would need to be monitored carefully to avoid an increase in one budget with no decreases in the others).

Some corporate executives, and especially chief executive officers who are in many cases almost singularly in control, may not welcome a call for accountability to stakeholders—or to anyone else. We would all probably relish great power without accountability. But even such executives must recognize, at least privately, that power without accountability is inequitable, inefficient, and promotes abuse. Our corporate system cannot fairly serve all stakeholders, all those who make it work, until it is accountable to all stakeholders. And it cannot bring forth full contributions from all stakeholders until all have the information they require to become full participants in the enterprise.

Some executives may cite "fiduciary responsibility to stockholders," an argument frequently invoked when it serves one's purpose.[7] By fiduciary responsibility they mean the idea that management holds corporate resources in trust for the stockholders and must always act in the stockholders' best interest. This may sound plausible until we recognize that, as we saw in Chapter 3, corporate managers not infrequently sacrifice stockholder interests for their own personal benefit, usually with impunity.

The courts, usually at the request of corporate management, have essentially rejected the fiduciary argument. Charitable contributions, even when they cannot be justified as contributing to goodwill and long-term profits, have been upheld.[8] Product price and quality decisions have been established as clearly within management's authority. Management can withdraw the corporation from a country because its government is undemocratic, or it can choose to stay, at its discretion, even though shareholders suffer as a consequence. Profits, purportedly earned for stockholders, may be shared with employees if management chooses. Recent cases have gone even further, allowing management to take defensive actions to fight takeovers and thereby protect their own jobs, even when these actions are opposed by a majority of the stockholders.[9]

The 1972 case of *Herald Co. v. Seawell*[10] appears to lay the "fiduciary responsibility to stockholders" argument firmly to rest. In this case the Tenth Circuit Court of Appeals upheld a rejection by the directors of a Denver newspaper of a takeover bid by the Newhouse chain, notwithstanding economic loss to the stockholders. The Court "upheld directors choosing the public interest in preference to shareholder interests in the absence of any possible basis for contending that shareholders might somehow be better off in the long run."[11] The Court noted:

> In this case we have a corporation engaged chiefly in the publication of a large metropolitan newspaper, whose obligation and duty is something more than the making of corporate profits. Its obligation is three-fold: to the stockholders, to the employees, and to the public.[12]

In other words, the corporation can serve the interests of all stakeholders and not just stockholders.

As noted, unrestricted autonomy is more fun than accountability. But most of us outside the realm of corporate management are held accountable—employees everywhere, teachers, public servants, soldiers, clergy, even politicians (although they demonstrate the desire of the powerful to exempt themselves). We must, in one forum or another, periodically account for our performance. We may not like to be held accountable, but accountability goes with authority and power. Power without accountability leads inevitably to abuse, a principle repeatedly demonstrated the world over by governments and mighty corporations.

## Other Proposals for Corporate Reform

A variety of other ideas have been put forward to bring the corporate system under control. A brief review may be helpful to put my proposal for corporate accountability into perspective.

Ralph Nader would "constitutionalize" the corporation through *federal chartering*.[13] John Kenneth Galbraith advocates *greater regulation*.[14] Robert Heilbroner first considers and then dismisses the idea of *breaking up* large corporations and finally proposes *nationalization* of those that are not socially responsible.[15] The ethical investing movement seeks to *encourage responsible and discourage irresponsible corporations* through selective investing.

*Worker control* of the company is often advocated, and, as a result of leveraged buyouts and employee stock option plans, is now a fact in a few corporations.

The Peoples Bicentennial Commission offered a more apocalyptic prescription: they would *abolish* the giant corporation.[16]

Some earlier proposals have also advocated greater disclosure. In the mid-1970s Nader, Green, and Seligman proposed the creation of a *Corporation Register* to be published by the SEC as a repository of information too voluminous to be included in the corporation's annual report.[17] While not addressing the problem of defining "profit" solely in terms of stockholder interests, they did call for disclosure of a number of items of information that are proposed here for inclusion in the *Corporate Report*.

Congress has, on occasion, shown an awareness that the level of corporate disclosure is inadequate. In 1976 it had an interagency committee draft a model corporate disclosure regulation. The rationale behind this effort was similar to that for the *Corporate Report*: to provide more useful corporate information while simultaneously reducing, through more uniform reports, the reporting cost.[18]

Also in 1976 Professor Donald Schwartz advocated a federal corporation law. It would have explicitly recognized stakeholders and would have required disclosure of certain employment, occupational safety, and environmental information.[19]

Then in 1980 the Corporate Democracy Act was introduced in Congress. This act called for disclosure of limited equal employment opportunity data, air pollution emissions, occupational injuries and illnesses, the chemical constituents of each chemical product manufactured, and corporate spending on political activities. Disclosure would have been part of the annual report to stockholders, which would also have been made available to the public. Although a good effort, this approach would still have accorded primacy to stockholders, while allowing other stakeholders to, in essence, look over the stockholders' shoulders. The Securities and Exchange Commission staff, apparently then more concerned with the interests of Wall Street than those of the broader public, opposed the Corporate Democracy Act, and it was never adopted.[20]

These and other proposals have been offered to address problems caused by large corporations. With few exceptions, they have been opposed by corporate lobbyists, corporate PACs, and corporate dollars. Many members of Congress have at least one large corporation in their district, and its campaign contributions and influence with local opinion leaders can be most persuasive. So such bills are routinely defeated. Meanwhile corporate abuses continue and the need for accountability grows.

The corporate accountability approach builds on the legacy of these earlier efforts, but differs from them in important respects. The most important difference lies in the recognition that corporations were originally created to serve the public purpose, but largely because of the adoption of an inappropriate scorekeeping system they have lost their way—their purpose has been perverted. A scorekeeping system is needed, by corporate management as well as by stakeholders, that will permit evaluation of the total performance of the enterprise. We need a system that will show how well the corporation has performed in serving the public that endows it with a charter, as well as in providing a return on investment to all of its stakeholders and not just to stockholders. Such a scorekeeping system is described in Chapter 11.

Stockholders have an investment in the corporation and a right thereby to accountability. But so do customers. So do workers. So do suppliers and lenders. So does the community and society. The bias inherent in accounting's profit and loss statement is here exposed—a bias that ostensibly favors stockholders but in practice leaves corporate managers accountable, by and large, only to themselves.

## Notes

1. Securities and Exchange Commission, *Staff Report on Corporate Accountability* (Washington, D.C.: U.S. Government Printing Office), 4 September 1980, 33.
2. John Kenneth Galbraith, *American Capitalism: The Concept of Counter-vailing Power,* rev. ed. (Boston: Houghton Mifflin, 1956).
3. Merino and Neimark argue that these laws were actually essential for the survival of capitalism, rather than being inspired primarily by a philosophy of providing information that would then allow market forces to regulate companies. See Barbara Merino and Marilyn Neimark, "Disclosure Regulation and Public Policy: A Sociohistorical Reappraisal," *Journal of Accounting and Public Policy* (fall 1982): 33–57.
4. Deborah A. DeMott, ed., *Corporations at the Crossroads: Governance and Reform* (New York: McGraw-Hill, 1980), 2.
5. Russell B. Stevenson, Jr., *Corporations and Information: Secrecy, Access, and Disclosure* (Baltimore: The Johns Hopkins University Press, 1980), unnumbered page preceding Table of Contents.
6. Stevenson, *Corporations and Information,* 6.
7. Proponents of this argument often cite *Dodge v Ford Motor Co.* [204 Mich. 459, 170 N.W. 668 (1919)], a case long since emasculated. For example, see the A. P. Smith Mfg. case cited in the following note.
8. See, for example, *A. P. Smith Mfg. Corp. v Barlow,* 13 N.J. 145, 98 A.2d 581, appeal dismissed, 346 U.S. 86 (1953). In this case a $1,500 contribution by a small New Jersey manufacturing company to Princeton University was upheld as contributing to the preservation of the free enterprise system and the availability of college-trained persons for managerial positions.

9. "In Takeover Wars, A Battle Is Won by Managers," *The New York Times,* 16 July 1989, International/National edition, citing recent Polaroid and Time/Warner cases.

10. *Herald Co. v Seawell,* 472 F.2d 1081 (10th Cir. 1972).

11. Phillip I. Blumberg, *The Megacorporation in American Society: The Scope of Corporate Power* (Englewood Cliffs, N.J.: Prentice-Hall, 1975), 9.

12. Blumberg, *The Megacorporation,* 9, citing 472 F.2d at 1090.

13. Ralph Nader, Mark Green, and Joel Seligman, *Taming the Giant Corporation* (New York: W. W. Norton, 1976).

14. John Kenneth Galbraith, *Economics and the Public Purpose* (Boston: Houghton Mifflin, 1973).

15. Robert L. Heilbroner, *In the Name of Profit* (Garden City, N.Y.: Doubleday, 1972), 245–47.

16. The Peoples Bicentennial Commission, *Common Sense II* (New York: Bantam Books, 1975), 101.

17. Nader, Green, and Seligman, *Taming the Giant Corporation,* 139.

18. Senate Committe on Commerce, *Corporate Rights and Responsibilities: Hearing before the Committee on Commerce,* 94th Cong., 2nd sess., June, 1976.

19. Securities and Exchange Commission, *Staff Report on Corporate Accountability* Committee on Banking, Housing, and Urban Affairs, United States Senate, 4 September 1980.

20. Securities and Exchange Commission, *Staff Report on Corporate Accountability.*

# 10

# *What The Scorecard Should Contain*

THE *CORPORATE REPORT* should provide the information needed by stakeholders for rational resource allocation and other decisions involving associations and transactions with the corporation. This information is diverse, extensive, and often specific to the stakeholder group. Appropriate groups, including business, the accounting profession, and stakeholder organizations, will want to engage in ongoing assessment of these needs. If a Corporate Accountability Commission is established as described in Chapter 9, it would likely find it appropriate to conduct recurring hearings and inquiries that involve the stakeholder groups themselves.

But we already know, on the basis of prior investigations and research, a great deal about the information presently needed.

## Accountability to Customers

In his first consumer message to Congress, President Kennedy proposed certain basic rights for consumers, including:

> The *right to be informed*: To be protected against fraudulent, deceitful, grossly misleading information, advertising,

labeling, or other practices, and to be given the facts to make an informed choice.[1]

Several measures have responded to customers' legitimate needs for fair product information. For example, the U.S. Food and Drug Administration and the Food Safety and Inspection Service of the Agriculture Department announced new food labeling regulations in May 1994 under the Nutrition Labeling and Education Act.[2] These are intended to substantially improve the information available to consumers in evaluating packaged and canned food purchases.

Other agencies and laws with significant consumer information components include the Consumer Product Safety Commission; the Freedom of Information Act; the Federal Insecticide, Fungicide, and Rodenticide Amendments and Regulations; the Motor Vehicle and School Bus Safety Amendments; the Truth-in-Lending Act; the Pension Reform Act; the Real Estate Settlement Procedures Act; the Federal Food, Drug, and Cosmetic Act; the Consumer Product Safety Act; and the Toxic Substances Control Act. Thanks to these, consumers now have a fair degree of useful product ingredient information, automobile gas mileage ratings, access to accurate interest rate information on loans, unit pricing in the supermarket, and clearer warnings on dangerous and toxic products. Such efforts have made consumers relatively better off, in terms of the availability of fair information, than either workers or local communities.

Progress has been made, but customers need, and should have a right to, important information not now available. Appendix 2 presents examples of additional information disclosure that consumers and customers may need for informed market choices.

The *Corporate Report* should contain a full section devoted to information required by customers. Much of the product and customer information that corporations must now report could be combined in this section, thus making it more accessible to the public while reducing the cost to the corporation (this would not replace, of course, the information that should be provided on product labels or at the point of sale). To ensure fair access, the *Corporate Report* could be made available to the public at company facilities, the city clerk's office, and the public library in each community in which the corporation has a facility.

Full and fair disclosure to customers is at least as sound, and most would say *more* defensible, than the disclosure to stockholders that now receives such costly attention. (At least one corporation has set a good example by voluntarily providing a "Customer Report," mailed directly to its customers. British Telecom's eight-page booklet included six broad sections with a mixture of narrative, charts, and photographs.[3])

Full and fair disclosure will ensure that customers, whose stake in the corporation is often greater than that of stockholders, receive the information they need to make safe and informed market choices.

## Accountability to Workers

Employees are stakeholders. They invest their effort, creativity, sweat, careers, and not infrequently their health and safety for the benefit of the enterprise. As decision makers in the economic marketplace, they must have full information on which to make informed career and work choices.

Information needed by employees is outlined in Appendix 3 and includes data on:

- Layoffs, plant closings, and employment stability
- Health and safety
- Company employment record
- Employee grievances
- Impact of technology
- Pension programs
- Future plans

Despite the efforts of labor unions, corporations do not now account systematically to their workers. This is so even though a worker's investment in the corporation, measured in years of commitment or risk to health and safety, may be considerably greater than that of the average stockholder. It is true as well despite the efforts of such agencies as the Equal Employment Opportunity Commission and the Occupational Safety and Health Administration. Although these agencies exist to seek the protection and well-being of employees and potential employees, neither agency requires corporations to provide the essential information individuals need to make informed personal choices regarding their workplace safety and their careers.

Take the EEOC's required report, Form EEO-1. Though minimal in content, it is not even available to present or potential employees and was specifically excluded from the provisions of the Freedom of Information Act. OSHA's required report is posted on the premises and so available to workers, but its contents are as meager and uninformative as the EEOC's; OSHA's summary form that must be posted in the workplace shows only the number of incidents in the two or three broadest categories. So-called "worker right-to-know" legislation requires posting of information about toxic and dangerous substances in the workplace but, like OSHA's reporting, the disclosure is not sufficient. In establishing these requirements, Congress and the regulatory agencies appear to have given greater attention to serving the corporation's desire for secrecy than to protecting workers.

The EEOC and OSHA reporting forms are evidence of a recognized *need*—a need by workers for fair information about the corporation and their jobs, so that their exposure to safety risks and barriers such as the "glass ceiling" can at least be conscious and informed. Gradually, corporations have been required to give workers some of the information they need, but not nearly enough and virtually always over the opposition of management.

For example, Congress finally passed in 1988, over Corporate America's resolute opposition, the Workers' Adjustment and Retraining Notification Act requiring sixty days' notice for plant closings. (This law applies only to companies with 100 or more full-time employees at any one site and requires notice when fifty or more workers will permanently lose their jobs. It also requires notice of layoffs when a third of a plant's workers or 500 people, whichever is less, are affected.) The bill supported the philosophy of the proposed *Corporate Report*, to provide stakeholders with information necessary for them to make rational, informed choices. But it has not worked; workers are not receiving the notification intended by Congress. Labor economists who studied this law's effects after four years concluded that it has had "no effect whatsoever,"[4] because of "too many loopholes, too many exceptions and virtually no enforcement."

The history of the plant-closing law shows how a weak, piecemeal approach to disclosure, with administration by agencies that lack the experience and the enforcement and audit capabilities of the SEC, holds only false promise. Employees and potential employees have a legitimate need for substantial information about the company, the workplace, and the job. Most of this information should be included in the *Corporate Report* (although site- and job-specific information may be provided on-site).

Some will resist such requirements: "unjustifiable cost," "trade secret," "proprietary information," "undue legal exposure," and similar rationale will be offered. Generally these will not be valid. A company that cannot provide safe and healthy working conditions does not warrant the special benefits conferred by a charter of incorporation granted by the public. We should not, as a civilized society, casually and without accountability trade workers' well-being and workers' lives for consumer goods and stockholder profits.

Day in and day out, employees put their careers, and often their health and safety, on the line—a line so tenuous it can be snapped by a manager in bondage to the bottom line. Workers with twenty years of seniority, loyal to a company they thought was equally loyal to them, can go to work in the morning and be without a job that evening, their few possessions from their desk or work station carried home in a cardboard box, now facing an uncertain future that may leave them effectively discarded on the economic sidelines—especially if they are over the age of forty or so. A third of those affected in a shutdown face *long-term* unemployment. But women are twice as likely as men to stay unemployed for longer than a year, and blacks are especially hard-hit.[5] In other words, the effect of plant closings is just the opposite of what

> Since I was laid off, two weeks before Christmas, I have lost my family health insurance, life insurance, and accident insurance coverages as well as the termination of my retirement plan.... My husband is now working three jobs to try to make ends meet and still our finances are in dire straits.... I was given no time to prepare for this, nor was the loyalty with which I approached my job returned in kind.... I performed in the spirit of the social contract that structured the security of my job. McDonnell Douglas, I feel, betrayed this spirit.
>
> **Susan Holler, former employee of McDonnell Douglas Corporation, testifying during Senate hearings[6]**

most people would expect national social policy to be, because it falls most heavily on those who have already suffered from discrimination.

Before people take a job, shouldn't they have a right to a fair disclosure of the corporation's record on layoffs and "downsizing" so they can make an informed choice? Before they risk their health, shouldn't they have a right to know the hazards they may face?

It is hard to understand why any company that seeks to be responsible, that would speak of its employees as "our most important assets," would resist disclosing the basic information employees must have to make informed career and risk choices. A few do try to provide reasonable disclosure, and to treat their employees as true stakeholders—instead of as consumable, disposable resources.

Pitney Bowes, for example, is well-known for its responsiveness to employee concerns. This company not only has an annual meeting for its common stock stakeholders; it has one for its worker stakeholders as well.

> Stockholders meetings are usually tame compared with the annual jobholders meetings. Held in theaters near all of the main sites, the meetings give every employee a chance to ask

management questions or air personal gripes. Senior officers . . . sit on the stage while groups of up to 500 attend.
Prizes—$50 U.S. Savings Bonds—are given for the best
questions. The meetings date from 1947. The company also
has an employee-management council, comprising an equal
number of management representatives and workers, that
meets monthly.[7]

Through hearings and research, a Corporate Accountability Commission could continuously monitor full and fair disclosure to workers. Only with such information can workers protect themselves
through informed market choices.

## Accountability to Communities

Corporations often seek special benefits from communities, benefits
that can cost taxpayers substantially. A company will frequently take
the position that it, not the community, is the one providing benefits in
the form of jobs, with little or no acknowledgment that workers *earn*
their jobs with their labor, or that the workers and community pay for
their education and for the infrastructure that support the corporation
with their taxes. Corporations routinely seek special tax breaks, zoning
exemptions, free utility line extensions, industrial development bonds,
and anything else the community may be able to provide. They may
even seek outright gifts, such as free land, buildings built by taxpayers,
and cash donations.

As shown in Chapter 8, corporations cost communities—cost
small businesses, families, neighborhoods, and other taxpayers. These
costs show up in school and university budgets as taxpayers pay for the
training the corporation wants in its future employees. They show up
in street construction and maintenance from the damage done by the
corporation's vehicles. They show up in sewer and water lines and
access roads extended to new plants. They show up in police and fire
protection provided to the corporation; in the court system the corporation needs to enforce its contracts, protect its patents, collect its

> Large new manufacturers almost always drain a community's
> existing infrastructure—its streets, water, sewers, schools. . . .
>
> *The Wichita Eagle-Beacon*[8]

accounts, and prosecute shoplifters; and in all the rest of the government infrastructure.

Public costs of private corporations may take the form of wastes and toxic emissions that pollute the air and water and, as we discover more and more frequently, can effectively poison the land. Excessive, wasteful product packaging not only costs consumers but also clogs dumps and landfills.

Despite the costs they impose, corporations continue to ask for more. Often to merely ask is to receive. For example, a study for one year in Michigan found that 97.2 percent of tax abatements that corporations sought were granted.[9] Frequently a corporation will, if turned down on some special favor, threaten to pack up and move to "a more favorable business climate."

Because local governments license businesses, because they grant them special favors, because governments purchase goods and services from corporations,[10] and because corporations often impose a tremendous cost on the community and its taxpayers, cities and communities have a legitimate claim to appropriate information to guide their decision makers.

Community leaders *need* information, but they often do not know what to ask for or what might be possible to obtain. Elected city and county commissioners rarely have business, finance, or accounting backgrounds. They are often "citizen-legislators," meeting once a week and holding down full-time jobs elsewhere. With too much to learn and too little time to give to the job, they rely heavily on city staff. Unfortunately, staff members are usually not much help when it comes to information about corporations. They rarely have significant work experience in corporations and seldom have appropriate training in accounting.

So most often it is a one-sided debate when the corporation wants something from the community. Corporate financial reports are publicly available (but only for publicly held corporations, of course; almost never for the corporations whose shares are not traded publicly), but these reports are not particularly useful. The numbers can be overwhelming to the nonaccountant, and even if they were understandable, they usually are not particularly relevant to the issues at hand.

In responding to corporate demands, city commissioners and staff need to know what questions to ask, what information to require; most of the time they don't. And they are usually reluctant to ask many questions anyway, since to do so might be made to appear, by political opponents or corporate spokespersons, as anti-business, anti-jobs, or anti-economic-growth—and in most communities, these are hot buttons, dangerous charges in electoral politics.

Take Chanute, Kansas, for example. Rose Chemical Company of Kansas City, Missouri, wanted to come in and build an incinerator to burn polychlorinated biphenyls (PCBs). According to State Representative Ed Bideau, Chanute officials "invited these people to the city without so much as making a phone call to the EPA to check their track record." It turned out that the EPA had levied more than $200,000 in fines against Rose Chemical at its Holden, Missouri, PCB storage facility, and the company was "embroiled in suits and countersuits with Holden city officials." The Chanute city manager lamented,"I certainly did not know anything about that when I contacted the company, and I don't believe that we at the city ever had any knowledge of it until citizen opponents raised the question at public meetings."[11]

If communities are going to provide benefits to corporations at taxpayer expense, they need to be able to fairly evaluate the probable return, the gain, to the community. To do this they need information, but more importantly, they need to know *what* information to seek. A Corporate Accountability Commission could survey local elected officials, meet with citizens' groups, interview officers of professional associations, hold hearings, and conduct other research to identify information that communities need. The commission could then provide guidance to business to ensure that communities receive this information in a timely manner; if business was not forthcoming, the commission might find it necessary to promulgate mandatory reporting standards.

Communities that seek to make rational decisions about corporations in their midst must now try to obtain the information needed at taxpayer expense, or do without. Mostly they do without. Communities should not have to make costly choices without fair information, and taxpayers should not have to pay to collect this information. The corporation that stands to benefit should provide the needed information freely and willingly.

Community decision makers and opinion leaders are often uninformed about large corporations and without fair information they can be manipulated to do the corporation's bidding. But research indicates that they do pay attention to relevant information, *when it is available.* Fletcher concluded that social responsibility disclosures by corporations were studied carefully by community leaders, and their decisions were clearly affected by those disclosures.[12]

Local government officials and community leaders who must respond to requests by corporations for special treatment and benefits must now do so with precious little relevant information. Corporate executives will make claims, often in the press, that cannot be evaluated because of lack of data. Most of these data must come from the corporation, from its internal documents. But in many cases corporate executives have pressured and even threatened a community while withholding the very information the community needs for a rational response. Full and fair disclosure will facilitate sound public resource allocation decisions and will permit residents and taxpayers to better use their resources for real, not fanciful, returns.

Appendix 4 lays out some of the kinds of information that community stakeholders need for decisions regarding their relations with corporations in their midst. Most of this information should be presented in the comprehensive *Corporate Report* that would be freely available from all large corporations; it can be supplemented with localized information placed in the city clerk's office and in the community's library.

## Accountability to Society

The nation—society at large—is an investor, a stakeholder, in the corporation. Corporations receive the benefit of a civilized, orderly society and a functioning economic system. Their profits are possible partly because of the security provided by the billions in taxpayer dollars spent on national defense. Corporations benefit from an open society that permits them to move into any state, any area, and count on finding an educated workforce, police protection, and an organized government.

In the United States corporations receive even more direct benefits. Our tax laws are frequently redrawn to "stimulate business"—which invariably translates not into improving the purchasing power of consumers, but into direct favors for corporations such as investment tax credits and accelerated depreciation provisions.

Corporations are also the beneficiaries of direct government expenditures, in the form of purchases, contracts, subsidies, and outright grants. And they obtain special value from the heritage of technological developments and accumulated knowledge of the past. The profits corporations reap are not only a product of their own efforts but of this heritage as well, even when it cost them nothing.

The nation is thus an investor, in both the corporate system generally and in individual corporations. In return the nation is entitled to an accounting. Much of this information should be provided in the *Corporate Report* and supplemented otherwise as necessary.

As a society we need much of the same information required by communities—taxes paid, pollution and waste generated, political involvement such as PAC activities and campaign contributions, and a history of legal actions. But we also need additional information reflecting the national impact of corporate actions. Examples of corporate information that should be disclosed in the *Corporate Report* to serve national needs are presented in Appendix 5.

This chapter, along with Appendices 2 through 5, has reviewed briefly the information needs of stakeholders—what should be considered for inclusion in the *Corporate Report*. In Chapter 11 we will see how to achieve corporate accountability—in our lifetimes!

# Notes

1. "Consumer Interests—Message from the President of the United States (H. Doc. No. 364)," *United States of America Congressional Record,* 26 February 1962-15 March 1962, vol. 108, Part 3, 4263.
2. "A Healthy Amount of Verbiage to Define What's Good for You," *The Washington Post,* 5 May 1994, A24.
3. Vivien Beattie and Mike Jones, "Telecom Publishes First Customer Report," *Management Accounting* (UK) (March 1987): 24–26.
4. "Layoff Law Is Having Slim Effect," *The New York Times,* 9 August 1993.
5. Barry Bluestone and Bennett Harrison, *The Deindustrialization of America* (New York: Basic Books, 1982), 49ff.
6. Kary L. Moss, "Devising Solutions to Capital Flight: The WARN Act," *Poverty and Race,* a publication of the Poverty & Race Research Action Council (May/June 1994): 3.
7. Lorraine Dusky and Baila Zeitz, "The Best Companies for Women," *Savvy,* May 1988, 47ff.
8. "Incentive Packages Stir Questions Among Taxpayers and Consultants," *The Wichita Eagle-Beacon,* 26 June 1988.
9. Louis Nemeth, "Giving Away the Store: Tax Abatements in Michigan," *Multinational Monitor* (31 March 1986): 7.
10. Berkeley, California, for example, imposes specific performance requirements on all companies doing business with the city. See "Berkeley: Matching Its Image," *Newsweek,* 11 February 1985, p. 11.
11. "Kansas Assuming Major Role in Disposal of PCBs," *The Wichita Eagle-Beacon,* 22 April 1986.
12. John Cameron Fletcher, "A Delphi Evaluation of a Railroad's Social Costs and Benefits" (D.B.A. diss., University of Colorado, 1981).

# 11

# *How Do We Get There?*

A PROGRAM TO bring about corporate accountability will require action on a number of fronts. The starting point is to mobilize stakeholders to call for disclosure, in a comprehensive annual *Corporate Report*, of the information they need to make rational decisions regarding their transactions and relationships with business.

The author is working with The Center for Advancement of Public Policy (P.O. Box 33608, Washington, D.C. 20033; FAX 202-265-6245) to build a broad national Stakeholder Alliance of public interest groups to bring about full and fair corporate accountability. Assistance is provided to participating organizations in seeking and obtaining disclosure from corporations in their separate areas of concern (e.g., the environment, civil rights, pay equity, the glass ceiling, and workplace safety), as well as in researching corporations when firms are not forthcoming with the information needed.

For example, environmentalists are encouraged to call on corporations to publicly disclose full information about their emissions and environmental record, including fines and assessments. A model corporate environmental report has been developed as a standard for corporate disclosure. This information will empower environmentalists as they seek greater pollution prevention and cleanup efforts from corporations.

Similarly, assistance is being provided to community organizations and local governments in identifying and requiring relevant information from corporations as a basis for evaluating decisions such as granting industrial development bonds or tax abatements. These groups are also being advised on researching information when it is not forthcoming from the corporation, as well as in estimating needed information from related data.

Complete voluntary disclosure models are being developed to assist individual corporations to begin voluntary disclosure to stakeholders. Some companies are now providing some good information in particular areas, especially on environmental issues; these "best practices" will be publicized as examples to guide other companies (and *solid* examples of stakeholder disclosure are welcomed). Corporate reporting standards will be developed, along the lines of the author's *Management Accounting* article, "Standards for Corporate Social Reporting."[1] Additional books and manuals to provide guidance to managers are also planned.

The accounting profession has a potentially major role to play in advancing corporate reporting to stakeholders. During the 1970s professional accounting associations were in the forefront of exploring new ways in which accounting could serve stakeholders and the public. The American Institute of Certified Public Accountants' Committee on Social Measurement developed an important guidebook, *The Measurement of Corporate Social Performance.*[2] The National Association of Accountants (now the Institute of Management Accountants) sponsored committees and research studies, including *The Measurement of Corporate Environmental Activity.*[3] The American Accounting Association appointed several committees including the Committee on Accounting for Social Performance; these usually issued reports. The international accounting firm of Arthur Andersen & Co. devoted substantial resources to develop the internal procedures that were spelled out in its *Practice Guidelines for Social Impact Planning and Reporting.*[4] (Many of these and similar efforts are described in the author's

*Corporate Social Accounting.*[5]) Unfortunately, during the recent movement toward stakeholder accountability, the accounting profession has been on the sidelines. It will be encouraged to once again assume a significant role.

If this multifaceted program does not produce an appropriate level of voluntary accountability from Corporate America, the Corporate Accountability Act will be introduced in Congress. Indeed, at some point impatient members of Congress may move precipitously with this act or a similar bill. I believe it would be better, though, to first try to bring about full and fair disclosure through the voluntary cooperation of public interest and stakeholder groups, exemplary corporations and business associations, and accounting firms and professional accounting organizations. If this approach fails or does not move rapidly enough, the act can then be taken up.

## What You Can Do

There is much that the individual can do—now—to advance corporate accountability to stakeholders and contribute to the overthrow of the tyranny of the bottom line. You can obtain information about corporations, make public statements about their actions, and build an organization to seek greater corporate accountability.

### Obtain Information

Much of the information you need may be available from reference sources, although it may not be easy to find in a convenient form. The business reference section of your city or university library should have such useful sources as:

- *The Wall Street Journal Index* (cites companies by name)
- *Business Periodicals Index*
- *How to Find Information About Companies: The Corporate Intelligence Source Book*
- The EPA's *Toxic Release Inventory*
- *America's Corporate Families and International Affiliates*

- *Directory of Corporate Affiliations*

- *Directory of American Firms Operating in Foreign Countries*

- *Directory of Foreign Firms Operating in the United States*

- *Who Owns Whom*

- *How to Find Business Intelligence in Washington*

- *Business Rankings Annual*

- *Multinational Corporations: The E.C.S.I.M. Guide to Information Sources* (European Centre for Study and Information on Multinational Corporations)

- *Europe's 15,000 Largest Companies*

- *Asia's 7500 Largest Companies*

- Corporate annual reports

- Financial reporting services such as Dun & Bradstreet, Moody's, Predicasts, Standard & Poor's, Thomas, Value Line, and Wards

Get a copy of the company's annual report, or better, its Form 10-K. Both can usually be had for the asking from the corporate stockholder relations office, and both are filed with the SEC.

Search local newspaper backfiles (usually called the "morgue") for stories mentioning a corporation of interest.

Seek interviews with corporate executives.

Use electronic media to find and exchange information rapidly and efficiently. A tremendous amount of information about corporations, and not just financial information, is available on-line through LEXIS, DIALOG, Compuserve, America Online, Prodigy, and other such electronic services. You may be able to draw on law students and attorney friends for access to LEXIS, probably the largest repository of news and financial and statistical information available.

Use the Internet. More and more corporations are setting up World Wide Web home pages; some provide annual reports and other documents, although you shouldn't expect to find information critical of the corporation. Corporate SEC filings are expected to be available for no additional charge on the Internet, and you may find useful discussion groups there as well (these are called "newsgroups"; see Eric Braun's *The Internet Directory*, published by Fawcett, for an extensive listing of newsgroups). Some of these newsgroups will have useful comments, but you're pretty much on your own about verifying the information. In particular take a look at the newsgroup that I've set up at *alt.corporate.accountability*.

Also check the discussion sections of bulletin board systems— BBSs. A sampling of BBSs is provided in the back of each month's *Computer Shopper* magazine.

## Make Public Statements

Buy a share (or more) of a target company's stock, then go to the annual stockholders' meeting. Plan and prepare to speak. You will probably be suppressed, but give the press a copy of your remarks ahead of time and warn them that you may be silenced. If appropriate, hold an impromptu press conference outside the meeting hall.

Use the media. Write letters to the editor calling for corporate accountability and reciting the consequences, especially those that are local, of unaccountable corporations. Publish op-ed columns; call the op-ed editor of your newspaper first because many local papers welcome submissions on local issues (they generally want about 750 words, although some will let you go up to twice or even three times that length). Call in to radio and television talk shows. Go further: contact producers of local talk shows and volunteer as a guest. If you or your organization have a particular perspective, expertise, or standing, call the newspaper, radio, and television news editors and offer comment on current corporate abuses or misbehavior. Or FAX them a press release. Always explain how full corporate accountability would have prevented or reduced the likelihood of the abuse.

## Build An Organization

Build organizations and coalitions to promote your particular concerns and add corporate accountability to your agenda. When corporations are fully accountable, they will be much less likely to commit the kinds of abuses described in Chapters 5-7; accountability may thus be the most cost-effective way available to your group to achieve its goals. Consider affiliating your group with the Stakeholder Alliance cited earlier.

These suggestions are only a beginning. Remember that, ultimately, you and your neighbors are the marketplace that is extolled in a free market system. And you are the citizens that empower your state government to issue charters to corporations. Corporations, in a very real sense, owe their existence to your acquiescence; it seems only proper that they provide an accounting to the authority, the citizens, that endows them with life.

## The Consequences of Corporate Accountability

Accountability works. Of numerous examples that could be cited, consider simply the toxic release inventory required by the 1986 Superfund law. Under this law manufacturers must make public an inventory of chemicals they stock and report the quantities of some 300 toxic chemicals released each year. The effect of this disclosure has been dramatic: for example, chemical makers, the largest producers of these poisons, reduced their emissions by 35 percent in only four years. An EPA official stated: "We could never have gotten here so fast" with regulation. Monsanto Company executive Nicolas Redding reflected industry's response: "We knew the numbers were high, and we knew the public wasn't going to like it."[6]

The consequences of corporate accountability will be substantial: less air and water pollution, less toxic waste, fewer workplace injuries and illnesses, less racial and sexual discrimination, more equitable compensation, more stable and secure jobs, fewer product-related injuries and illnesses, communities that are stronger both economically and socially, and a better quality of life for all those affected by corporate behavior.

As employee morale and commitment are improved, as customer loyalty to products is again developed, as communities become respected partners with their corporate residents, American companies will become more productive and more competitive in the global marketplace.

As corporations become accountable to their stakeholders, the corporation will come to be managed more in behalf of their balanced

A critical review of research on the compatibility of social responsibility and financial success has been conducted by the Center for Advancement of Public Policy. This review indicates that companies that treat customers, employees, communities, and the environment in a responsible and reciprocal manner do somewhat better on financial dimensions over the long run, with exceptions in specific circumstances. For example, the Domini 400 Social Index, which uses social responsibility screens for its investment decisions, has outperformed the Standard & Poor's 500 since its inception in 1990 (see Peter Kinder, Steven Lydenberg, and Amy Domini, *Investing for Good*, New York, Harper-Business, 1993, and their *The Social Investment Almanac*, New York, Henry Holt and Co., 1992). Similarly, Kravetz found that companies that scored high on a human resource progressiveness scale experienced considerably higher growth in sales, profits, and equity than less progressive companies (Dennis Kravetz, *The Human Resources Revolution*, San Francisco, Jossey-Bass Publishers, 1990). In another study, Spicer correlated companies' pollution control against their investment value; he found that companies with better pollution-control records show higher profitability, lower risk, and higher price/earnings ratios (Barry Spicer, "Investors, Corporate Social Performance and Information Disclosure: An Empirical Study," *The Accounting Review*, January 1978, pp. 94–111). A number of other studies reached similar conclusions, while some have not found such a positive correlation.

interests instead of solely to enhance the wealth of stockholders. But stockholders do not necessarily lose: accountable corporations that practice stakeholder management are more likely to be the successful survivors in the twenty-first century (see box), while the corporations that exploit and consume, rather than nurture, their stakeholder resources fall by the wayside.

Corporate managers, the ones to be held accountable, ultimately gain as well. In the present corporate culture, managers feel that their responsibility to the bottom line requires them to take actions they would consider unacceptable outside the corporation—in their homes, neighborhoods, or churches. Corporate accountability to stakeholders will allow corporate managers to be as moral and ethical within the corporation as they try to be outside it.

## The "Aftermarket" for Corporate Information

As additional information, information needed by corporate stakeholders, becomes routinely available, it will be assembled, reported, and criticized by independent enterprises. This is of course what happened with the financial information that must be reported to the SEC as a consequence of the 1933 and 1934 securities acts. Services like Dow Jones, Moody's, Standard & Poor's, and Value Line swarm over SEC filings—dissecting, diagnosing, comparing, and analyzing. These enterprises then provide summaries and critiques to users that are referenced far more frequently than the original documents. Analyses from these "aftermarket" services are commonly reported in newspapers and in business-oriented magazines, as well as on radio and television, often with the evening news.

This same process will occur when information is provided for other stakeholders—except that in today's media age it will develop much more rapidly. In the days following the annual publication of the *Corporate Reports*, independent services will rank the polluters, the discriminators, the recyclers. Workplaces will be rated for safety. Breakdowns will appear for individual communities and states. Cumulative tabulations of a corporation's several plants and subsidiaries will be developed. The nightly business report will then tell us more than bond prices and stockholder profits; it will give us product recall summaries, listings of the most-sued corporations, which corporations with local facilities try to avoid layoffs, and which ones treat employees as exploitable and expendable goods.

The need and the interest are there (see box for examples); all that is lacking is the information. Even when information is not readily accessible, aggressive enterprises already try to dig it out and make it available to the public. For example, the Council on Economic Priorities has performed thorough, responsible, and well-received studies of companies in several industries, including steel, paper, and defense. Executive compensation, of particular interest to workers who want to compare executive salaries to pay in the plant, is regularly gleaned from current SEC filings and reported by the business press. And a number of organizations and magazines are devoted to giving consumers relevant product information.

As companies begin to systematically provide more of the information needed by stakeholders, the accounting profession, which has effectively been delegated the authority to set reporting standards under the securities acts, will be pressured to adopt the standard of disclosure proposed for the *Corporate Report*. Even smaller companies will come under pressure to follow suit or to explain why they are not providing the disclosure needed by their stakeholders.

As stakeholders become empowered with information, they will be able to direct their labor, resources, and support toward corporations that present a responsible demeanor—as well as withhold these from corporations whose behavior is not acceptable. Thus will the "free market" be brought much closer to the model imagined in freshman economics classes, in which economic decision makers are assumed to have access to full and fair information.

## The National "Bottom Line"

As this important information about the corporations that dominate so much of our society enters the public domain, the real consequences

Sampling of some publications demonstrating an interest in broader, nonfinancial measures of corporate performance:

*The Better World Investment Guide*, Myra Alperson (Prentice-Hall)

*Companies That Care: The Most Family-Friendly Companies in America*, Hal Morgan and Kerry Tucker (Fireside/Simon & Schuster)

*Corporate Social Accounting*, Ralph Estes (John Wiley & Sons)

*Corporate Social Performance*, Ariane Berthoin Antal (Westview Press)

*The Council on Economic Priorities Guide to Corporations*, Joe Zalkind (Council on Economic Priorities)

*Disclosure of Corporate Social Performance*, Harold L. Johnson (Praeger)

*Green Reporting: Accountancy and the Challenge of the Nineties*, Dave Owen (Chapman & Hall)

*The Measurement of Corporate Social Performance: Determining the Impact of Business Actions on Areas of Social Concern* (American Institute of Certified Public Accountants)

*Measuring Business's Social Performance*, John Jay Corson et al. (Committee for Economic Development)

*The 100 Best Companies to Work for in America*, Robert Levering et al. (Addison Wesley)

*Rating America's Corporate Conscience*, Steven D. Lydenberg et al. (Council on Economic Priorities)

*Research in Corporate Social Performance & Policy— A Research Annual* (JAI Press)

*Shopping for a Better World* (Council on Economic Priorities)

*Social Auditing: Evaluating the Impact of Corporate Programs*, David H. Blake et al. (Praeger) will come in the form of a better economic system and a better society. Corporate managers will become accountable to all stakeholders. Their decisions will reflect a balance among the corporation's several constituencies, instead of constantly favoring financial investors at the expense of other kinds of investors.

With corporate accountability, customer well-being will be elevated to the level of a prime corporate objective and will not be merely a means to an improved profit and loss statement. Workers will be treated with greater respect and dignity; they will be seen as co-investors in the corporation and not simply as its servants or tools.

Managers who become accountable to communities and to society will seek to make the corporation truly a good citizen, instead of doing good deeds merely for their public relations value. Programs and investments to control pollution and waste, for example, will be desirable because they will appear as pluses in the *Corporate Report*'s accounting to the community; they will no longer be viewed simplistically as costs to be avoided.

Corporate accountability will not magically cure all the ills of our corporate and economic system. Venal managers can still make venal decisions. But corporate accountability will allow honorable managers to make honorable choices. Honorable choices—choices that balance the interests of all stakeholders—cannot easily be made today, when the organization's objective, as defined by the accounting scorecard and believed and practiced by management, is to maximize the bottom line at whatever cost to stakeholders.

Free to behave as most decent people would prefer to behave, and be held accountable to all stakeholders, most corporate managers will reject the costly choices of the past—choices that have given us the tobacco company coverups, unsafe silicone breast implants, Dalkon Shields, defense contracting scandals, Love Canals, runaway plants, and devastated communities.

## Overthrowing the Tyranny of the Bottom Line

Corporations have grown from small affairs hardly different from family businesses to great monoliths with enormous power. Their power is not "merely" in the economic domain; it reaches to the remotest corners of our nation and, indeed, of the world. Unconstrained, it can do great harm.

Corporations were first chartered to serve a public purpose. Over time, and with the help of a skewed scorekeeping system, that public purpose has been perverted into a singularly private purpose—maximization of profit, the "bottom line." This publicly spoken purpose serves the private interests of top management but can lead to the abuse of corporate stakeholders, even including the stockholders.

Today great corporations have vast power, but are not accountable for that power. Citizens will not accept this arrangement forever. As problems with the corporate system continue to grow—and without accountability, they will certainty grow—a backlash will develop. The public will demand that corporations be brought under control.

The limitations that may develop in response to this backlash could very well hamstring corporations to the point that they would not be able to function effectively. It is not inconceivable that a politician will someday—possibly very soon—ride a populist tide of resentment to the presidency on a pledge to smite down the mighty corporations.

Full accountability is the best, and the most appropriate, way for corporations to stave off a public backlash. No entity can continue forever to have it both ways, with enormous power on the one hand but no accountability to those affected on the other. The disclosure proposed in an annual *Corporate Report* to stakeholders is a reasonable prescription for providing accountability while retaining the corporation's full operating flexibility.

Wise corporate leaders, those who are not obsessed with their own short-term gain but who would seek a long-lasting, responsible corporate system, will support corporate accountability. They will support full and fair disclosure in an annual *Corporate Report* as far more desirable than restrictive, and potentially punitive or even vengeful, legislation and regulation.

But the wisest corporate leaders, those who have the ability to see the future and to stay ahead of the curve, will move to provide leadership in accountability to stakeholders. They will influence other corporations by their actions and their examples. Their leadership may head off action by Congress. If a Corporate Accountability Act is introduced, their record will give them the credibility to speak to the form that legislation might take. They will recognize what every corporate stakeholder already knows—that corporate accountability is necessary, fair, and long overdue.

The bottom line has exercised its tyranny for too long. It is a historical accident that has hurt good people, both corporate managers and stakeholders affected by corporate actions. This tyranny must be overthrown and replaced with a reasonable system of corporate accountability, lest the abuse it encourages brings down the whole corporate system.

## Notes

1. Ralph Estes, "Standards for Corporate Social Reporting," *Management Accounting* (November 1976): 19-22, 26.
2. American Institute of Certified Public Accountants, *The Measurement of Corporate Social Performance* (New York: American Institute of Certified Public Accountants, 1977).
3. Loren A. Nikolai, John D. Bazley, and R. Lee Brummet, *The Measurement of Corporate Environmental Activity* (New York: National Association of Accountants, 1976).
4. Arthur Andersen & Co, *Practice Guidelines for Social Impact Planning and Reporting* (Chicago: Arthur Andersen & Co., 1975).
5. Ralph Estes, *Corporate Social Accounting* (New York: John Wiley, 1976).
6. "An Embarrassment of Clean Air," *Business Week*, 31 May 1993, 34.

# Appendix 1
# The Corporate Accountability Act

Presented below is a draft of an act that might be proposed to Congress to require full and fair corporate disclosure to stakeholders, as discussed in Chapter 9.

### The Corporate Accountability Act

*Purpose:*

The purpose of this act is to secure corporate accountability to stakeholders, through full and fair disclosure of information required by employees, customers, communities, investors, suppliers, and others in society as a basis for rational and informed economic choices.

*Whereas:*

The corporate form was originally devised to serve the public interest; and

corporate charters were initially issued solely for pursuit of public purposes; and

corporations are now chartered by each of the several states, under their authority to promote the common welfare; and

a corporate charter provides benefits not available to other forms of business organization, including unlimited life, limited liability of shareholders, divisibility and transferability of ownership shares, and authority to make contracts and to sue for their enforcement; and

required corporate reporting to federal agencies is fragmented, inefficient, and costly; and

the Constitution provides that Congress shall have the authority to regulate interstate commerce;

*Be it therefore ordered that:*

The Securities and Exchange Commission is hereby designated the Corporate Accountability Commission; and

the Corporate Accountability Commission is charged with implementing regulations and procedures to ensure that corporations engaged in interstate commerce are accountable, through an annual comprehensive *Corporate Report* to be filed with the Commission and through filings at community and facility level, to their several stakeholders, viz., their employees, their customers, their stockholders, their suppliers, their neighboring communities, and the nation at large; and

the Corporate Accountability Commission shall consolidate corporate reporting to federal agencies (excluding income tax reporting), to the greatest degree practical, into the *Corporate Report* to be filed with the Commission; and

information reports required in implementation of this act shall be freely and publicly available at the Corporate Accountability Commission, through electronic media such as the Internet and public bulletin board systems, and at such other locations as necessary to satisfy the purpose of this Act; and

the Corporate Accountability Commission shall hold hearings among stakeholders and conduct other research and inquiries from time to time to identify stakeholder information needs and to determine the information that corporations shall be required to provide.

# Appendix 2
# Customer Information Needs

More attention has probably been given to disclosure to consumers than to the information needs of other stakeholders. Yet as noted in Chapter 10, important gaps still exist, and new information needs will arise with the development of new products and processes. These information needs fall generally into three major categories.

I. **Record of legal and regulatory actions and claims brought against the corporation**

A. To judge the safety and reliability of products, customers should be able to see the record on product liability, injury, and wrongful death claims that have been brought against a company. For example, if numerous lawsuits have been brought against the manufacturer of a powerful vaccine charging that the vaccine causes brain damage, parents of a child about to receive that vaccine ought to know this.

B. A comprehensive legal record covering all jurisdictions should be provided for at least the past five years. Each claim should be fully described, along with its current status or disposition. Claims should be tabulated and identified by specific product since this is where the customer's market choice is made.

C. Similarly, a corporation's record of indictments and citations for regulatory violations should be published. Because errors by medical and financial institutions can be devastating to patients and customers, these organizations should provide a complete record of the complaints and claims that have been filed against them. This information will allow consumers to make informed decisions and to better control their risks. It will also serve those who have bought the corporation's products or services in the past and who may be eligible for recalls or for damages.

Most of this information will already be in the public record, although not accessible to the average consumer; its disclosure to stakeholders would thus not place a significant burden on the corporation nor breach appropriate requirements for confidentiality.

II. **Product information**

    A. Despite truth-in-packaging regulations, consumers are missing important product information. They need to know what pesticides are on fruits and vegetables and what hormones and chemicals have been used in growing and processing the meat they're about to eat. As new chemically formulated products become available and as medical science advances our knowledge of diet, nutrition, and health, our information needs will continue to develop. Increased knowledge has, for example, produced a demand for food product labeling that discloses the fat, cholesterol, and sodium content—but these needs will grow as we learn more about health and nutrition.

    B. With a growing strain on and concern for the environment, product packaging should be identified as to biodegradability.

    C. Automobiles, trucks, farm equipment, vans, campers, and other vehicles are large investments for consumers. Progress has been made in providing relevant information for these products, but before purchasers have to commit such a large expenditure, they should have full recall data for each vehicle model: when and what it was recalled for, along with evidence as to whether the problem has been corrected in the present unit. Air pollution emissions ratings should be provided as well for each specific vehicle model; in a world increasingly concerned with acid rain and the "greenhouse" effect, customers must have information that will permit them to make investments that are environmentally responsible.

D. In more general terms, disclosure should be considered for:

1. Significant characteristics of products that are expensive or purchased only infrequently.

2. "Well-hidden characteristics," those important qualities of any product, regardless of expense or frequency of purchase, that remain hidden even after use—such as the amount of toxic chemicals and nicotine in cigarettes, the nutritional values of foods, and potentially hazardous properties that are not evident on inspection (proposed by Russell B. Stevenson, Jr. in *Corporations and Information: Secrecy, Access, and Disclosure*; Baltimore: The Johns Hopkins University Press, 1980, 123).

III. Social responsibility information

A. Many customers, in choosing among competing producers and vendors, prefer to avoid those that do not follow appropriate standards of social responsibility. Some would rather not purchase shoes, for example, that were manufactured in other countries under abusive, exploitive labor conditions. Some seek to spend their money with companies that are environmentally clean. Some don't want to support multinational conglomerates that market tobacco products or provide weapons to tin-horn dictators. Some would rather avoid patronizing companies that have injured customers or workers in the past, especially if those companies managed to develop convoluted legal techniques to prevent those harmed from receiving fair compensation for their losses.

B. Decisions thought to be "merely" economic are, to many customers, reflections of their personal religious, moral, political, and social philosophies. We may disagree with each other regarding these views, but it is surely the pre-rogative of individuals to apply their personal convictions to purchase decisions as much as they are applied to other areas of life. Persons with such preferences, and that may mean most of us, require information beyond that con-cerned directly with the product—information that reveals how companies treat their stakeholders.

Fortunately, a comprehensive *Corporate Report* will provide this information in the sections concerned with workers, communities, and society; additional information in the customer section should not be required, except for unusual circumstances that require ad hoc disclosure.

# Appendix 3
# Worker Information Needs

As noted in Chapter 10, workers need much information not now available to them in order to make appropriate decisions regarding their jobs—i.e., labor market decisions. They need information about plant closings, layoffs, and employment stability; health and safety; employment data; employee grievances; the impact of technology; pension programs; and the company's future plans.

I. Employment security and stability

   A. Plant closings: To protect their economic lives, workers need real information about plant closings, including:

      1. Company plans for transferring local employees to other locations or for helping them find jobs when transfers are not available.

      2. What plans, if any, the company has to help with the sale of workers' homes.

      3. Full information, as up-to-date as possible, about jobs available at other company sites (because of the costs of a shutdown to affected workers, some effort and expense to the corporation in this instance are justified).

      4. Before kids are pulled out of school, spouses quit their jobs, and homes are sold, workers contemplating transfer need a statement of the company's future plans for its other sites, the ones to which they might be transferring.

      5. Perhaps above all, workers should have readily at hand the company's past record of facility closings—where, when, how many employees affected, how many successfully relocated, how much notice was given. With this

information workers could make more informed decisions about which company to go to work for.

A company's history on shutdowns, while it may be a matter of public record, is difficult for an individual worker to obtain. Corporations should accumulate this information over time and across facilities, and disclose it in the *Corporate Report*. Any worker who is considering a job change, and who may be about to give up years of seniority and security in her or his present job, should have access to this information before taking such a step. A person who is giving up years of seniority should have at least this much of a basis for judging whether the new job may be wiped out in six months.

B. Layoffs: While *potentially* temporary, layoffs often have the same devastating effect on individual workers as a shutdown. Those who aren't called back within a prescribed period, often eighteen months, lose all recall priority and seniority; they are like any other job applicant who comes in off the street. Older workers in particular may find themselves not just out of a job but permanently unemployable. Corporations should publicly report their layoff record for the previous five years, showing the following information for each layoff:

1. The site of the layoff.
2. Number of employees affected by broad employment categories (e.g., managerial, clerical, production, support; or other, more relevant classifications) and by departments.
3. Total person-days involved in the layoff, along with first, second, and third quartile days (e.g., "Of 180 employees affected, 25 percent were out seventy-eight days or more, 50 percent were out sixty-two days or more, and 75 percent averaged forty-seven or more days off").

4. A statement of the company's *layoff policy* should be available to present and potential employees. Does the company use worker layoffs as a cheap tool for managing inventory and manipulating quarterly profits, or does it seek to maintain a no-layoff policy?

C. The company's unemployment compensation rating and record should be publicly reported since this can provide a prospective employee with valuable insight into the company's record of employment stability.

## II. Health and safety

Layoffs and shutdowns can cost workers their careers and end their economic livelihood, but dangerous working conditions can end their lives, leave them crippled, sick, or in lifelong pain.

Workers may accept such risks in return for employment; many feel they must mortgage their life expectancy and future health against the availability of a job today. That may be acceptable as long as it is a worker's free choice. But workers must have the information necessary to make it an informed choice.

A. Job risks: Employees and potential employees should be provided with information about the risks on each job:

1. Exposure to radiation, noise levels, chemicals, fumes, toxic substances, fibers, and emissions, and to inhalation of smoke, chemicals, and dust.
2. Risks associated with the use of tools and equipment.
3. Dangers of prolonged exposure or repetition of movement.
4. Incidence of carpel tunnel syndrome, headaches, hernias, back problems, and tendonitis/bursitis by specific jobs.
5. Computer monitor (VDT/CRT) exposure; radiation levels from laser printers, televisions, and microwaves.
6. Risks to pregnant women.

B. Medical statistics: Detailed data on past accidents, injuries, illness, and medical complaints, broken down by specific job, department, date, and nature of the problem.

### III. Employment data

In addition to information about layoffs, shutdowns, and safety issues, workers need information that describes the corporation in its role as an employer. Data should be provided in such areas as equal opportunity, employee turnover, opportunity for internal promotion, grievances, and technological change.

A. Equal opportunity: Equal employment opportunity is now monitored, with reporting required to the Equal Employment Opportunity Commission. But the standard report required by this agency, Form EEO-1, is not routinely available to present and prospective employees, unless the company chooses to provide it to them (and this is by no means the norm). The government gets the report, but the workers, the ones suffering from discrimination, often are not allowed to see it.

It hardly matters, though. The report to the EEOC does not give enough information to be of real use anyway. It reports numbers of women and minorities employed in a few broad categories.

Workers need much more information to decide whether to risk their career with a corporation. They need information classified by gender and race about:

1. New hires during the year.
2. Promotions during the year.
3. Number in position at year end.
4. Average total compensation levels (including stock options and other benefits) broken down by such categories as:

   a. Top executives (Corporations already have to report, in proxy statements, the compensation and benefits of top executives).

b. Other top management.

c. Second level management.

d. Middle management.

e. Line.

f. Clerical.

g. Custodial.

Other classifications may be necessary, such as professional, research, supervisory, or entry-level. These data should be provided for at least the prior five years.

Providing this information should require little additional expense for the employer. Any corporation that does not already routinely collect and analyze the data described cannot fairly claim to have an affirmative action program, or to truly care about equal employment opportunity.

B. Turnover: Statistics about employee turnover can be important to potential employees deciding among corporate employers. Data classified by department, job level, gender, race, and age categories can help one identify troublesome work areas as well as provide insight into possible discrimination.

C. Promotions: Career opportunities will be reflected to a fair degree in statistics showing promotions from within as opposed to external hires. These data are difficult to interpret for a single corporation, but they become meaningful when employees are able to make comparisons across several companies. A large number of managerial appointments from outside may indicate a high percentage of jobs that dead-end in middle management or lower.

## IV. Employee grievances

Comparative data on employee grievances filed can help reveal whether a corporation is the kind of employer that exploits workers and fights them over every benefit or one that treats its employees with respect and dignity. Data should include

grievances of all sorts, whether filed internally (with the personnel office or a corporate "ombudsman"), with labor unions, with
state agencies, or in the courts. A standard format should be
developed to permit summarization of incidents in a manner
that will reveal the broad nature and significance of complaints.

Of course some complaints will be frivolous, but people understand that. They also understand that where there's smoke there
may be fire, and a company with a hundred or a thousand
complaints raises concerns about management's policies and
fairness, which are not raised to the same degree for a company
with, say, a couple of complaints. The approach used by better
business bureaus, which does not seem to have kept corporations from operating competitively, might be adopted. The
BBBs report the number of complaints received about the business practices of specific firms, along with the number not sat-
isfactorily resolved. And they report this to anyone who asks.

## V.  The impact of technology

New technology can cost workers not only their jobs but their
lifetime careers as well. We may find, in the too near future, that
production jobs require skill and education levels beyond those
available to a large majority of the population. Most workers in
the next generation may be qualified only for generally menial
jobs in the ever-growing service sector. To ameliorate the
impact of new technology, legislation has been proposed by
European labor unions that would require advance notification
to workers of technological change, as well as provide for specific benefits to those workers displaced by new technology.
Similarly, several unions in the United States have called for a
"New Technology Bill of Rights for American Workers" ("New
Technology," *Meeting the Corporate Challenge: A Handbook
on Corporate Campaigns*, Transnational Information Exchange
Report 18/19, February 1985, 17–21).

If employees cannot be protected from advancing technology,
they at least deserve the best information that can be made

available so they can try to protect themselves—so they can invest, for example, in education and training appropriate for the new technology. These and similar proposals need to be studied to identify the nature and form of information that corporations should provide relative to technological change.

## VI. Pension programs

An employee's pension plan is likely to be his or her largest single asset, and a crucial support for sustenance during retirement. When these programs are mismanaged, the loss to employees may be devastating.

Fair reporting of complete information will not keep companies from going under and may not completely prevent misuse of pension plan assets, but it will allow employees to better protect themselves through planning and informed choice. Workers should be provided with full information concerning their pension programs, including the extent to which past and current benefit liabilities are funded as well as changes in market value of the program or fund's investments (some of this information is now reported to employees under the Employee Retirement Income Security Act).

## VII. Future plans

Most of the information called for here will be a matter of historical record, but workers, just like stock investors, have indicated that they are most interested in future projections and plans. The future is of course difficult to project; nevertheless, corporate executives do make projections, they certainly make plans and long-term commitments, and they often reveal these to security analysts. Why shouldn't employees be able to plan for their future too? Why shouldn't they be told about significant expansions, technology introductions, plant closings, product changes, and divestiture of whole units?

The reason employees cannot effectively plan for their own future is because the corporation keeps *its* plans secret from them. Managers will of course maintain that any disclosure of future plans will get into competitor's hands, to the corporation's detriment. But what is the corporation? Isn't it as much its employees as anything else? This is the general view in Japan, and Japanese corporations do not seem to have been hampered from effectively competing in the global economy.

Certainly there will be some plans whose disclosure may justifiably be limited to the smallest number on a "need to know" basis, but many corporate plans can be shared with employees. The tradeoff might indeed be some small loss in competitive advantage, producing a minute drop in stockholders' return on investment, against opportunities for employees to seek alternative arrangements and to cushion themselves against technological obsolescence. Whether this is a fair tradeoff can be debated; but it is clear that *some* balance between the benefits to other stakeholders is appropriate, in contrast to the present arrangement where most decisions are made in behalf of stockholders only, while workers bear most of the cost.

# Appendix 4
# Community Information Needs

Little attention has been given by Corporate America, professional associations of local government officials, or community activists, to the information corporations should provide to allow communities to make informed decisions in response to corporate requests for special favors. As Chapter 10 notes, communities need information regarding corporate ownership, the corporation's financial record, relevant corporate history, school impaction, water consumption, waste creation, vehicular activity, taxes paid, materials used, facility construction, materials sourcing, pollution emissions, job creation, investments, contributions, and lobbying and political activities.

I. **Ownership Information**

Who owns the corporation? Who has the large blocks of stock? And not just individual blocks, but by groups. (For example, if no one person or organization holds a large number of shares of a company, but oil interests or members of organized crime, or developers, or foreign interests collectively hold a significant or controlling interest, then this information should be available.) "Street names," through which investment companies hide the true beneficial owners, would be unacceptable for identification of stock owners. The people, in chartering a corporation and allowing the charter to continue, should be able to see just who is benefitting from the charter.

This information is needed to assess the direction in which the corporation is headed and what its goals are likely to be. It may be especially relevant at the state level, given the concern in some states about foreign corporations buying up local real estate, farms, and businesses.

II. **Financial data**
Financial information, equivalent to present SEC Form 10-K filings, for the past five years is needed for a general assessment of the corporation's size, capability, capacity, and staying power.

III. **Relevant corporate history**
  A. The corporation's legal history is often the strongest basis community decision makers can have for predicting the corporation's behavior in the community. An enumeration should be provided of legal actions brought against the corporation during the past five years, from whatever source and in whatever jurisdiction, describing the nature of the claim or charge, parties involved, and status or disposition.

  B. Historical data should be reported about industrial development bonds previously authorized, showing the actual use that was made of the funds. Since these bonds are often authorized in return for a promise of new job creation, the actual jobs created from past development bond issues should be reported, and classified by general job type and compensation levels. For example, were the jobs primarily part-time and minimum wage?

  C. Additional history should be provided about tax exemptions, abatements, or deferrals; zoning changes previously sought; city condemnation and acquisition of land that is then leased or sold to a corporation; land cleared for the corporation at public expense; grading for drainage or flood control; discounts on water and sewer charges; cutting, paving, or rerouting streets; and installation or modification of traffic controls for a corporation's special benefit.

IV. **School impaction data**
Corporations moving into a community should provide data about the impact on local schools from the families of its

its employees. This is similar to that used by the federal government in providing impacted area assistance where there are large federal facilities. The information is important to school administrators in budgeting and planning for a large influx of students.

V. **Water and waste data**

Corporations should project annual water consumption and the quantities of waste and sewage that will be generated. Separate estimates should be provided for amounts and types of waste from consumption of the company's products (for example, how much styrofoam packaging will be added to the waste stream each year from consumption of a fast food chain's carry-out products).

VI. **Vehicular activity**

To permit projection of the effects on streets and traffic, it may be appropriate to ask larger corporations to estimate the number of vehicles, annual mileage, and annual ton-miles driven in the city.

VII. **Taxes paid**

Corporations should report the taxes paid to all jurisdictions: property, corporate income, unemployment, workers' compensation, Social Security, severance (wellhead; natural resource extraction), sales, and franchise. While this information can be readily assembled within the corporation, it is next to impossible for any one level of government to put it all together.

> Wichita's City Hall was consumed by the search [for incentives to offer Gates Learjet to keep it in Wichita] Thursday, with staffers there and at the Sedgwick County Courthouse spending much of the day digging for information about how much Gates Learjet pays in taxes to governments and in leases to the Wichita Airport Authority ("Cities Scurry to Woo Learjet," *The Wichita Eagle-Beacon*, 15 October 1985).

Comparative data on total taxes paid among the corporations in an area can be highly revealing. Not infrequently smaller businesses pay proportionately more, and sometimes many times more, than the corporate giants, yet the larger corporations usually place a much greater burden on the community's infrastructure.

Any corporation that is paying its fair share in taxes will presumably be pleased to publicize this information. Opposition to disclosure, on the other hand, may lead community leaders to question whether the enterprise is properly supporting the cost of public services.

VIII. Materials used

Corporations should provide information on raw materials, chemicals, cleaning and curing agents, and other potentially hazardous or toxic materials used, transported, or stored.

Some may believe that the need for information on hazardous materials was resolved by Title III of the Federal Superfund Amendments and Reauthorization Act of 1986, the "Emergency Planning and Community Right-to-Know Act of 1986." But this does not appear to be the case—even the EPA cannot get the information it needs:

> The survey data received by the [EPA] did not give information vital to an assessment of health risks, such as concentrations of the substances, the timing of releases or the number of people exposed. . . . Only manufacturers that use more than 10,000 pounds or produced more than 75,000 pounds of the substances were required to report. Moreover, about 25 percent of manufacturers required to report their releases into the environment did not do so. . . . ("Toxin Levels Unacceptable, EPA Reports," *The Wichita Eagle-Beacon*, 13 April 1989).

It is even more difficult for communities to obtain the information they need to protect health and property. For example:

The lack of information about health has been a constant source of tension between neighbors of Vulcan [Chemical Co.] and the local, state and federal agencies. The EPA says health is the state's responsibility; the state says it doesn't have the staff to develop its own information on health effects.

Dean Wencl lives near the Vulcan Chemicals plant outside Wichita. The information required under the community right-to-know act and EPA's risk assessment can't tell Wencl what dose of chemicals, if any, he and his family are breathing or what health problems could result from the levels found in the air in his back yard. "Wencl said he just wanted to know what it was his children smelled coming from the plant two miles south of their home" ("Rough Health-Risk Estimate is All Vulcan Neighbors Have," *The Wichita Eagle-Beacon*, 13 April 1989).

On a current and continuous basis, corporations should disclose information regarding radioactive, toxic, hazardous, and dangerous materials used or stored at sites within the community or transported, by or on behalf of the corporation, through or within a designated distance of the city limits. Complete information should be provided on any chemicals known to cause cancer or reproductive toxicity (California's "Safe Drinking Water and Toxic Enforcement Act of 1986," passed by voter initiative, could be a useful model). Sources, destinations, and routes should be identified for transported materials.

Corporations should also provide complete information about waste materials that result from the production process. Are any dangerous? Where and how are they disposed of? Are there risks in transport and disposal of corporate waste (waterways pollution, ground water pollution, dangerous fumes, fibers, radiation)? How does the corporation now dispose of its waste? Is any buried in covered ground sites and, if so, what and where?

IX. **Facility construction data**

Information about plant construction should be reported to city officials and maintained on an up-to-date basis for any modifications. Data should include whether any asbestos, lead, or other potentially hazardous materials were used, whether there are any known structural defects, how the ground surface was prepared, and prior uses if known—for example, was the facility built on a waste dump?

X. **Materials sourcing**

Community leaders may have a strong interest in the proportion of materials that corporations purchase from local sources, especially in communities that have given corporations large tax breaks.

XI. **Pollution emissions data**

Along with waste, corporate air and water pollution represent a tremendous cost to many communities, one that is often uncompensated—that is, the citizens pay the cost, not the corporation. Regular estimates should be reported of air and water emissions, by specified category and quantity. Waterways should be identified for water discharges. Comparative data should be provided for prior years to enable community leaders and citizens to gauge progress or deterioration.

XII. **Job creation data**

Corporations often defend their tax breaks and other subsidies on the basis of job creation. They should therefore provide communities with statistics about jobs, including:

A. Employment data showing numbers of employees and annual changes, by major categories.

B. Historical layoff statistics at all corporate sites for the prior five years, reporting for each layoff:

1. Site of layoff.

2. Number of employees affected, classified by broad job categories (e.g., managerial, clerical, production, support;

or other, more relevant classifications) and by departments.

3. Total person-days involved in each layoff, along with first, second, and third quartile days (e.g., "Of 180 employees affected, 25 percent were out seventy-eight days or more, 50 percent were out sixty-two days or more, and 75 percent averaged forty-seven or more days off").

C. Company unemployment compensation rating and record (since this provides insight into the company's record of employment stability).

D. Record of plant closings for the prior five years, in all jurisdictions. The 1988 federal plant closing bill requires sixty days' notice to the local government's chief elected official and the state's dislocated workers' director, with smaller companies exempted. As noted earlier, this law has not been effective. Even if it were, in many cases two months' notice would not allow sufficient time to adjust budgets for such programs as police, schools, traffic administration, and unemployment assistance. Communities need to be prepared by making their own projections. To do this they need the corporation's history of plant relocations or closings. They also need to be informed of the corporation's current plant relocation *policy*, if it has one.

XIII. Investments

State and local governments as well as citizens may have a legitimate interest in whether a corporation is making an effort to invest in entities located in the state or community, and whether it seeks to avoid investment in countries with oppressive regimes. Corporations should therefore disclose a breakdown of corporate investments and provide a statement of their investment policy.

XIV. Contributions

Corporate charitable contributions should be detailed with each recipient's location identified. A community that provides special benefits to a corporation may have a reasonable interest in the proportion of the company's charitable contributions that are distributed in that community.

XV.  Lobbying and political activities
Efforts of a corporation to influence public policy, in the form of political contributions to candidates or parties, or in behalf of particular issues (such as a referendum or charter ordinance) should be disclosed. Data should be provided for any corporate-controlled political action committees (PACs). In deciding how to vote and what issues to support, citizens need to be able to determine how much a corporation may be spending to influence legislation or policies favorable to it.

# Appendix 5
## Society's Information Needs

Stakeholder needs for information are briefly described in Chapter 10. The nation, the greater society, is shown to be a stakeholder in corporations, and as such entitled to an accounting. These needs will be partly served by the disclosure suggested for communities listed in Appendix 4. Additional national disclosure needs might include information such as the following:

I.   Taxes paid and collected at all levels of government

II.  Air and water pollution generated

III. Information about where materials are stored and where they have been and are being disposed of, especially radioactive and other dangerous waste

IV.  Data about transportation of radioactive and other dangerous materials, giving routes, quantities, and frequency

V.   Political efforts such as PAC activities, campaign contributions, and lobbyists used (including fees paid)

VI.  A history of legal actions

VII. Amount and content of trade with nations that is officially discouraged as a matter of national policy (because of, for example, hostile relations with the United States, or abuse of human rights)

VIII. Foreign exchange generated and used to permit an assessment of the extent to which the corporation is contributing, favorably or unfavorably, to our balance of trade

IX.  **Major government contracts,** by nature and dollar amount
This disclosure might be described somewhat as follows: "Any
bidder on a U.S. government contract valued at [specified minimum, such as $1 million] or more shall provide, in a memo-
randum accompanying the bid, an accounting of government
contracts awarded and executed over the past five years indicating *original* contract amount and total *actual* payments
received, with cost overruns or underruns identified."

X.  **Fines levied against the corporation** by federal regulatory
agencies and courts, including those for malfeasance associated
with government contracts

# References

"A Healthy Amount of Verbiage to Define What's Good for You." *The Washington Post*, 5 May 1994.

"A Plea for Corporate Conscience." *Harper's*, June 1984.

"A Top G.M. Official Is Reported Chosen to Succeed Iacocca." *The New York Times*, 16 March 1992.

ABC News. "20/20." 20 September 1991.

"Ads Could Hit School Halls." *USA Today*, 30 July 1993.

"Air Force Temporarily Suspends GE from Defense Contracts." *Waco Tribune-Herald*, 29 March 1985.

"Air Midwest Grounds Planes, Lays Off 30." *The Wichita Eagle*, 3 October 1989.

Alperson, M. *The Better World Investment Guide*. Prentice-Hall, 1991.

"American Home Plans to Cut 4,000 More Jobs." *The New York Times*, 25 January 1995.

American Institute of Certified Public Accountants. *The Measurement of Corporate Social Performance*. New York: American Institute of Certified Public Accountants, 1977.

"An Embarrassment of Clean Air." *Business Week*, 31 May 1993, 34.

"Are Tampons Safer Now?" *Consumer Reports*, May 1986, 332–34.

Armstrong, J. Scott. "Social Irresponsibility in Management." *Journal of Business Research* 5 (1977): 185–213.

Arthur Andersen & Co. *Cost of Government Regulation Study* (Prepared for the Business Roundtable). Chicago: Arthur Andersen & Co., 1979.

———. *Practice Guidelines for Social Impact Planning and Reporting*. Chicago: Arthur Andersen & Co., 1975.

"Asbestos Pact: Legal Model or Monster?" *The Washington Post*, 11 May 1994.

"Atlanta Firm Plans to Launch 'Video Kiosk' Advertising At High School Pay Phones." *Education Hotline (Teacher Magazine Education Week)* (October 1990): 2.

Baggerman, Lisa. "The Futility of Downsizing." *Industry Week,* 18 January 1993, 27, 29.

"Bankruptcy Can Make Survival Costly." *The Wichita Eagle-Beacon,* 13 November 1988.

*Bartlett's Familiar Quotations,* 15th ed. Boston: Little Brown, 1980.

Beattie, Vivien, and Mike Jones. "Telecom Publishes First Customer Report." *Management Accounting* (UK) (March 1987): 24–26.

Becker, J. "Toward a 'Real' Value Accounting." *Advances in Public Interest Accounting* 2 (1988).

"Berkeley: Matching Its Image." *Newsweek,* 11 February 1985, 11.

Berle, Adolf A. Jr. *Power Without Property.* New York: Harcourt, Brace & World, 1959.

———. *The 20th Century Capitalist Revolution.* New York: Harcourt, Brace & World, 1954.

Bernstein, Dennis, and Connie Blitt. "Lethal Dose." *The Progressive,* March 1986.

"Big Business is Plagued by Greed and Stupidity." *The Atlanta Journal and Constitution,* 29 April 1991.

Blake, D., W. Frederick, and M. Myers. *Social Auditing.* Westport, Conn.: Praeger, 1976.

Bluestone, Barry, and Bennett Harrison. *The Deindustrialization of America: Plant Closings, Community Abandonment, and the Dismantling of Basic Industry.* New York: Basic Books, 1982.

Blumberg, Phillip I. *The Megacorporation in American Society: The Scope of Corporate Power.* Englewood Cliffs, N.J.: Prentice-Hall, 1975.

"Boeing to Close Mississippi Plant." *The Wichita Eagle-Beacon,* 30 November 1988.

"Bored Directors." *The Economist,* 27 January 1990.

Borkin, Joseph. *The Crime and Punishment of I. G. Farben.* New York: The Free Press, 1978.

Braithwaite, John. *Corporate Crime in the Pharmaceutical Industry.* London: Routledge & Kegan Paul, 1984.

Braverman, Harry. *Labor and Monopoly Capital: The Degradation of Work in the Twentieth Century.* New York: Monthly Review Press, 1974.

Brenner, Harvey. "Estimating the Social Costs of National Economic Policy: Implications for Mental and Physical Health and Clinical Aggression." A report prepared for the Joint Economic Committee, U. S. Congress. U.S. Government Printing Office, 1976.

Breslin, Catherine. "Day of Reckoning." *Ms. Magazine,* June 1989, 46–52.

Broder, D. "'Corporate Welfare' Next Tax Target." *The Wichita Eagle-Beacon,* 17 February 1985.

Brodeur, Paul. *Outrageous Misconduct: The Asbestos Industry on Trial.* New York: Pantheon Books, 1985.

Brown, Lester R. *World Without Borders.* New York: Random House, 1972.

Brown, Michael H. *Laying Waste: The Poisoning of America by Toxic Chemicals.* New York: Pantheon Books, 1980.

"Business Goes to School Looking to Give Some, Gain A Lot." *The Wichita-Eagle,* 20 November 1989.

Buss, Terry E., and F. Stevens Redburn. *Shutdown at Youngstown.* Albany: State University of New York Press, 1983.

"Carbide Chief Says Company Took Too Long to Tell of Leak." *Reno Gazette-Journal,* 17 August 1985.

"Carbide Violations Draw Fine." *The Wichita Eagle-Beacon,* 2 April 1986.

Chamber of Commerce of the U.S. *Handbook of White Collar Crime.* Washington, D.C.: Chamber of Commerce of the U.S., 1974.

"Channel One, Round Two." *The New York Times,* 19 May 1993.

Chen, Edwin. *PBB: An American Tragedy.* Englewood Cliffs, N.J.: Prentice-Hall, 1979.

"Cities Scurry to Woo Learjet." *The Wichita Eagle-Beacon,* 15 October 1985.

"Clifton Teenager Hits the Big Time: Broadcast News in L.A." *The Bergen Record,* 21 February 1995.

Clinard, M., and P. Yeager. *Corporate Crime.* New York: The Free Press, 1980.

Cobb, Sidney, and Stanislaw Kasl. "Termination: The Consequences of Job Loss." Public Health Service, Center for Disease Control, National Institute for Occupational Safety and Health, U.S. Department of

Health, Education, and Welfare, Washington, D.C.: U.S. Government Printing Office, June 1977.

Conference Board. *Handling Protest at Annual Meetings.* New York: The Conference Board, 1971.

"Consumer Interests—Message from the President of the United States (H. Doc. No. 364)." *United States of America Congressional Record.* Vol. 108, Part 3. 26 February 1962–15 March 1962.

Corbett, Dave, and Thea Lee. "Learning for Sale: Will Business Set the Agenda for School Reform?" *Dollars & Sense* (October 1989): 13–15.

"Corporate Crime: The Untold Story." *U.S. News & World Report,* 6 September 1982.

"Corporate Dumping." *Washington City Paper,* 11 December 1992.

Cotton, J. "Discrimination and Favoritism in the U.S. Labor Market: The Cost to a Wage Earner of Being Female and Black and the Benefit of Being Male and White." *American Journal of Economics and Sociology* (January 1988): 15–28.

Coulter, Harris L., and Barbara Loe Fisher. *DPT: A Shot in the Dark.* New York: Warner Books, 1985.

"Crime in the Suites." *Dollars & Sense* (November 1989): 5.

"Criticism of Leak Increases." *The Wichita Eagle-Beacon,* 13 August 1985.

Dahl, Robert A. "Governing the Giant Corporation." In *Corporate Power in America.* Edited by Ralph Nader and Mark J. Green. New York: Grossman Publishers, 1973.

"Data Show G.M. Knew for Years of Risk in Pickup Trucks' Design." *The New York Times,* 17 November 1993.

Davis, John P. *Corporations: A Study of the Origin and Development of Great Business Combinations and of Their Relation to the Authority of the State.* Vols. I and II. New York: Capricorn Books, 1961.

"Defense Contractor is Accused of Fraud." *Fort Worth Star-Telegram,* 16 July 1986.

Dembo, David, Ward Morehouse and Lucinda Wykle. *Abuse of Power: Social Performance of Multinational Corporations, the Case of Union Carbide.* New York: New Horizons Press, 1990.

DeMott, Deborah A., ed. *Corporations at the Crossroads: Governance and Reform.* New York: McGraw-Hill, 1980.

"Derby Mothballing 2 Refineries." *The Wichita Eagle-Beacon*, 5 February 1987.

Dierkes, M., and R. Bauer. *Corporate Social Accounting*. Westport, Conn.: Praeger, 1973.

"Dioxin Puts Dow on the Spot." *Time*, 2 May 1983, 62.

Domini, A., and P. Kinder. *Ethical Investing*. Reading, Mass.: Addison-Wesley, 1984.

"Donations Land Charities in Trouble." *The Wall Street Journal*, 27 October 1989.

"DOT Rejects Lorenzo's TX Bid; Cites Safety, Compliance Problems." *Air Safety Week*, 11 April 1994.

Dowie, Mark. "The Corporate Crime of the Century." *Mother Jones*, November 1979, 23–25, 37–38, 49.

————. "How Ford Put Two Million Firetraps on Wheels." *Business & Society Review* (fall 1977): 46–55.

Dowie, Mark, and Theodore A. Brown. "Taking Stock: The Best and Worst of American Business." *Mother Jones*, June 1985, 25.

"Downsizers Chalk Up a Record First Half." *Business Week*, 25 July 1993, 20.

Drucker, Peter. *Management: Tasks, Responsibilities, Practices*. New York: Harper & Row, 1973.

Dusky, Lorraine, and Baila Zeitz. "The Best Companies for Women." *Savvy*, May 1988, 47.

"E. F. Hutton Co. Pleads Guilty to 2,000 Fraud Counts." *The San Diego Union*, 3 May 1985.

"Eastern Air Indicted on Inspections." *The Washington Post*, 26 July 1990.

"Eastern Denies It Has Weight Problem." *Washington Times*, 24 August 1988.

*Economic Report of the President*. Washington, D.C.: U.S. Government Printing Office, various years.

*Economic/Social Impact of Occupational Noise Exposure Regulations: Testimony Presented at the OSHA Hearings on the Economic Impact of Occupational Noise Exposure*. Washington, D.C.: U.S. Environmental Protection Agency, September 1976.

*Environmental Health Issues Including Toxic Site Profiles*. Visalia, Calif.: Central California Health Systems Agency. February 1986.

Estes, Ralph. *Corporate Social Accounting.* New York: John Wiley, 1976.

———. *Dictionary of Accounting.* 2nd ed. Cambridge, Mass.: The MIT Press, 1985.

———. "Standards for Corporate Social Reporting." *Management Accounting* (November 1976): 19–22, 26.

———. *ESTES Economic Loss Tables.* 1991 Edition. Washington, D.C.: A.U. Publishing, 1991.

"Executive Pay: The Party Ain't Over Yet." *Business Week,* 26 April 1993, 56–79.

"Final Payments on the Bailout." *Business Week,* 27 February 1995, 34.

"Finding a Bad Night's Sleep with Halcion." *The New York Times,* 20 January 1992.

Finn, David. *The Corporate Oligarch.* New York: Simon & Schuster, 1969.

Fletcher, John Cameron. "A Delphi Evaluation of a Railroad's Social Costs and Benefits." D.B.A. diss., University of Colorado, 1981.

Folk, Ernest. "Does State Corporation Law Have a Future?" *Georgia State Bar Journal* (February 1972): 311–12.

"For Many Dalkon Shield Claimants Settlement Won't End the Trauma." *The Wall Street Journal,* 9 March 1988.

"Fortune 500." *Fortune,* 24 April 1989, 354.

Fossedal, Gregory. "Corporate Welfare Out of Control." *The New Republic,* 25 February 1985, 17–19.

Freeman, A. *Air and Water Pollution Control: A Benefit-Cost Assessment.* New York: John Wiley, 1982.

Friedman, Milton. "The Social Responsibility of Business Is to Increase Its Profits." *The New York Times Sunday Magazine,* 13 September 1970.

"The Fugitive Accuser." *Time,* 8 April 1985.

Galbraith, John Kenneth. *Economics and the Public Purpose.* Boston: Houghton Mifflin, 1973.

———. *The Age of Uncertainty.* Boston: Houghton Mifflin, 1977.

———. *American Capitalism: The Concept of Countervailing Power.* Rev. ed. Boston: Houghton Mifflin, 1956.

———. *The New Industrial State.* 4th ed. Boston: Houghton Mifflin, 1985.

———. *Annals of An Abiding Liberal.* Boston: Houghton Mifflin, 1979.

———. *Almost Everyone's Guide to Economics.* Boston: Houghton Mifflin, 1978.

"GAO Study on Plant Closings." *DH&S Review,* 14 September 1987, 30.

"GE Admits Defrauding Pentagon." *The Wichita Eagle-Beacon,* 14 May 1985.

"GE Faces Charges of Fraud." *Dallas Times-Herald,* 27 March 1985.

"GE Is Fined $10 Million in Criminal Case." *The Wall Street Journal,* 17 July 1990.

"General Dynamics Accused of Lying." *The Wichita Eagle-Beacon,* 1 March 1985.

"General Dynamics Under Fire." *Business Week,* 25 March 1985, 70–76.

"General Motors: Exploding Gas Tanks." *Multinational Monitor* (December 1992): 13.

"General Motors: Reckless Homicide?" *Multinational Monitor* (December 1994): 10–11.

Getz, Bob. "Would You Hire This Man? Even If He's 45 Years Old!" *The Wichita Eagle-Beacon,* 2 July 1989.

Gibbs, Lois Marie. *Love Canal: My Story.* Albany: State University of New York Press, 1982.

Glover, Jonathan. *Causing Death and Saving Lives.* Harmondsworth, Eng.: Penguin, 1977.

"GM Hopes Suit Settlement Translates to Truck Sales." *The Washington Post,* 21 July 1993.

"GM Settles Truck Suits With Coupon." *USA Today,* 20 July 1993.

"G.M. Unit Settles Mortgage Escrow Suit." *The New York Times,* 28 January 1992.

"G.M.'s Profits a Record in Quarter and Year." *The New York Times,* 1 February 1995.

Gray, R., D. Owen and K. Maunders. "Accountability, Corporate Social Reporting, and the External Social Audits." *Advances in Public Interest Accounting.* 4(1991).

———. *Corporate Social Reporting: Accounting and Accountability.* Englewood Cliffs, N.J.: Prentice-Hall International, 1987.

*The Great Quotations.* New York: Pocket Books, 1967.

Green, M., and N. Waitzman. *Business War on the Law.* Rev. 2nd ed. Corporate Accountability Research Group, 1981.

Grostoff, Steven. "LTV Pension Funds Double PBGC Deficit." *National Underwriter* (19 January 1987): 3, 50.

Guthrie, J., and L. Parker. "Corporate Social Disclosure Practice: A Comparative International Analysis." *Advances in Public Interest Accounting.* 3(1990).

Haas, Gilda, and Plant Closures Project. *Plant Closures: Myths, Realities and Responses.* Boston: South End Press, 1985.

"Halal, W. E. "A Return-on-Resources Model of Corporate Performance." *California Management Review* (summer 1977): 23–33.

"Halcion Lawsuit Alleges FDA, Upjohn Conspiracy." *The Houston Chronicle,* 7 January 1994.

Handlin, Oscar, and Mary F. Handlin. "Origins of the American Business Corporation." In Donald Grunewald and Henry L. Bass. *Public Policy and the Modern Corporation.* New York: Appleton-Century-Crofts, 1966.

Hankin, Samuel F. "PBGC Cracks Down on Funding Waivers." *Pension World* (January 1986): 10.

"Hazards of a Toxic Wasteland." *Time,* 17 December 1984, 32–34.

Heilbroner, Robert L. et al. *In the Name of Profit.* Garden City, N.Y.: Doubleday, 1972.

Herman, Edward S. *Corporate Control, Corporate Power.* Cambridge, Mass.: Cambridge University Press, 1981.

"Hole in Fuselage Forces Plane to Make Landing." *Christian Science Monitor,* 27 December 1988.

Holzner, B. *Reality Construction in Society,* Rev. ed. Cambridge, Mass.: Schenkman, 1972.

"How Lawless Are Big Companies?" *Fortune,* 1 December 1980, 56–64.

"How Much For a Life? Try $3 Million to $5 Million." *The New York Times,* 29 January 1995.

Hurst, James Willard. *The Legitimacy of the Business Corporation in the Law of the United States: 1780-1970.* Charlottesville: The University Press of Virginia, 1970.

"Iacocca Pay Climbs to $4 Million." *The Washington Post,* 14 April 1990.

"In Takeover Wars, A Battle Is Won by Managers." *The New York Times* (International/National ed.), 16 July 1989.

"Incentive Packages Stir Questions Among Taxpayers and Consultants." *The Wichita Eagle-Beacon,* 26 June 1988.

"India Sues Union Carbide." *The Wichita Eagle-Beacon,* 9 April 1985.

*Infact Brings GE to Light.* Boston: INFACT: 1988.

"Is Disney Ready for School?" *Business Week,* 2 August 1993, 22.

"Israeli Military Scandal Jolts GE; Company to Settle Fraud Charges, Defends Ethics Program," *The Washington Post,* 20 July 1992.

Jacoby, N., P. Nehemkis, and R. Eells. *Bribery and Extortion in World Business.* New York: Macmillan, 1977.

"Jeans Fade But Levi Strauss Glows." *The New York Times,* 26 June 1989.

"Jeans Plant to Be Closed; 835 Workers to Lose Jobs." *The Wall Street Journal,* 12 September 1988.

Johnson, J., and J. Douglas, ed. *Crime at the Top: Deviance in Business and the Professions.* Philadelphia: J. B. Lippincott, 1978.

Johnson, Samuel. *The Idler.* Pafraets Book Co., 1903.

Jonson, L., B. Jönsson, and G. Svensson. "The Application of Social Accounting to Absenteeism and Personnel Turnover. *Accounting, Organizations and Society.* 3, 3/4(1978).

Josephson, Matthew. *The Robber Barons.* New York: Harcourt, Brace & World, 1962.

"Judge Ready to Approve Robins Plan." *The New York Times,* 19 July 1988.

"Jury Awards $15 Million in DPT Case." *The Wichita Eagle-Beacon,* 15 October 1987.

Kahn, E. J. Jr. "We Look Forward to Seeing You Next Year." *The New Yorker,* 20 June 1970, 40–2t.

"Kansas Assuming Major Role in Disposal of PCBs." *The Wichita Eagle-Beacon,* 22 April 1986.

Kapp, K. *The Social Costs of Private Enterprise.* New York: Schocken Books, 1971.

Klein, T. *Social Costs and Benefits of Business.* Englewood Cliffs, N.J.: Prentice-Hall, 1977.

Knight, S., and D. Knight. *Concerned Investors Guide: Non-financial Corporate Data.* Hopkins, Minn.: Resource Publishing Group, 1983.

"Last Car Rolls Off Line." *USA Today,* 22 December 1988.

"Layoff Law Is Having Slim Effect." *The New York Times,* 9 August 1993.

Lehman, C. *Accounting's Changing Roles in Social Conflict.* New York: Markus Wiener, 1992.

Letters. *Time,* 13 December 1993, 11.

Levering, Robert, Milton Moskowitz, and Michael Katz. *The 100 Best Companies to Work for in America.* Reading, Mass.: Addison-Wesley, 1984.

"Levi Strauss Closing Plant." *The New York Times,* 18 January 1990.

"Levi Strauss." *The New York Times,* 2 February 1989.

Liebert, Robert M. "Effects of Television on Children and Adolescents." *Developmental and Behavioral Pediatrics* (February 1986): 43–48.

Lindblom, C., and T. Tinker. *Social Accounting for Corporations: Private Enterprise Versus the Public Interest.* Manchester: Manchester University Press, 1984.

"Living Dangerously, with Toxic Wastes." *Time,* 14 October 1985, 86–90.

Lydenberg, Steven D., Alice Tepper Marlin, Sean O'Brien Strub, and the Council on Economic Priorities. *Rating America's Corporate Conscience.* Reading, Mass.: Addison-Wesley, 1986.

Mace, Myles L. *Directors: Myth and Reality.* Rev. ed. Boston: Harvard Business School Press, 1986.

*Meeting the Corporate Challenge: A Handbook on Corporate Campaigns.* TIE (Transnational Information Exchange) Report 18/19. February 1985.

Merino, Barbara, and Marilyn Neimark. "Disclosure Regulation and Public Policy: A Sociohistorical Reappraisal." *Journal of Accounting and Public Policy* (fall 1982): 33–57.

Miller, A. *Socially Responsible Investing: How to Invest With Your Conscience.* New York: New York Institute of Finance, 1991.

Mintz, Morton. "A Crime Against Women: A. H. Robins and the Dalkon Shield." *Multinational Monitor* (15 January 1986): 1–7.

———. *At Any Cost: Corporate Greed, Women, and the Dalkon Shield.* New York: Pantheon Books, 1985.

Mintzberg, Henry. *Power In and Around Corporations.* Englewood Cliffs, N.J.: Prentice-Hall, 1983.

Moberg, David. "Shuttered Factories—Shattered Communities." *In These Times,* 27 June 1979, 11.

Mokhiber, Russell. *Corporate Crime and Violence.* San Francisco: Sierra Club Books, 1988.

————. "Corporate Crime and Violence (editorial)." *Multinational Monitor* (April 1987): 4.

————. "The Ten Worst Corporations of 1994." *Multinational Monitor* (December 1994).

Mokhiber, Russell, and E. Virgil Falloon. "The 10 Worst Corporations of 1988." *Multinational Monitor* (December 1988).

"Money Woes Ground Braniff." *The Wichita Eagle,* 28 September 1989.

Morris, Charles R. "The Stock Market Is Far Removed from Reality." *The Wichita Eagle,* 6 November 1989.

Moss, Kary L. "Devising Solutions to Capital Flight: The WARN Act." *Poverty and Race,* a publication of the Poverty & Race Research Action Council (May/June 1994): 3.

Nader, Ralph. ed. *The Consumer And Corporate Accountability.* New York: Harcourt Brace Jovanovich, 1973.

Nader, Ralph, Mark Green and Joel Seligman. *Taming the Giant Corporation.* New York: W. W. Norton, 1976.

"Nature or Nurture? Study Blames Ethical Lapses on Corporate Goals." *The Wall Street Journal,* 9 October 1987.

"Navy Freezes Future Deals with Firm." *The Wichita Eagle-Beacon,* 22 May 1985.

"N.C. Plant Fined $808,150 After Fatal Fire." *The Washington Post,* 31 December 1991.

Neimark, M. *The Hidden Dimensions of Annual Reports.* Princeton, N.J.: Markus Wiener, 1992.

Nemeth, Louis. "Giving Away the Store: Tax Abatements in Michigan." *Multinational Monitor* (31 March 1986).

————. "Mendacity in Michigan." *Multinational Monitor* (31 March 1986): 3–7, 12.

"News of the Weird." *City Paper,* 22 June 1990.

Nikolai, Loren A., John D. Bazley, and Lee R. Brummet. T*he Measurement of Corporate Environmental Activity.* New York: National Association of Accountants, 1976.

Nocera, Joseph. "Delaware Puts Out." *Esquire,* February 1990.

"No More Smoke Screens." *The Washington Post,* 4 March 1995.

Norris, Floyd. "Market Place." *The New York Times,* 7 June 1989.

Nussbaum, Bruce, and Judith Dobrzynski. "The Battle for Corporate Control." *Business Week.* 18 May 1987, 76.

"Occidental Liable for Love Canal." *The Wichita Eagle-Beacon,* 24 February 1988.

Office of Noise Abatement and Control, U.S. Environmental Protection Agency. *Public Hearings on Noise Abatement and Control. Vol. VIII: Technology and Economics of Noise Control; National Programs and Their Relations with State and Local Programs.* 9–12 November 1971.

"'Office Politics' is Taking on a New Wrinkle." *The Washington Post,* 11 September 1994.

"On Cigarettes, Health and Lawyers." *The New York Times,* 6 December 1993.

"$1 Billion Lawsuit Filed Against Maker of Halcion." *The Houston Chronicle,* 30 December 1993.

"Outcry Grows Over Defense Purchases." *The Wichita Eagle-Beacon,* 14 April 1985.

"Overruns Unearthed in Contractor Audit." *The Wichita Eagle-Beacon,* 5 April 1985.

Owen, D. *Green Reporting: Accountancy and the Challenge of the Nineties.* New York: Chapman & Hall, 1992.

"The Pay-for-Performance Myth." *The Washington Post,* 22 July 1990.

"Pensions May be Built on Illusions." *The Wichita Eagle,* 14 November 1989.

"Pentagon to Probe Overbilling." *The Wichita Eagle-Beacon,* 3 May 1987.

The Peoples Bicentennial Commission. *Common Sense II.* New York: Bantam Books, 1975.

"Piercing the Dalkon Shield." *National Law Journal* (16 June 1980): 13.

Plato. *Dialogues, Apology.* Cited in *Bartlett's Familiar Quotations.* 15th ed. Boston: Little Brown, 1980.

Pollay, Richard W. "The Distorted Mirror: Reflections on the Unintended Consequences of Advertising." *Journal of Marketing* (April 1986): 18–36.

"The Posner Principle: When Goliath Controls the Company, Look Out." *Business Week,* 29 October 1990, 34.

"Probe Grounds 43 Eastern Airlines Jets." *San Francisco Chronicle,* 20 April 1988.

Proxmire, W. "Oligopoly Investigation." *Antitrust Law and Economics Review,* Vol. 3, no. 1 (fall 1969).

"Questionable Defense Bills Widespread, House Panel Says." *The Wichita Eagle-Beacon,* 16 May 1985.

"Racial Discrimination Has Become a Major Drain on the U.S. Economy." *The Washington Post,* 7 January 1993.

Ramsey, Peter. "Some Tudor Merchants' Accounts." *Studies in the History of Accounting.* Edited by A. C. Littleton and B. S. Yamey. Homewood, Ill.: Richard D. Irwin, 1956.

Readers Report. *Business Week,* 24 October 1994, 14.

Regenstein, L. *America the Poisoned.* Washington, D.C.: Acropolis Books, 1982.

"Reich, Redefining 'Competitiveness.' " *The Washington Post,* 24 September 1994.

Robertson, Ross M. *History of the American Economy.* 2nd ed. New York: Harcourt, Brace & World, 1964.

Rosenthal, A.M. "The Real Revolution." *The New York Times,* 6 January 1995.

"Rough Health-Risk Estimate is All Vulcan Neighbors Have." *The Wichita Eagle-Beacon,* 13 April 1989.

"Rupture Discovered in Another Boeing 727." *Washington Times,* 29 December 1988.

Sadgrove, K. *The Green Manager's Handbook.* Aldershot, Eng.: Gower, 1992.

Scherer, F. M. "Corporate Ownership and Control." In *The U.S. Business Corporation: An Institution in Transition.* Edited by John R. Meyer and James M. Gustafson. Cambridge, Mass.: Ballinger, 1988.

Schreuder, H. "Corporate Social Reporting in the Federal Republic of Germany: An Overview." *Accounting, Organizations and Society.* 4, 1/2 (1979).

Seavoy, Ronald E. *The Origins of the American Business Corporation: 1784–1855.* Westport, Conn.: Greenwood Press, 1982.

Seidler, L. J., and Seidler, L. L. *Social Accounting: Theory, Issues, and Cases.* Los Angeles: Melville, 1975.

Shapiro, Mark. "William Tell's New Targets." *Mother Jones,* August 1983, 50.

"Shareholders Block Kmart Stock Issue." *The Washington Post,* 4 June 1994.

Silk, Leonard, and Mark Silk. *The American Establishment.* New York: Avon Books, 1980.

Simon, D., and D. Eitzen. *Elite Deviance.* Boston: Allyn and Bacon, 1982.

Skornia, Harry J. *Television and Society.* New York: McGraw-Hill, 1965.

Sloan, Allan (column). "Drexel Wiggles Through a Tax Code Loophole to Shed Its Felonious Past." *The Washington Post,* 30 March 1993.

"Smokers' Health Toll Put at $52 Billion." *The New York Times,* 21 February 1990.

"Smoking-Related Medical Care in '93 Estimated at $50 Billion." *The Washington Post,* 8 July 1994.

"Some Firms Urging Workers to Oppose Health Care Bills." *The Washington Post,* 20 August 1994.

Spicer, Barry. "Investors, Corporate Social Performance and Information Disclosure: An Empirical Study." *The Accounting Review.* January 1978.

Stevenson, Russell B. Jr. *Corporations and Information: Secrecy, Access, and Disclosure.* Baltimore: The Johns Hopkins University Press, 1980.

"Stop Capital Flight: A Strategy for Corporate Accountability." *Multinational Monitor* (June 1993): 12–15.

Strobel, Lee Patrick. *Reckless Homicide: Ford's Pinto Trial.* South Bend, Ind.: And Books, 1980.

Summa, John. "Union Carbide." *Multinational Monitor.* (October 1988): 23–24.

"T. Boone Pickens: 'Clearly a Phenomenon.'" *The Wichita Eagle-Beacon,* 24 February 1985.

"10 Million Severance Package." *The Washington Post,* 28 June 1990.

"These Board Members Aren't IBM-Compatible." *Business Week,* 2 August 1993, 23.

Thurow, Lester. "The New World of Work." *The Boston Globe,* 16 August 1994.

Tinker, T. *Paper Prophets.* Westport, Conn.: Praeger, 1985.

Toffler, Alvin. *The Third Wave.* New York: William Morrow, 1980.

"Toxic Time Bomb Ticks Away in Local Dumps." *Fort Worth Star-Telegram,* 21 October 1986.

"Toxic Waste Risk Rated Above EPA Estimates." *Austin American-Statesman,* 10 March 1985.

"Toxin Levels Unacceptable, EPA Reports." *The Wichita Eagle-Beacon,* 13 April 1989.

Trum, Dara Lynn. "Civil Procedure—Remittitur of Punitive Damages in Exchange for Product Recall—O'Gilvie v. International Playtex." *The University of Kansas Law Review.* Vol. 34, No. 4 (Summer 1986). The case is found at 609 F. Supp. 817, 818 (D. Kan. 1985).

"25 Die as Fire Hits N.C. Poultry Plant." *The Washington Post,* 4 September 1991.

"2 Expected to Leave I.B.M. Board." *The New York Times,* 22 July 1993.

U.S. Bureau of the Census, *Statistical Abstract of the United States.* Washington, D.C.: U.S. Bureau of Census. Various years.

U.S. Internal Revenue Service. *1985 Statistics of Income: Corporation Income Tax Returns.* 1989.

*U.S. PIRG Citizen Agenda.* Vol. 10, No. 3 (Winter 1995).

U.S. Securities and Exchange Commission. *Staff Report on Corporate Accountability.* Washington, D.C.: U.S. Government Printing Office. Committee on Banking, Housing, and Urban Affairs, United States Senate. 4 September 1980.

U.S. Senate Committee on Commerce. *Corporate Rights and Responsibilities: Hearing before the Committee on Commerce.* 94th Cong., June 1976.

"Value of Intangible Losses From Exxon Valdez Spill Put at $3 Billion." *The Washington Post,* 20 March 1991.

"Video Ads by Phones Ring Up School Funds." *USA Today,* 3 December 1991.

Votaw, Dow. *Modern Corporations.* Englewood Cliffs, N.J.: Prentice-Hall, 1965.

Wallace, Henry A. *Whose Constitution—An Inquiry Into The General Welfare.* New York: Reynal & Hitchcock, 1936.

"We Forgot to Write a Headline, But It's Not Our Fault." *The New York Times*, 19 February 1995.

Weir, David. *The Bhopal Syndrome*. San Francisco: Sierra Club Books, 1987.

White, Larry C. *Merchants of Death: The American Tobacco Industry*. New York: Beech Tree Books, 1988.

Will, R. *Shopping for a Better World: A Quick and Easy Guide to Socially Responsible Supermarket Shopping*. Washington, D.C.: Council on Economic Priorities, 1988.

"Winchester Foods Wins Ruling." *The Wichita Eagle-Beacon*, 22 March 1989.

Winjum, James Ole. *The Role of Accounting in the Economic Development of England: 1500–1750*. Urbana, Ill.: Center for International Education and Research in Accounting, 1972.

"The Yamaguchi-gumi Goes to the Mattress." *Newsweek*, 11 February 1985, 49.

# Index

# About the Author

RALPH ESTES has seen corporations from the inside out, as a CPA and auditor with Arthur Andersen & Co.; consultant to business, the professions, and government regulatory agencies; expert witness on economic loss in cases in which people died or were injured by corporate acts; and chief financial officer of several corporations. He has also studied corporations as a university professor, since 1990 with The American University in Washington, D.C. (He thinks Washington is great, but Texas is still home!)

This work has led to many scholarly and popular articles and eleven previous books. These include *Corporate Social Accounting*, which early on (in 1976) laid out a program for corporate accountability; *Accounting and Society*, which showed how accounting could go beyond the needs of individual clients to serve the broader public interest; and *Who Pays? Who Profits?*, an analysis of what has gone wrong with our national tax policy and what needs to be done to make it both simple and fair. He is a national authority on the social costs of business and the economic consequences of public policy decisions.

Ralph is committed to bringing the results of academic scholarship to bear on issues of public policy. He serves as resident scholar at The Center for Advancement of Public Policy, a nonprofit organization that fosters a more humane corporate system. There he, along with some really great people, is organizing the Stakeholder Alliance, bringing together members of stakeholder groups and public interest organizations, throughout the nation and around the world, to work for the stakeholder accountability proposed in *Tyranny of the Bottom Line*.

He spends most of his time working, but not all. Life must include time for guitar and autoharp, bluegrass music, flowers, poker, Texas

Bar-B-Q, and chiles rellenos (with New Mexican Chimayo—or, second best, Hatch—chiles).

Ralph can be contacted at the Kogod College of Business Administration, The American University, Washington, D.C. 20016-8044; FAX (202) 265-6245. His E-MAIL address, which he is not very good about checking, is restes@american.edu.